SAMPLING THE UNIVERSE

The growth, development and influence of market research in Britain since 1945

Colin McDonald and Stephen King

Edited and introduced by
John Goodyear

NTC PUBLICATIONS LIMITED

IN ASSOCIATION WITH

THE MARKET RESEARCH SOCIETY

First published 1996

NTC Publications Ltd
Farm Road
Henley-on-Thames
Oxfordshire RG9 1EJ
United Kingdom
Telephone: 01491 411000
Facsimile: 01491 571188
E-mail: 100144.3037@compuserve.com

in association with
The Market Research Society

The authors and publisher acknowledge the kind permission of
Rex Audley to reproduce in this book some of his cartoons that have
appeared over the years in issues of *Admap*

A CIP catalogue record for this book is available
from the British Library

ISBN 1-899314-51-2

Typeset in 12/14pt Garamond
by NTC Publications Ltd
Printed and bound in Great Britain by
Biddles Ltd, Guildford and King's Lynn

The Market Research Society gratefully acknowledges the generosity of the following companies, all of which have made financial contributions to the costs of producing this book and to the various 50th Anniversary celebrations.

Kantar Group

Research International

Millward Brown
  International

BMRB International

MBL Group

The MBL Group Plc

BJM Research &
  Consultancy Ltd

Market Behaviour Ltd

Marketing Blueprint Ltd

NOP Research Group

NOP Market Research

Bulmershe Research

The Research Business
  Group

CRAM International

Research Services Ltd

Harris Research Centre

Pegram Walters Associates

Parker Tanner International

Laybourne Valentine
  Research Group

Research & Auditing Services

Simon Godfrey Associates

Audits & Surveys Europe

The Added Value Company

Martin Hamblin Research

Gordon Simmons Research
  Group

The New Fieldwork
  Company

Semiotic Solutions

FDS Market Research Group

Facts International Ltd

GfK Marketing Services Ltd

Network Research

The HPI Research Group

DVL Smith Ltd

Peter Southgate & Associates

City Research Group

Numbers Market Research

Lansdowne Market Research

Ulster Marketing Surveys

PHD Research Ltd

Hugh Bain Research

IFF Research

AUTHORS' ACKNOWLEDGEMENT

Many people have had a hand in this book, either through talking to us, or reading and commenting on earlier drafts, or because we have quoted from their speeches, writings or published interviews. We are very grateful to them all, but it would be far too lengthy to name everyone.

However, there is one source which we feel we must acknowledge specifically. Ian Blythe's history of the Market Research Society is an immensely detailed record of the Society's structure and development – personalities, functions, committees, services, annual events, anecdotes, everything you could think of – taking us up to 1986. Sadly it was never published, but for us it has been a goldmine. It has saved us hours and hours of work, and we are painfully aware of the time it must have taken Ian to comb through and organise so much material. We owe a particular debt of gratitude to him for hacking down the jungle so effectively in front of us, and leaving us a much smoother path than we would have had without his pioneering.

Colin McDonald
Stephen King

CONTENTS

Introduction

This is not just a book about market research, although – more than any other book I know of – it provides a really thorough appreciation of how such research has developed, what it has involved over the last half century, and what it involves today.

Nor is it simply a celebration of the value and importance to the research industry that the Market Research Society has demonstrated over the last fifty years – although the Society's contribution to education and training, and its critical rôle in setting, reviewing and maintaining standards of professionalism and codes of conduct is clearly recognised and deserving of celebration.

Equally, this book is not intended to be a 50-year 'history' of the Market Research Society in the UK – although, again, more than any book I know of, it recognises and records key figures and key developments and sets them clearly in context.

Most of all, however, this book sets out to show how professional, objective market, social and opinion research – in all its many manifestations – has affected, influenced and helped shape the Britain that we know today through its influence on product and brand development in consumer and business markets, and through the input that has been provided to government, local government and other bodies.

The fact that, along the way, the book will also serve to inform and educate even the most experienced marketer, market researcher, advertising agency planner and interested, open-minded observer of the world around us, is a bonus.

For some years now, the British research industry has been handling significantly more than its proportional share of the worldwide market research market. Despite having only around 1 per cent of the world's population, and only some 5 per cent of the world's advertising spend, the UK's market research industry has almost 10 per cent of the world's market research market.

Britain's research industry can trace its history back to the 1930s – one of the world's earliest professional research markets – with companies such as Sales Research Services, British Market Research Bureau, Mass-Observation, British Institute of Public Opinion and the BBC's own Research Department all in full swing well before World War II.

But being long-established, and operating within one of the world's developed economies, are not the only factors underlying the success of the British research industry. The founding of the Market Research Society in London in November 1946, in the immediate post-war period, marked the beginning of the professional growth and development that has taken today's research industry in Britain to its current turnover level, well in excess of £600 million per annum, and growing healthily.

The handful of people who got together in November 1946 to form the Market Research Society in London set in motion a process which has led, fifty years later, to a Society of almost 7,000 members: the largest professional market research body of individual members anywhere in the world. But Britain's market research industry is not only extremely sophisticated and large, it is – and has been – also extremely influential.

Britain's heritage of Commonwealth and Empire, linked with its general orientation to look beyond its borders for market growth, led the British research industry to develop internationally at an early stage – not only in Europe, but on a worldwide basis.

British researchers can be seen to have had a significant rôle to play in the development of the research industries of Canada, India, South-East Asia, Africa, the Middle-East, and many other countries.

British-owned and headquartered research companies, in turn, own subsidiary research operations around the world and, over time, the 'international business' element of the UK research industry's revenues has grown significantly to become the fastest-growing sector of those revenues – proportionately greater than that of any other country around the world.

This book was conceived, planned, commissioned and produced to honour one of the most successful of Britain's service industries of recent years, and to celebrate the 50th anniversary of its professional society.

As a by-product, it will serve to enlighten and educate a whole new generation of researchers and provide insight and understanding to many hundreds of others.

John R Goodyear
Editor

1

The Rise and Rise of Market Research

The story begins in 1946. In that year, a small group of people decided to start a luncheon club, to exchange ideas about what they were doing. They were working in market research, a strange, new activity which virtually nobody else, at the time, knew anything about.

World War II was over, but Britain was a very different place from today. We were still a traditional, stratified society with inherited values. Most people were more limited in their options, especially after the wartime experience. They were not very mobile: they had to buy at the local shop and accept what it had to offer. The shops in turn had to sell what they could get, and had little leverage, by today's standards, to provide a choice for their customers. Goods were mass-produced, and production led. Rationing did not completely finish until 1954.

Fifty years on, things are very different.

Traditional structures and beliefs have been, and are still being, increasingly questioned. We have become a much more complex, less stratified, more individualistic society. More people have more money, and are free to spend it as they choose. Reflecting this, there is more choice. It is commonplace to say that social structure has ceased to be a hierarchical pyramid and become more like an onion, with a small top slice and bottom slice and a wide, amorphous, equivalent middle.

Those who reach the top in this onion do not necessarily come from a limited stratum, as once they would have been expected to do. Almost everything about people is less predictable than it was, and conflict within society has grown.

During these same fifty years, the fledgling discipline of market research, practised by a mere handful of companies and advertising agencies, has grown to become, in the United Kingdom alone, a £600 million plus industry, growing in real terms throughout that period, and accelerating its growth especially during the last two decades, when it has quadrupled in real terms; in the same period, it has spread out to cover every economically active country in the world.

The growth of market research over these fifty years not only reflects the growth, developments and changes which have taken place in British society: to a considerable extent, market research has itself been a factor in helping to influence, shape and bring about these changes. Market research has been an engine of change, whirring quietly away in the background. It has been a principal means of enabling people's wants and needs to be perceived, understood, and taken into account by businesses and policy-makers, thus contributing to a more efficient, more democratic and more satisfying society.

In the public sector, it has been fundamental to all branches of government in coming to grips with an increasingly complex and demanding society. If government is to work effectively these days, it has to understand more about the attitudes, motivations and behaviour of individuals, and assume less about them, than used to be acceptable in pre-war days. As a result, as will be seen, the commitment of all branches of government to expenditure on research has survived and, indeed, increased, irrespective of economic crises or political philosophies.

When research has been published, either directly or through media interpretation, it has helped to build people's knowledge of what is going on, so that they can make more balanced judgements about what they are told by individual journalists, politicians or pressure groups. At its best, research can stimulate public debate about issues at a higher level than was ever possible before.

In commerce, where companies have had to face increasing competition, their success has depended more and more on being able to woo their customers effectively, which in turn has depended on knowing the subtleties of their customers' wants better than their competitors do. Had it not been for market research, the inefficient sellers' market which obtained immediately after the war might have continued much longer than it did. Market research was instrumental in placing the consumer firmly in the centre of the picture, and thus bringing about the development of the new disciplines of marketing.

Increasingly sophisticated research has, over the years, led marketing companies and their advertising agencies to understand the attitudes that motivate consumers, and how their usage and purchase of products fits into their lives; to understand them as people, not as merely the end link in a distribution chain. It has thus contributed to developing the expertise of a wide range of professionals – product designers, marketers, retailers, advertising executives and many others – thereby increasing the precision and efficiency with which marketing is done. Companies which cut back their research spend in a recession, as many did in the mid-1970s, came to regret it, and never repeated the mistake.

In all these areas, public sector and commercial, market research has a better record than other methods, and is therefore increasingly valued, in spite of having a lower profile than some other forms of information (such as the daily print and broadcast media) and for the same reason: it is (if done properly) objective, it does not seek to dramatise, it is reliable, and in these ways it directly serves the interests of those who commission it.

Market research in Britain is a post-war success story. Some claim not to understand it. Others refuse to believe its findings – especially if they differ from their own beliefs. Many grumble about its cost, even while, at the same time, they may be spending twenty times as much on the advertising campaign which the research is monitoring. But, over the years, more and more have come to rely on it.

Today there are few manufacturing companies of any substance, or retailers, media houses or advertising agencies, government departments, public bodies or academic institutions which do not, in some way at least, integrate research into their decision-making processes. It is not confined any more to 'markets', if indeed it ever was (although nobody has been able to find a better phrase for it). Corporate activities, services as well as goods; health, housing, employment and other social needs; the planning of our towns and cities; the financial world, the arts, sports and leisure pursuits; indeed everything that affects people's lives as citizens or families can be and is touched in some way by what we know as 'market research'.

The luncheon club that first met on November 5th, 1946, was the start of what later was to become the Market Research Society. For the successful and sophisticated research industry which has since developed, and for the quality and integrity of the product which it provides for its ever-broadening circle of users, this was an event of seminal importance.

This book traces the history of that development over the last fifty years, showing how market research has become an industry serving other industries and businesses, and the part it has played in the social and economic development of Britain.

At the same time, it is a celebration of the Market Research Society, whose 50th anniversary this is, and recognises its unique role in promoting professionalism, encouraging training and skill development, setting and monitoring standards, and generally helping to establish market research as a valued discipline which is respected and trusted all over the world.

The New Enfranchisement

The twentieth century, in spite of all its faults, can be seen as the one in which most people in the West have achieved a genuine independence for the first time. In Britain, it was not until the first half of the century that people acquired full *political* freedom, in the shape of all citizens irrespective of sex or race having the vote, together with freedom of *information* in the shape of a free press, choice of reading and listening matter and lack of censorship. But freedom is a three-legged stool. Up to the end of the second world war, it could be argued that the third leg – *economic* freedom – was still (for most people) largely missing. Economic freedom requires success, with the spreading of wealth and disposable incomes to ever wider circles. But it requires something more. It is fuelled by, and inevitably accompanied by, the enfranchisement of people *as consumers.* With the freedom to choose and the power to buy comes the influence of being listened to. Increasingly, in such a climate, the successful product or service is the one whose provider has taken the trouble to find out what his customers really want. To begin with, they may hardly know themselves, but gradually, as they get used to their economic power, they gain confidence and enter into a relationship with producers: there is "evolution of the dialogue... between the manufacturer (and service agencies) and the consumer", as Mary Goodyear has put it. This process started seriously in the post-war years in Britain and most of Europe (somewhat earlier in America), and is maturing: it is at various stages of development in many other parts of the world, in some cases (e.g. the 'tiger' economies) catching up very fast. Market research is a principal vehicle, mechanism and accompaniment of this process of 'economic enfranchisement', wherever it occurs.

Put like this, the name '*market* research' often seems something of a misnomer. It suggests a rather passive activity – studying a 'market' as one might study a cadaver laid out on a slab. It seems to put the consumer in the position of an object to be looked at, rather than (preferably) as an influential partner in a dialogue. Also, it is not a very satisfactory portmanteau description of the huge variety of activities that it in fact encompasses.

However, the name has stuck, and there seems little we can do about it, because it has simply not been possible to find a better. It has not been for want of trying. Sir Harold Wilson, when he was President of the Market Research Society in 1979, commented in his speech at the annual luncheon that 'market research' was inappropriately named, and should more properly be described as 'attitude research', because "politics is not a market"; he also implied (according to the report of his speech in the Society's Newsletter) that in what he termed the 'social sphere' there was "some conflict of perspective between the activities of fact-finding and attitude measurement on broad important society issues and the rather narrow label we bear".

The Market Research Society has considered on a number of occasions whether it should change its name, and at one point the Society's Newsletter held a competition. There were only a few entries, none thought 'very compelling', and the Newsletter commented that either the issue was not a very burning one, or the problem was too difficult. The candidates were:

- The Demological Society
- The Institute of Information Technologists
- The Social Research Society
- The Marketing and Survey Research Society
- The Social and Marketing Research Society
- The British Social and Marketing Research Society

The difficulty is that market research is a bundle of techniques which has expanded ('exploded' might be a better word) in both scope and method since the first adoption of the term. In the beginning, market research (as brought over from America in the 1920s and 1930s) was undoubtedly about 'markets', and largely driven by the requirements of advertising. The Journal of Marketing (vol XII) produced the following definition:

> Market Research may be defined as 'the gathering, recording and analysing of all facts about problems relating to the transfer and sale of goods and services from producer to consumer'.

But by the time of the Society's foundation, post-war, such a definition was already out of date. The instruments were being used to serve government as well as markets. And 'facts' soon became too limiting, as commercial interests of all kinds, not merely producers of manufactured goods (and not to mention government), became concerned with understanding behaviour, attitudes and responses to communication.

There were many who wanted to change the name to The Survey Research Society, on the grounds that what distinguishes its professional membership is expertise in gathering information by sample surveys (whether in 'markets' or not). But this again has always proved too limiting. Sampling of people and asking them questions is indeed the core discipline, but, as Gerald Goodhardt wrote in the Newsletter in 1979:

> ... at the same time as the growth in non-commercial uses of survey methods we have also had a growth of non-survey market research and developments in what is, perhaps, more properly called *marketing* research: the scientific study of all aspects of marketing over and above the collection of facts about markets; sales analysis, desk research, academic interest.

New technology since then has opened up other toolkits: database management, simulation experiments, scanners in retail stores, all kinds of computer-based analytical techniques. There is no simple phrase which encompasses all this.

We are stuck with 'market research', because everybody is used to it. Derek Martin, when Chairman of AMSO (the Association of Market Survey Organisations, the premier suppliers' trade association in Britain collectively responsible for some 60% of the total UK MR turnover), in his speech at AMSO's 1995 AGM, set market research in its modern context as information provider:

> No manager at any level in a corporation assumes that they can do without research to help them make decisions on many aspects of their business. Whether it is what we sometimes too narrowly define as market research is another matter. Taking advice from IT consultants, management of change consultants, re-engineering or any of the multitude of advice-givers is an everyday experience, and frequently a rather high-profile one for the givers and receivers of the advice. Market research performs its role in a wide spectrum of activities, sometimes with the high profile of the consultant, but also frequently as part of the ongoing stream of management information from many sources, and the analysis and interpretation of it.

The Growing Profession

We have already noted how the Market Research Society started with a handful of people meeting for a monthly lunch (there will be more about these pioneers in the next chapter). As one of them, Mark Abrams, said (in a 1978 interview): "we didn't really have any professional objectives, except that we liked to meet each other, talk about what we were doing." Six years or so later, it was decided to turn it into a proper professional society. By 1950 the numbers had risen to 90, and the following table shows how the total has risen, give or take some fluctuations:

1955	216
1965	1,599
1975	2,586
1985	4,829
1995	ca 6,000

Harry Henry (another of the original founders) said in a speech to the inaugural meeting of the Dutch Market Research Society in 1963:

> You will be interested to know that the graph of membership of the British Market Research Society, plotted semi-logarithmically, is an almost perfect straight line. I have been able to calculate from this that if the present trend continues, in fifty years' time the membership of the Market Research Society of Great Britain will be equal to the whole population of the United Kingdom. Frankly, I welcome this as it looks like giving a final answer to the problem of how to deal with 'don't knows'.
>
> *Harry Henry: 'Some Observations on the Market Research Society of Great Britain', The Hague, 1963*

In 1946/47 (the authorities seem to disagree about the precise year), as Henry puts it, "the whole operation was extremely informal since we all knew each other extremely well, we were not at that time concerned with the niceties of constitution and procedure". By 1995, the Society had acquired (as listed in the Yearbook):

- an educational Diploma (besides providing the new National Vocational Qualifications or NVQs);
- a Code of Conduct, to which all members must adhere;
- five serial publications, three annual publications, and a wide range of occasional publications;
- an annual Conference;
- an "extensive programme of courses and seminars that cater for all levels of staff and encompass a wide range

of topics", together with evening meetings, lectures, luncheons and social events throughout the year;
- five categories of membership (soon to be increased);
- a Research Development Foundation;
- a President, Chairman and two Vice-chairmen, together with a Secretary/Treasurer and a nine-strong Council;
- a Director-General;
- a Managing Editor of Publications, with three staff;
- a Head of Membership Services, with one staff;
- a Head of Training, Education and Conference Services, with three staff;
- a Head of Marketing and Membership Development, with two staff;
- a Manager of Field Activities and Interviewer Membership (including the interviewer identity card scheme);
- a Financial Controller, with two staff;
- an Office Manager (also the DG's assistant), and a receptionist;
- twelve standing Committees;
- eleven special interest groups;
- eight regional branches;
- an Award Structure of eight different medals and awards.

And the total annual income of the Market Research Society, just £345 (according to Harry Henry) in 1948/9 ("the first year for which I have found detailed records still available"), had become, for the year ending 31st March 1995, £2,595,993.

And this professional growth has run in parallel with the emergence of an industrial structure. At the start of our period, in 1946, outside the government service, there were only a small handful of companies specialising in market research, modest in size and all privately owned. By 1996, market research had acquired the full structure and appurtenances of a serio industry. There are today no less than ten research companies based in Britain, not including Nielsen, with annual turnovers from their UK operations alone of more than ten million pounds. Two of these are plc, four are owned by large plc groups (WPP, United News & Media), one is American-owned and two under French ownership. Six out of the ten feature among the top ten research companies in the European Union.

How the Market Research Spend Has Grown

Until AMSO began to collect and publish turnover statistics in 1977, it is impossible to form a good estimate of research turnover. We can presume that, after the war, commercial expenditure started again more or less from scratch. Louis Moss tells us, in his history of the Government Social Survey, that its annual budget was put up from £63,000 to £133,000 per annum in 1951 (only to be cut back again to £112,000 by Winston Churchill on his election). Most commercial work was private, within the consumer goods companies which needed it. BMRB, the first independent agency, had (according to its historian John Downham) a turnover of £65,300 in 1946, which trebled to £181,500 by 1956. On this evidence, it seems unlikely that total expenditure on research can have averaged more than £500,000, if that, during the first ten post-war years, apart from the Nielsen retail audit business and the BBC's own audience research.

Up to the 1970s, few figures are quoted. There is an estimate of £5 million for 1963; this comes after the establishment of the National Readership Survey and the TAM television audience measurement system. By 1973, AMSO (founded 1968) had begun to provide estimates. The first serious attempt to estimate the turnover of the industry was made by Martin Simmons (one of the founders of Gordon Simmons Research Ltd) in a specially commissioned survey which was reported in the Society's Journal in July 1978.

Simmons took AMSO turnover figures from 1973 and inflated them by estimates for non-AMSO agencies based on their number and turnover ranges as quoted in the MRS *Yearbook*. This revealed that in 1969 turnover stood in the range £14m-17m. By 1973 this had doubled, to £31m, but then showed minimal increase during the years of recession: £34m in 1974, £36m in 1975, £43m in 1976 and £55m in 1977. Simmons comments:

> Research expenditure in real terms, adjusted for inflation, grew by nearly half (47%) between 1969 and 1973. In 1977, despite its recent recovery, the industry was still below the 1973 real level, having been set back at least half a decade.
>
> During the recession period of 1974 and 1975 retail prices rose by 44% whereas research turnover increased by only 16%. Consequently, the industry declined by 1975 in real terms to four-fifths of the 1973 level.
>
> Since 1975, research turnover at current prices has increased by half (53%) whilst retail prices rose by one third. The real growth during that period was 17%.

This is illustrated by the following charts.

Figure 1: AMSO Turnover, 1978-1994

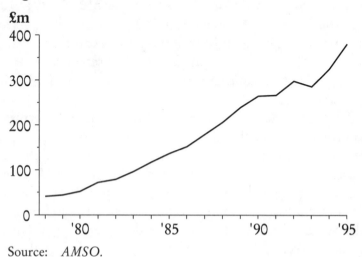

Source: *AMSO.*

Figure 2:   Real Research Growth UK, 1973-1994
Indexed to 1973 = 100

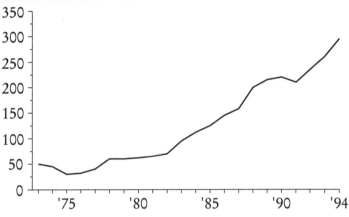

Source: *AMSO.*

From 1978 onwards we have properly collated statistics for the AMSO companies. Figure 1 shows how they (AMSO only) increase year by year from £41m (1978) to £325m (1994). If the 'approximately 60%' formula is applied, the total turnover estimate ranges from about £60m (1978) to more than £500m (1994). In 1995, the AMSO audited turnover increased by a further 10% (in real terms) to £380 million. In this year, for the first time, the turnover for ABMRC (the Association of British Market Research Companies, which includes most of the remaining smaller companies which are not members of AMSO) has been estimated accurately, and can be added to the AMSO figure. The ABMRC estimate is £144 million, and combines with the AMSO figure to produce a combined total for the two main industry supply bodies of £515 million for the 1995 year. If Nielsen, IRI, IMS (the medical statistics company) and other consultancies not in the two trade bodies are added, the total estimate for the market research industry of Great Britain in the 1995 year amounts to something well in excess of £600 million.

The graph is relatively flat only in the 1978-1980 period (the 'Winter of Discontent') and 1990-91 (the recession years). The 1992-93 dip was due to the resignation from AMSO of AC Nielsen, which took some £42m out of the total.

That the growth was real is shown by Figure 2. Derek Martin has modelled the AMSO statistics against inflation from 1978 (the first year of consolidated statistics) and also projected them backwards (based on the Simmons estimates from the turnovers of non-member companies during those years, a method he acknowledges as 'somewhat crude'). The resulting graph reveals a real drop during the serious recession years of the mid-70s, recovery by 1978 to about the level of 1973, little real change until 1982, and staggering real growth thereafter, broken only by the 1990-1 recession (paradoxically, the defection of Nielsen from AMSO in 1993 enhanced the growth rate of the remaining members).

Where the Growth Has Come From

The source of the business is as interesting as the increase in value, as is demonstrated in the table below, which compares the breakdown in AMSO figures between 1984 and 1995.

Percent unless otherwise indicated

	1984	1995
Total AMSO turnover	£117m	£380m
Consumer goods		
Food & soft drinks	23	13
Health/beauty aids	8	6
Household durables	4	1
Alcoholic drinks	4	4
Household products	3	4
Tobacco	2	1
Total	**44**	**29**
Other Clients		
Media	10	9
Advertising agencies	7	3
Public services/government[1]	7	13
Pharmaceutical	5	6
Vehicles	4	7
Industrial/business	3	6
Financial	4	7
Retailers	4	5
Tourism/travel	3	4
Agricultural	1	..
Oil companies	1	1
Total	**49**	**61**
Others[2]	**6**	**11**

Notes: [1] Public service/government figures refer to that which is subcontracted to AMSO companies and does not include the major expenditure for government handled by OPCS and SCPR (see Chapter 3). The 1995 figure includes 'utilities'.

[2] Including other AMSO subcontracted.

In the last decade there has been a notable shift in profile away from consumer goods companies to other services and interests. Consumer goods are still the main source of research revenue, but their relative importance has sharply declined, as have the advertising and media services dependent on them: in contrast, other sectors have grown, especially cars, financial services, pharmaceutical services and retailers.

International Growth

International research, defined as research conducted by UK research agencies by subcontracting to, and supervising, agencies in other countries (including the overseas subsidiaries of UK agencies), has also shown remarkable growth particularly in the last decade. By 1978 the international research conducted by AMSO companies appeared to have reached £3m, about 8% of total turnover. By 1989 (when AMSO started formally recording this component) it had reached £36m (15% of turnover). In 1995 it had grown to £103m (27%); more than a quarter of all research done by AMSO agencies is therefore international, i.e. subcontracted overseas, and the proportion is still increasing.

The essential element which has characterised British international research, and is responsible for its leading position, has been the combination of centralised design and control within the UK with multi-country co-ordination (i.e. fieldwork done by local agencies under the central control). British companies were helped in developing this service by the fact of speaking English, which made them a natural 'conduit' for American multi-nationals into Europe and farther afield. Most American research companies, even today, are concerned much more with the internal markets in the United States than with markets outside. In addition, many British companies set up subsidiaries in other countries at an early stage: for example, companies such as Research International (formerly owned by Unilever) have subsidiaries throughout Europe; Research

International, Millward Brown and NOP have companies in the USA. The MBL Group has companies throughout the Middle East, Asia and South East Asia, and so on. Advertising agencies like J Walter Thompson, by the 1960s, were setting up research subsidiaries such as JMRB in Japan and IMRB in India, which later became operationally relatively independent of their ad agency parent. In more recent years, many UK research companies have formed cross-country alliances with like-minded companies abroad – another way in which British influence spreads through the world-wide industry – and certain local consortia, such as the SRG Group in Asia and South East Asia (formed in the 1970s and since acquired by Nielsen) were from the start (and to some extent still are) managed by senior executives trained in Britain.

ESOMAR, the European Society for Opinion and Marketing Research, was founded in 1948, two years after the British Market Research Society. British members were influential in ESOMAR from the beginning, and the ESOMAR International Code of Practice bears many resemblances to the MRS one. Of the 24 ESOMAR Presidents to date, six have been British; but it is significant that four of these (Henry Durant, A. Graeme Cranch, Michael Lyster and Paul Berent) held office before 1970, and are thus counted among the first eleven: just one instance of how Britain in those early days led the development of research in Europe, but has dropped back to a more proportionate level as the profession has matured elsewhere. Today, out of a total ESOMAR world-wide membership (in some 80 countries) of over 2900, the United Kingdom accounts for 396 (in the 1994/5 year), or about 14% – this excludes a number of members of British origin who are working permanently in other countries.

By any standard, this growth and international spread, from a handful of people to a multi-million pound world-wide industry, is an achievement in a mere fifty years. It deserves an explanation. In the rest of this book, we shall be looking at how it has happened, and how it has affected all our lives.

2

Research and the Changes of the Last Fifty Years

Since market research is the business of understanding people, we should expect it to reflect closely the changes that have taken place in society during the last five decades.

The growth described in Chapter 1 has been strong, but not uniform: it has occurred in spurts, with pauses in between, just like the economy in which it is embedded. The growth itself has brought significant operational changes with it: from cottage industry to stock exchange listings and take-over targets; from labour-intensive businesses to ones requiring capital investment drawn in by new technology. At the same time, certain things have remained constant: a principled code of conduct, a commitment to high standards of objectivity, and a sense of responsibility to both informants and clients. All of these have continued, resisting all temptations, to mark out the research business from others involved in marketing.

This sense of professional integrity has been arguably the most important achievement of the Market Research Society, founded at the start of the period we are considering.

For all these reasons, the best way to understand the development of market research during the past fifty years is to set it in its historical context, so that one can see the influences to which it has had to respond. We will attempt to do this now in general terms; in the following chapters we shall be looking, in the same sort of way, at specific aspects of the research business in more detail.

History is messy, and does not fall neatly into discrete sections. However, we can divide the period we are considering roughly into four *phases*, which more or less represent the spirit of the time (which market research and the uses made of it reflect). We propose to call these phases as follows:

1. *Recovery and Consensus:* roughly the period from the end of the war to the Treaty of Rome, 1945-57.

2. *The New Freedom:* ending with the miners' strike, 1958-73.

3. *The Past catches up with us:* ending as we emerged from the second recession in ten years, 1974-82.

4. *Experiments with Enterprise and the New Uncertainty:* 1983 to date.

The Appendix gives a detailed timetable of events, and how research fits in.

PHASE 1: Recovery and Consensus, 1945-57

The chrysalis stage – 1946-52

After the end of the war, Britain still had a pre-war economic structure and social attitudes. The long period of austerity meant that the 'seller's market' was maintained for some time; shortages and rationing, lack of disposable incomes, and the need to give priority to exports all combined to delay recovery. But by the early 1950s the feeling had changed: greater prosperity and economic confidence based on the welfare state, a final recognition of the end of empire after the Suez fiasco, an accelerating change to a buyer's market and the growth of the 'marketing culture' in consumer goods companies, the start of rebellion against traditional social conventions and modes of thought.

At the end of the war the UK was essentially bankrupt. The economy had only been kept going by Lend-Lease, and that came suddenly to an end in 1945. New US loans and Marshall Aid were a welcome relief, but were not enough to prevent a series of sterling and balance of payments crises, with a 30% devaluation in 1949. Stop-Go became the norm for economic management. At the same time there was a new Labour government with aspirations to change what had been wrong with society before the war. They wanted the UK to remain a world power: one of the top trading nations, with its sterling area and its commonwealth. But they also wanted to introduce 'the new Jerusalem' of a modern welfare state. The resources to do all of this were not really there. Compromises were unavoidable, and meant that the economy, and market research too, had little scope to grow during these initial years.

Britain was still dominated by the traditional industries of the 19th century – shipbuilding, coal, steel, rail, textiles and utilities. Most of them were nationalised in the late 1940s, which brought some 2 million new workers into a protected public sector, itself greatly expanded for managing the war effort. But little could be afforded on investment in modern plant and machinery, and it was assumed too easily that public ownership, freed from profit-hungry entrepreneurs, would automatically guarantee the best service to the public.

Meanwhile the need to give priority to exports led to controls and allocation of raw materials for manufacturers in the private sector; again, investment suffered. There was also a shortage of manpower, as 2 million people were still in the armed forces in 1950. The result of all this was that the seller's market went on for a long time in the UK. Most of industry worked on the basis of make-and-sell. Marketing departments were a rarity until the mid-1950s, and there seemed little need to spend money on challenging the maker's accepted wisdom about what the public wanted.

The seller's market in international trade lasted only two or three years, and although British exports regained their 1938 level in 1946, they did not do very well in share of world trade after that. This period was the beginning of a long refrain of complaints about designs unsuitable for overseas markets, high prices, long delivery dates and inadequate marketing/service organisations. It is perhaps not too surprising that manufacturers, more concerned with supply than demand in their home market, showed signs of weakness in marketing and market research abroad.

However, the public accepted the seller's market and the need for rationing and austerity with what might seem today a surprising equanimity. There was a great feeling of consensus; everyone wanted a fair society. People's attitudes still seemed to be governed by traditional thinking, with a strong element of complacency and romantic idealism – 'we won the war', a major world power, the glories of empire, the inevitability of the social class structure, leadership of the industrial revolution, a great trading nation, and so on. The traditional family was seen as the basis of a civilised society, and the ending of the war meant that families could be reunited. Values could again be handed down from parents to children.

This consensus was shared by politicians, many of whom had worked together in the wartime coalition government. The one new element was a determination to eliminate the unfairness of pre-war mass unemployment and poverty in an otherwise quite prosperous economy. The Labour government's major achievement was the setting up of the welfare state. It covered 'full' employment, social security, health, education and housing. An important aspect was that of universality of benefits, a reaction against crude methods of means-testing before the war. Most of the costs were under-estimated and there was a certain amount of folie de grandeur; but the patterns were set here for the state's contribution to society for the next fifty years. The new Conservative government of 1951 kept the main structures of the welfare state, on the grounds of both equity and public opinion. It was clearly a very popular institution; so maybe there seemed little need to probe people's feelings about it too deeply.

Market research, during these early post-war years, can be seen as in a sort of chrysalis state: the basic methods established, endorsed by the wartime experience, but still with very few practitioners, and, outside a handful of large advertisers, generally unknown. Most company executives, if they thought about it at all, were as likely as not to do so with suspicion and alarm.

Market research techniques had been brought to the UK already in the 1920s and 1930s, mostly in the service of a few advertising agencies (especially J Walter Thompson and the London Press Exchange) and their clients, mainly to measure aspects of consumer behaviour. Some media surveys were being done, and the BBC had set up its own regular listener survey. Henry Durant had brought the Gallup poll to Britain in 1937 and continued running it throughout the war, and Tom Harrison and Charles Madge had established Mass-Observation.

During the war, the usefulness of these sample survey techniques was recognised by the government, who employed them initially to assess morale and later to provide information about people's basic needs and responses to wartime conditions and government communications. Thus, at the start of peace, there was already in place a tried and tested toolkit of sample survey methods which emerging industry could, if it wished, pick up and use. There were a small number of trained practitioners, some returning from war service elsewhere and some who had continued to apply these methods in the Government Social Survey or in those few private organisations, like BMRB, which had continued in business serving government requirements.

Under their guidance, market research quietly came together, from a collection of (sometimes maverick) entrepreneurs into a coherent, professional discipline. Standards were set; the values and correct use of research began to be promoted, and its development encouraged. In all this, the most crucial factor was the foundation of the Market Research Society.

Foundation of the Society

Twenty-three individuals met on November 5th 1946, in the offices of the London Press Exchange, and started a luncheon club. Some of them had been involved in market research activities since before the war; some had returned from service elsewhere, whilst others had been fulfilling the wartime government's need for surveys.

Twenty-Three Founding Fathers and Mothers of the MRS

Dr M.A. Abrams	*Managing Director, Research Services*
T. Cauter	*Manager, British Market Research Bureau*
Mrs L. Chappell	*Manager, Market Research, W.S.Crawford*
W.N. Coglan	*Managing Director, Sales Research Services*
Mrs D. Darling	*Senior Research Officer, London Press Exchange*
I.W. Desbrow	*Senior Research Officer, London Press Exchange*
Dr H.W. Durant	*Director, British Institute of Public Opinion*
O. Ellefson	*Research Director, Foote, Cone & Belding*
Mrs R. Glass	*Director, Association for Planning & Regional Reconstruction*
J. Haydock	*Information Manager, Research, British Export Trade Organisation*
H. Henry	*Manager, Market Research Department, Colman, Prentiss & Varley*
A.G.Jones	*Director of Research, British Export Trade Organisation*
W.F.F. Kemsley	*Surveys Branch, Ministry of Food*
F. Lambert	*Market Research Director, Co-operative Wholesale Society*
Miss J.M. Ledgard	*Head of Presentation Department, British Market Research Bureau*

A.G. Lewis	*Senior Research Officer, British Institute of Public Opinion*
A.P. McAnally	*Head of Research Department, FC Pritchard, Wood & Partners*
C. McIvor	*Senior Research Officer, Social Surveys*
T.D. Morison	*Director, Mather & Crowther (representing A.Graeme Cranch, Director, Mather & Crowther)*
L. Moss	*Director, Government Social Survey*
H. Munt	*Market Research Manager, Lintas*
C.P. Scarborough	*Research Officer, Institute of Incorporated Practitioners in Advertising*
R.J.E. Silvey	*Director of Listener Research, British Broadcasting Corporation.*

Harry Henry recalls that no less than eight of these founder members (Mark Abrams, Tom Cauter, Henry Durant, Jack Haydock, Louis Moss, Dick Desbrow, Ruth Glass and himself) had all been students at the London School of Economics. The LSE still had a reputation for radicalism in those days, and no doubt this bias, if perceived at all, would not have helped to endear the new discipline to conservatively-minded businessmen.

It is proper to give the roll-call of these twenty-three founding fathers (and mothers) and their then occupations, not only because they deserve to be remembered, but also to illustrate the range of interests they represented (as shown above).

There is certainly no record of political affiliations with the exception of Mark Abrams, whose work for the Labour Party began early and continued with Research Services until MORI later took it over. Be that as it may, there continued to be a recurrent LSE connection. Five of the first six Chairmen of the Society were LSE men (Durant, Abrams, Haydock, Cauter, Moss); so was Andrew Elliott, the ninth Chairman; so also, after a gap of twelve years, were six Chairman who held office in the 1970s (Bert de Vos, John Parfitt, Gerald de Groot,

Frank Teer, Bryan Bates and John Barter). And after incorporation in 1953 the Society appointed five non-executive Presidents who were ex-LSE: Sir Arthur Bowley (1953-55), Lord Piercy (1955-60), Sir Ronald Edwards (1965-69), Sir Claus Moser (1969-74), and Sir Ralf Dahrendorf (1981-83).

David Pickard (Chairman in 1958-9) comments:

> There is little doubt in my mind that at least up until the mid-50s, Mark Abrams and Henry Durant 'were' market research in most people's minds. Henry held this position partly because his work was always in the public eye, partly because of the Gallup association (the best known name of the lot), and partly because he was obviously a shrewd commercial operator, running a successful and growing business. Mark's standing was intellectual and political – he was in active demand, through his Labour Party contacts, with ministers and senior civil servants during the ferment of rebuilding society that went on from 1945 onwards. He also enjoyed strong links with the academic world, in the States as much as in this country. Henry's would have been the best known name among the general public, Mark's among 'Top People'.
>
> *MRS Newsletter interview*

Each member paid an annual subscription of 3 guineas for a jealously guarded membership. The founders' view at the time was that membership was unlikely to exceed twenty-five, since the Society already encompassed "all existing research talent". *Advertiser's Weekly* welcomed the new Society with the hope that a society "formed of men of like mind" should "develop the passionless atmosphere of the laboratory and reveal as worthless the wishful thinkers and charlatans".

Harry Henry (Some Observations on the Market Research Society of Great Britain, speech to the Dutch Market Research Society at The Hague, 1963) noted that a driving motive for the founders was the need they felt to present a united front in order to protect the fledgling discipline, which was by no means universally accepted or understood:

Market research was an extremely new and very much an untried discipline. We desperately needed to get together to exchange information, to work together, to learn our business together. But there was more to it than that. Market research was a very long way from being the accepted tool of business that it is today. We needed to be able to present our credentials to the business world, to speak together on behalf of this infant science, and we judged – and I think rightly – that a Society would help us in this. Those of you who are of my generation will remember the hostility with which the claims on behalf of our techniques were met, and will appreciate what was in our minds.

In its early days the new Society continued to meet as a monthly luncheon club with invited speakers. It was, and has remained, a society of individuals practising research and not a trade association. From the beginning, an aim was to provide a forum through which members could express views and keep in touch with one another and with industry developments; perhaps more importantly, it provided a vehicle for controlling the style and direction of these developments.

The butterfly emerges – 1952-57

From approximately 1952, the post-war austerity began to end. People began to feel gradually more prosperous, and to look for greater choice. Incomes grew, and there was a sharp increase in expenditure on consumer durables. Economic recovery moved into a higher gear: industrial production grew, the balance of payments had a good spell, rationing was finally ended and 300,000 houses a year were built. Harold MacMillan felt able to say in 1957: "... most of our people have never had it so good". The seller's market ended, competition grew and the need for market research became much more pressing. According to Peter Chisnall:

> Consumer products were the first to experience the decline of a sellers' market and the strong development of a buyers'

market. These conditions were world-wide, moreover, and from the early 1950s, companies became increasingly aware of the need to know more about the preferences, prejudices and buying habits of those who bought their products and services. The days of easy trading were numbered, and no company could expect to survive for very long if customers' needs were not adequately met.

Consumer Behaviour, 3ʳᵈ edition, 1994

As disposable incomes increased, people began to explore new ideas, and rebel against what now came to seem constricting traditions. Up to the 1950s, culture in the UK had reflected the pre-war shape of society. Novels and plays used traditional forms. Mass media and entertainments predominated: cinema audiences, national newspaper circulation and attendance at football matches were at their peak. The BBC reorganised its radio services into Third/Home/Light to match the traditional social classes and resumed its rather sedate television broadcasting in 1946.

From about 1953 there were signs of real change. Kingsley Amis' Lucky Jim, John Osborne's Look Back in Anger and the emerging following of rock music and Elvis Presley suggested that tradition and deference were about to be modified. ITV was launched in 1955 to challenge the BBC's monopoly and style.

There was a culture change in market research too. The prediction that the Society's membership would never exceed 25 was soon overturned. By 1950 it had reached 90, and it was then decided to seek a more formal structure, by way of incorporation as a professional body. In 1953, the Board of Trade agreed to the Society becoming a company limited by guarantee. In 1957 (by which time membership had risen to over 300) the Society was recognised by the Board of Trade as an organisation with its own code of professional standards and rules, and allowed to drop 'Limited' from its title.

An early concern of the Society was to devise and adopt standards of good practice, which would distinguish market research as a respectable and professional business and separate it in people's minds from more dubious activities which could be confused with it. The hostility to which Harry Henry refers could come from many directions; research was (and still is) vulnerable on many sides.

In the first place, it was essential to explain the discipline to the general public. Market research depends uniquely on the goodwill of ordinary people who are contacted by interviewers and requested to give up some of their time to answering questions which may well seem strange, if not downright intrusive. They have to be reassured that the procedure is honest and above board, even when its purpose may not be made known to them. Above all, they have to know that they are free to refuse without being pressured, that the information they give will be confidential, that they will not be identified as individuals to anyone else (including the research sponsor), and that this interview is not a cover for trying to sell them something. This practice of 'sugging' (Selling Under the Guise of research) began to appear in the mid-fifties, and has bedevilled genuine market research ever since. There is no way of directly stopping it; the best that can be done is to try to prevent the irritations which may be caused by such deception from poisoning public attitudes to genuine research, by making the difference as clear as possible.

It was also necessary to convince clients that they were being treated honestly. Survey research is difficult to police. The buyers of the information have to be assured that the interviewers have really gone out on cold, wet evenings and persuaded a quota of persons previously unknown to them (and perhaps living in an area they would never normally visit) to answer their 30-minute questionnaire, instead of staying at home in the warm and making it up. Such dangers became apparent at a very early stage, and quality control methods to combat them were soon demanded from the new Society. Buyers also need to know that the information which finds its way to them in graphs and tables, presentations and reports is accurately compiled from the survey done, without distortions or omissions to make the results more palatable and without relevant information being concealed, and that the research agency has behaved properly as a confidential partner. There were obvious opportunities for the charlatan in many of the research techniques which had been in use since before the war; it was vital that controls should be in place, so that research users could be reassured.

The first members of the Society faced these problems straight away; undoubtedly, the wartime experience had helped to cement in their minds the importance both of statistical accuracy and of keeping research acceptable to the public. A brochure was produced, which became the first standard code of practice for the profession in 1954 (it has been revised and updated several times since). Adherence to the Code is a condition of Society membership, which in turn is a sign that the person to whom you are entrusting your research project works according to accepted professional practice. The original code dealt, in four main sections, with the rights of clients, responsibilities to informants, reporting standards, and the sanctions available (expulsion from membership or demotion) if a member is found to fall short of professional standards (as far as we are aware, this has hardly ever happened, but this probably matters little: what matters is that members value the good opinion of their peers and the protection given by the Code, and do their best to conform with it). The Code of Practice, if nothing else, justifies the existence of the Market Research Society; it is continually being revised to respond to new conditions and types of research, most recently 'mystery shopping' and databases (discussed more fully in Chapter 8).

Another early task the Society undertook was to try to formulate agreed social class classifications. A committee was set up in 1948-9 (with one eye on the 1951 Census) to "obtain some measure of agreement between the differing definitions now widely used". Some of these were pre-war and, of course, now radically out of date. For example, the system used by the

International Broadcasting Corporation in 1937 read as follows (besides some detail about occupations):

Class A: Have at least one maid; telephone; medium-priced car; detached or semi-detached house of more expensive kind in suburbs, with 8-10 rooms... or comfortable central flat in 'good district'. Children at private school or good secondary or grammar school...

Class B: Regular maid rare and usually no telephone; occasional domestic help; second-hand or cheap car; detached or semi-detached house, 5-8 rooms with garden..., flat in inner suburbs, or cottage dwelling in less congested parts of town. Children usually at secondary school...

Class C: No maid or telephone; occasional domestic help; house reasonably well-kept; house and street definitely superior in character to D; 4-5 room house; 3-5 room flat; house semi-detached in suburbs or more commonly in row; small garden in less congested areas; occasional motor-cycle and, very rarely, second-hand car; good push bicycle. Children usually at elementary school...

Class D: No telephone or maid. No paid domestic help. Cheaper council houses or older houses in row of tenements; 2-4 rooms. No garden as a rule. Poorer working class areas, excluding only the worst slum quarters...

How can you possibly suggest that we're incompatible, Daphne, seeing that we're in the same socio-demographic grouping?

This classification system is interesting in its reliance on perceived 'lifestyle' and therefore on the observations that would be made by interviewers on the spot. There was no separation, even in Class D, between white and blue-collar workers. The new MRS committee accepted that some degree of subjectivity is unavoidable, but proposed to base a system mainly on occupation, "the grouping being so arranged as to provide for different social levels within the same broad occupation" (eg the difference, for market research purposes, between an 'office worker' paid a monthly salary and one on a weekly wage). Three main groups were proposed, each with further subdivisions. The three groups were 'salaried and employers' (subdivided into proprietors of shops or businesses, professional and managerial, and salaried clerical workers), 'weekly wage earners' (with four subdivisions), and 'not gainfully employed' (with five subdivisions, one of which was 'housewives'). There was a further suggestion that this last group could also be classified by the job they used to do, if retired, or (if housewives) by the jobs of husbands or chief wage earners. Within 'salaried clerical workers', it was thought it might be helpful to make a further division by income ('£1,000 a year and over' versus 'under £1,000 a year').

If this proposal were ever adopted, it did not last long. By 1947, the Hulton Readership Survey and the IPA were defining social class in the A – E terms which have since become familiar, although the descriptions (as in this example from the 1955 Hulton Readership Survey) still seem somewhat condescending by today's standards:

	Pop. (%)	Typical Income	Typical Occupation
A. The Well-To-Do	4%	more than £1,300	Doctor/ headmaster of public school
B. The Middle Class	8%	£800-£1,300	Veterinary surgeon/ headmaster of smaller school
C. The Lower Middle Class	17%	£450-800	
D. The Working Class	64%	£250-£450	
E. The Poor	7%	less than £250	

Source: *Dawn Mitchell, 'Forty Years On', AMSO Annual Conference paper, 1995*

Dawn Mitchell comments that in terms of eligible occupations the distinction between headmasters of public schools and other headmasters seems quaint today. She notes also that the £1,300 annual income for As, indexed to current values, would today be worth only £17,550, which is below the *average* of current male earnings, an indication of how living standards have improved.

As the commercial climate was transformed, so were the opportunities for the new industry. Martin Simmons has described the climate at the time when the Society was born:

> At that time, there were only a dozen market research agencies in the country. Most were subsidiaries of advertising agencies whilst a few were run by successful entrepreneurs. Unlike today, those research agencies operated in a seller's market. There was little active promotion. Competitive tendering for assignments was

virtually unknown. Most research was ad hoc rather than syndicated, continuous services. The life of a research agency executive was dominated by data output which, in pre-computer days, was tedious, time-consuming and prone to error. This left relatively little time for interpretation and communication of research findings. Few user companies employed experienced executives for market research. Consequently they relied heavily on their advertising agencies who acted as middlemen with the research agencies.

Survey, June 1983

By 1957, the picture had changed markedly. As markets moved from seller to buyer, new ideas of 'marketing' were taking hold. Companies began to grasp the importance of understanding what the consumers *really* wanted; it could no longer be assumed to be the same as it had always been. Major consumer goods companies were setting up their own research departments, sometimes doing their own fieldwork; market research was regarded seriously by these companies as an aid to product development, advertising and merchandising, and above all to understanding their true competitive position in the market. The market research function was in some cases represented directly on the board.

Consumer panels were in place with the Attwood service (founded 1947), and competitors to Nielsen's retail audit (a pre-war survivor) were appearing. The first regular readership surveys had begun, and, with the introduction of commercial television in 1955, the first industry Joint Committee to measure it. New agencies were entering the market, among them MIL in 1956 and NOP in 1957; others followed quickly. Political opinion polling began to be taken seriously, supported by the press, and (so far) appeared to be reasonably accurate: the debacle of 1970 was still to come.

And finally, it was a time when new ideas began to be grafted onto the perception of research as primarily about statistical description. Users started to be interested in understanding attitudes and feelings; motivation research and the use of qualitative techniques began, not always with sufficient rigour. As Winston Fletcher puts it:

> It was the era of Dichter, Schwerin and Vance Packard's Hidden Persuaders; it was the era of the market research hucksters – brilliantly entrepreneurial, creative, self-publicist salesmen. It was an era of imaginative metaphors, sweeping generalisations, and gross over-simplifications
>
> *Newsletter, February 1981*

It is another tribute to the training and discipline put in place by the founders of the Society that the wilder excesses of these characters were curbed and a new toolkit labelled loosely 'qualitative research' was enabled to grow, within the framework of the same standards. This important development is covered more fully in Chapter 5.

But some aspects of market research were still relatively easy, more so than they are today. Interviewing was mostly done face-to-face, in homes, in the street, or after invitation to a hall; a limited amount was done by post, and virtually none by telephone, which relatively few possessed. Interviewing was seen as an attractive opportunity, especially for women whose children had reached school age or were otherwise off their hands; the hours might be a little unsocial, but they needed something they could fit flexibly into their ordinary lives:

> Market research had developed in a climate in which there was a limitless supply of middle class ladies willing to earn pin money through part-time interviewing. The public liked and respected them, and market research was generally (by 1954) regarded as an important and valued activity. Whatever the facts about relative levels of crime, there was less fear of crime 40 years ago: the door was opened, and the interviewer came in.
>
> *Dawn Mitchell, 'Forty Years On',*
> *AMSO Conference Paper, 1995*

In these years, the Society became preoccupied with the question of its membership, a matter which has continued to exercise it at regular intervals. It ties up with the deeper question: what sort of Society should this be? Michael Lyster, the Chairman in the 1957-58 year, describes the debate:

> At that time, as now, membership in the MRS was strictly on an individual basis. But I and other officers found ourselves being be-devilled by requests from certain members to involve the Society in matters which were really the concern of a trade organisation (such as AMSO, today) and not with a society of 'professional' individuals... It was, perhaps, not at all surprising that such requests for representation came up, because at that time there was no other society looking after market research interests in the UK. But such requests certainly put me and others in a considerable dilemma. How could the MRS – a society of individuals – possibly act effectively for, say, contracts between research institutes and their clients. At that time, the MRS 'statutes' really gave no help. Further, none of the officers had any time to deal with such matters as we were all in full-time employment.
>
> As a result of such approaches, David (Pickard) and I sat down to try and analyse out what exactly should the MRS be trying to do. Rather, we did not sit down at all! We met, if I recall correctly, in my office, in the evenings, for several weeks in succession and 'orbited' in arguments as to what exact form the MRS should best take in the future. Should it be a purely learned society (à la Royal Statistical Society)? Should it become a real professional society (in which some form of professional qualification might be called for, together with an examination structure)? Or should it become a body representing the interests of companies (institutes)? In which case, there would be little case for individual members at all – only corporate members.

What they came up with was to keep the MRS a society of professional *individuals*, which would be complemented (later) by the foundation of the trade associations, which have *corporate* membership: first AMSO in 1964 (generally representing the larger suppliers and with strict membership rules) and, 18 years later, ABMRC (a looser organisation comprising a larger number and wider range of smaller and specialist agencies). This has led to a creative tension between the two 'sides' which has unquestionably been of great benefit. The MRS has been able to concentrate on education, training and professional development, on techniques and methodology and professional ethics, leaving the development of business and generating of revenue to the agencies themselves, and the lobbying of helpful interests to the trade associations. At about the same time, the MRS, in order to avoid being put in the awkward position of recommending market research services to enquirers, began to circulate a list of organisations offering these services, which turned into the present annual Year Book.

The MRS had created the new profession at just the right time. By the end of this phase, it was more widely realised that the customer had to come first. The early, tentative uses of research had begun to reveal a world which was not always as expected. As the economy continued to grow, so did the research-based learning curve, and this in turn stimulated new ideas and created new opportunities for appealing to increasingly adventurous customers.

PHASE 2: The New Freedom, 1958-73

Expanding confidence

The 1960s were a period of rapid economic growth by UK standards, about a third higher than in the inter-war years and twice as fast as pre-1914. Real incomes rose steadily, inflation and unemployment were low. The 'affluent society' became a reality. Ownership of durables, TVs, cars, central heating and houses took off; telephone ownership grew from a very low base. Most markets grew comfortably, and there was a promise of a new era when in 1973 the UK finally joined the EEC. Harold Wilson's 'white heat of technological revolution' proved a touch premature in 1964, but there were marked product improvements in cars, synthetics, electrical and electronic goods, frozen foods, convenience foods and detergents. It was altogether a good environment for the coming of age of marketing and market research. There was a steady increase in marketing departments and brand managers.

Market research grew with its clients. In this period, most of the remaining companies which now form AMSO were founded: Marplan in 1959, AGB (1962), Taylor Nelson and Market Behaviour Limited (1965), Martin Hamblin and MORI (1969); there were many other smaller companies, some of which have now disappeared. The major industry media research surveys were established, and a new media research vehicle, the Target Group Index, which could link together media exposure and product use, was introduced by BMRB. In the political field, the first British election studies were conducted, and Butler and Stokes prophesied that in future Labour would be the 'natural party of government'.

Below the surface all was not quite so well. Many economic cracks were being papered over by government fine tuning. Stop-Go intensified; there were frequent balance of payments problems, sterling crises and in 1967 a devaluation of nearly 15%. Growth in the EEC and Japan was a good deal faster, and in particular growth in manufacturing productivity. By 1973 the UK gross domestic product per head had been overtaken by France and Germany, and inflation was starting to grow disturbingly. Underneath the surface confidence, the ground was being laid for the troubles of the seventies.

However, while the economic problems were slowly coming to the boil, there was a feeling of great expansiveness and excitement. There was a boom in formal education: the school leaving age was raised to 16 and the numbers of A-Level passes, people doing teacher training and full-time undergraduates all doubled. In 1969 the Open University started, and there was growth too in informal education – from TV, evening classes, museums, art galleries, stately homes, holidays abroad and membership of clubs.

With this went a rampant new individualism. People were beginning to see a world of opportunity in which traditional social class barriers were coming down and they could all do their own thing (dress as they liked, go into a golf club or eat in a restaurant). The boom in cars and homes gave them more private space. There seemed to be especially a new world for women, their roles, employment and attitudes; the term 'women's lib' was freely used. Children too were starting to be regarded as individuals in their own right: mealtimes became less rigid and 'grazing' became the norm. The Pill and a new openness gave a promise of more sexual freedom. The illegitimacy rate grew somewhat, but marriage was as popular as ever, with the age of first marriage still coming down.

The new freedom was supported by a remarkable series of law reforms in 1967, liberalising the state's approach to abortion, homosexuality and divorce, and abolishing the death penalty. Theatre censorship was abolished in 1968, and words and activities common in real life were allowed to be shared in public. All this encouraged what was almost a cultural revolution. The arts boomed, and most of the new writers, directors and artists owed little to pre-war forms. Beyond the Fringe and Private Eye (1961) started a new wave of satire, and That Was The Week That Was took it onto TV.

New groups of like-minded people started to form, and society became much more complex. The whole nature of 'us and them' became much fuzzier than the traditions of the social classes and the boss v. the workers. It also included us v. the government, North v. South, private v. public sector, workers v. scroungers, us v. foreigners, skilled v. unskilled, owners v. tenants, real people v. civil servants, and so on. There was a feeling that everything had got too big – the State, the local authorities, big companies, trade unions, nationalised industries, supermarkets, pollution and the rat-race. This led to increasing activism, mostly peaceful – though there were riots in Notting Hill in 1958, based on racism and the new Rent Act, and ritual battles between Mods and Rockers on the beaches. Most protest was on a small scale – motorway action groups, parent power, factory sit-ins, kids' lib and consumer groups. But gradually organised single-issue pressure groups were set up. CND was founded in 1958 and held its first Aldermaston march. The Women's Liberation Movement was set up in 1970, Friends of the Earth in 1971, the Green Party in 1973 (originally called the People's Party, then the Ecology Party) and various bodies representing consumers (though people on the whole seemed to prefer looking after themselves).

'Youth culture' emerged. At first it was coffee bars, boutiques, photographers, jeans, miniskirts and Carnaby Street. But the key was the development of pop music. Bill Haley's 1957 tour inspired hundreds of skiffle groups, performing in clubs and pubs round the country. The Beatles set up in 1960; the Rolling Stones and many others followed. A huge record business grew up. The BBC introduced Pick of the Pops in 1962, and the media began to proliferate and fragment. Pirate radio stations came in 1964. BBC2 was launched in 1964, colour TV in 1966, Radio 1 and local radio in 1967, the first commercial radio – LBC – in 1973. Cosmopolitan and Spare Rib came in 1973, and the boom in specialist magazines had started.

So increasingly during this phase market research was dealing with a society very different from the stable and stratified population of the early 1950s. It was clear that the traditional forms of segmentation no longer reflected reality and that understanding people's attitudes would be both more difficult and more important.

Meanwhile there were significant changes in the commercial world. Resale price maintenance was abolished in 1964, and with the new freedom to cut prices retailers invested heavily in supermarkets and self-service, both of which grew rapidly, as did car-borne weekly shopping. The balance of power between manufacturers and retailers was changing dramatically. In response manufacturers' advertising grew as a percentage of GDP, and qualitative research showed that consumers were becoming increasingly expert in advertising and marketing methods. Agencies showed a new interest in planning advertising objectives more precisely and evaluating results against them; and in 1968 the first account planning departments were set up.

A time of innovation

In market research, this was a time of intense methodological development. Methods of measuring attitudes and brand images on a regular basis were invented, under the impetus of agencies like J Walter Thompson which needed this kind of service for their major clients, to supplement what they could learn from behaviour alone and to give early warning if their advertising treatment was on the wrong track (a notable case where this happened was Andrex toilet tissue, where it was found that a concentration on the product's softness had led to a belief that it would tear too easily; the image measurement discovered this in time, and future campaigns corrected it by combining the notion of 'strength' with softness). There was intense interest in trying to model how advertising works, so that one could identify the most useful measures to indicate success, and some agencies (notably JWT and LPE) poured considerable resources into the pretesting of commercials and print advertisements. There was a growing interest in sales modelling, the attempt to link sales movements to prices, promotional expenditure and other factors, and again certain advertising agencies carried out forecasting exercises for their clients. Unlike later, they were making enough money to offer these services in order to keep their best clients.

Multivariate statistics and market modelling techniques began to come into use, as people looked for more subtle ways of interpreting the data they collected. This was made possible by improvements in the technology available for analysing data. Previously, the fact that any manipulation of data had to be done by hand or by primitive mechanical sorters was in practice an insurmountable barrier. By the mid-1960s a much faster card sorter, the 101, became available; a few years on, there were electronic calculators (cumbersome at first, but then increasingly portable), and the first computers began to be used to produce tables directly. All this speeded up the pace and made much more complex calculations possible. Also, this period saw the first effective attempts to derive scientific generalisations about consumer behaviour from analysis of continuous panel data – Andrew Ehrenberg's theories of buying behaviour.

Education and training

In this period the educational activities of the Market Research Society could be said to have come to fruition. Setting a code of standards had been the first main plank in the Society's objective of establishing market research as a respectable profession; the second was education and training, and facilitating the development and spread of ideas.

The education and training programmes run by the MRS are superior to most other professional bodies. The Summer Schools started as early as 1955, to provide basic training in research methods. In 1968 Winter Schools were introduced, to cope with new autumn graduate intakes. In the Winter School, students are taken through a series of lectures and hands-on syndicate work covering the basic disciplines, including designing a survey, constructing a questionnaire, then doing some real interviews with that same questionnaire – an invaluable learning experience, specifying analysis and reporting the results. After the Winter Schools were established, the Summer Schools continued but eventually acquired a different emphasis, less concerned with the basic techniques and more with second-level training in how research is used in different marketing and business contexts.

The schools have a reputation which has attracted both client companies and agencies to send their new recruits each year, as well as several students from overseas. There are a number of training courses, at least one or two each month on average, which have evolved over the years and are now graded into basic, intermediate and senior levels: they may cover such matters as questionnaire design, qualitative research, business-to-business research, interviewing methods, multivariate analysis, understanding brands, international research, and so on. There are regular seminars, study groups and evening meetings, in addition to the main annual Conference. And there is the administration of the MRS Diploma Scheme, started in its present form in 1973, and now covering the market research element in a wide range of courses run by universities and colleges throughout the country. All of these activities are organised and actively run and taught by professional researchers, all of whom are fully occupied in their own businesses, who give their time (unpaid) to train new generations.

The 1959-60 year saw the first publication of *Commentary*, which later became the *Journal of the Market Research Society*. This is the only academic journal of market research in Britain (in contrast to America, which has at least three), and is respected; papers which appear in it are carefully reviewed. John Downham, then Chairman, wrote in a foreword to the first issue:

> This is the first issue of a new Journal which the Market Research Society plans to publish at least three times a year. Its purpose is to provide an opportunity for exchanging ideas and experiences relating to market research. Quite clearly, with a society membership which has grown to over 600, there is now an acute need for a regular journal devoted to the theory and practice of market research.

Asking the Embarrassing Question
by Allen H. Barton, University of Chicago

The pollster's greatest ingenuity has been devoted to finding ways to ask embarrassing questions in non-embarrassing ways. We give here examples of a number of these techniques, as applied to the question: *"did you kill your wife?"*

1. **The casual approach**
   "Do you happen to have murdered your wife?"

2. **The numbered card**
   "Would you please read off the number on this card which corresponds to what became of your wife?" (Hand card to respondent.)

   1   Natural death

   2   I killed her

   3   Other (what?)

   (Get card back from respondent before proceeding.)

3. **The 'everybody' approach**
   "As you know, many people have been killing their wives these days. Do you happen to have killed yours?"

4. **The 'other people' approach**
   a) "Do you know any people who have murdered their wives?"

   b) "How about yourself?"

5. **The sealed ballot technique**
   In this version you explain that the survey respects people's rights to anonymity in respect to their marital relations and that they, themselves, are to fill out the answer to the question, seal it in an envelope and drop it in a box conspicuously labelled 'sealed ballot box' carried by the interviewer.

6. **The projective technique**
   "What thoughts come to mind as you look at the following pictures?" (*Note:* The relevant responses will be evinced by picture D.)

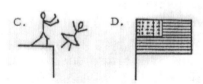

7. **The Kinsey technique**
   Stare firmly into the respondent's eyes and ask in simple, clear-cut language such as that to which the respondent is accustomed and with an air of assuming that everyone has done everything:
   "Did you ever kill your wife?"

8. **Putting the question at the end of the interview.**

Although *Commentary* was a vehicle for serious articles and comment, its contributors were not averse to a bit of fun occasionally, as the extract opposite (from Spring 1962) shows.

The first of the Society's annual Conferences had taken place in 1957, after incorporation, and this too, together with periodic seminars, has been an important forum for the publication of innovative papers. This has been buttressed over the years by a number of awards, including the Society's prestigious Gold Medal, first instituted in 1961 for 'contributions to the theory or practice of market research'. One paper a year was selected for the Gold Medal up to 1977, when it was discontinued and replaced by a Silver Medal (some might think this devaluation rather sad). A new Gold Medal was instituted in the 1980s, to be awarded only rarely for 'signal services to the profession'; to date four of these have been given (Mark Abrams, Leonard England, Harry Henry and Elizabeth Nelson).

By 1973, the Society's membership had grown to over 2,300, and the industry's turnover to over £30 million. It had been a stimulating period, in which great changes had taken place in British society. Research had helped to reveal what consumers wanted, and made it clear that satisfying those wants was the route to success both for business and government. But in the next phase it proved unexpectedly hard to apply these lessons.

PHASE 3: The Past Catches Up with Us, 1974-82

Recession

The 1970s were not a comfortable time. All the hidden economic problems seemed to come to a head at once.

The old consensus on full employment had already been eroded. Labour's In Place of Strife was dropped in 1969 after TUC opposition and its various voluntary incomes policies failed. In the early 1970s other attempts to control public sector wages led to two miners' strikes, states of emergency, power cuts, a three-day working week and the fall of the Heath government. Coupled with an international energy crisis, this led to the first severe post-war recession.

1973 had seen the most extreme Go stage yet, the Barber Boom. Stop was inevitable, but the new Labour government found it impossible to control public spending and paid hugely for peace in the mines. Stop-Go continued, but its fluctuations were more violent. It seemed that whatever policies any government followed, they did little to change the realities caused by years of low productivity compared with international competitors. The pound continued to decline, and there was a sterling crisis in 1976, requiring a £2.3bn loan from the IMF and £2.5bn cuts in public expenditure. Unemployment grew gradually at first, passing 1.5 million in 1976; then very rapidly indeed from 1981. In 1982 it was over 2.8 million and still rising.

Initially the most striking change was in inflation. Retail prices rose by some 240% between 1973 and 1982 (about four times the rate of the previous phase), much more than those of industrial competitors. Inflation fluctuated, with 25% the highest and 9% the lowest annual rate. Traditional Stop policies started bringing it down in 1976-8, but then Go policies put it up again in 1979. Increases in VAT in 1979 (the new Thatcher government's quid pro quo for cutting the very high marginal tax rates on income) helped speed it up to 16% in 1980, before Stop policies and the resulting recession returned it to 9% in 1982.

Productivity growth declined in most countries after the 1973 oil crisis, but particularly in the UK. Investment was somewhat lower, but the real problem remained the low extra output from investment compared with competitors. Causes given for this were government fine-tuning, over-powerful unions, restrictive work practices, weakness in production management and a failure to innovate and add value. It was a particularly bad time for the British car industry, in which long-established problems of design, manufacturing skill, labour relations, productivity and marketing finally came to a head. Equally the national press was in a state of recurrent financial crisis, plagued with overmanning, restrictive practices and high costs.

In 1974-5 marketing companies faced soaring commodity prices, increasing concentration and buying power among retailers, destocking in the retail trade and severe cash flow problems. Profits fell sharply, and most companies seemed to deal with the problem by keeping their heads down, taking a short-term view, cutting both prices and investment in the longer-term future of their brands. In real terms, for instance, manufacturers' consumer advertising and market research (the only elements of marketing effort properly measured) dropped by about a quarter between 1973 and 1975, though consumer spending went down only 3%. There was a real danger of a vicious spiral.

Research hits the buffers

Market research, responsive as ever to advertising, felt the freezing weather. Advertising agencies during this time (1973-6) had to respond to sharp cuts in revenue by widespread redundancies, including sometimes whole departments; these would include those providing 'ancillary services' to the core business, naturally including research. Client companies also slimmed down their research departments, if not abolishing them altogether. Under pressure, research was relatively easy for them to cut, before attacking other marketing expenditure. Research companies which depended wholly or mainly on ad hoc projects suffered severely; those with a large continuous service (retail audit, consumer panel, one of the main media or government contracts, etc.) had a useful cushion, since clients tended to be locked into these and would always drop ad hoc projects in preference. Nonetheless, even these companies stopped recruiting new staff and even suffered some redundancies. Membership of the Society stopped growing for two or three years. Turnover, for the first time, dipped in real terms.

In 1975, the worst year of the recession, Antony Thorncroft, who covered the Market Research Society annual Conference for the *Financial Times*, headed his report 'Nail Biting' at Bournemouth, and commented:

> There is no way in which 1975 can be a good year for the market research industry. Companies invest in research, in the main, when they feel in an expansive frame of mind, and past experience indicates very strongly that research expenditure, like advertising, moves in close parallel to industrial investment.

Thorncroft went on to note that market research costs had risen very rapidly in recent months:

> Postage and petrol, rent and rates, these are all important cost centres for research companies, and each week they seem to jump higher.

The cost of fieldwork (which could be 45% of the cost of a research project) had risen.

> The, admittedly underpaid, interviewers have received extra money, their petrol rates are up, and communicating with them is that much more expensive.
>
> It would be a remarkable research firm that did not face a 20 per cent plus rise in expenses this year. However, most companies have taken vigorous action to reduce costs. The most obvious has been to cut back on staff... There are few research companies who are not 10-15 per cent lighter in staff than they were nine months ago and... there are currently very few vacancies.
>
> It is research companies that look to ad hoc assignments for the bulk of their work that are suffering most. There are slightly fewer jobs, the competition is intense, and the profit is negligible... Companies with the well-established, continuous surveys are partly protected from the storm. Clients are locked in to long-term contracts, and are anyway dependent on data, like the Nielsen retail audits, and the TCA and JICTAR figures from AGB, for their marketing planning.

Thorncroft might have added that two of the biggest ad-hoc agencies, BMRB and Research International, were also somewhat cushioned, since they were wholly-owned subsidiaries whose owners (J Walter Thompson and Unilever respectively) valued them for their skills rather than their profit-earning power.

How were market research agencies able to survive? One advantage they had over other businesses was that the cost of field interviewers, the main category of persons employed, is variable: if there is no work, they are simply not used or paid that week. Research, said Thorncroft, "is an industry where companies can dwindle down and wait for the inevitable upturn." However, this period of retraction revealed significant weaknesses in the research business which were concealed in more expansionist times. It was time to pay more attention to research as a *business*, rather than merely a professional service.

The major problem was that research agencies (at least, those which depended on ad hoc business) were not profitable. "British companies receive what is probably the best research in Europe at around the lowest cost", according to Antony Thorncroft in 1973 ('The Prospects Do Not Please'); clients were used to a false notion of what they should have to pay. Increasing costs plus the downward pressure of competition and nil growth exacerbated this position:

> ... undoubtedly the very low profits made by most research companies, around 5 per cent before tax, are accounted for by their competitiveness when bidding for ad hoc assignments.
>
> *Antony Thorncroft, Financial Times, March 1975*

John Treasure complained that market research was not a business one could make money in.

The chief difficulty with ad hoc work is that, because each project brief presents a new set of problems, a considerable amount of expensive executive time is required to design the solution, run the project and present the results. It was in practice very hard, often impossible, to reflect this hidden cost in the price charged to the client, especially in a competitive tender. This cost would be multiplied by the number of tenders which would be unsuccessful, so that no return could be expected for this expenditure of expensive time. Research is unavoidably an 'executive intensive' business. It is not of course unique in this; advertising agencies and other consultancy-type businesses also have to spend long hours in new business pitches which fail. But traditionally the fees advertising agencies were able to charge under the commission system were large enough to compensate for these time costs, at least when business was good: this was not true of research. The continuous research contracts, which required comparatively little effort to maintain them once the investment had been made to set them up, suffered much less from this problem.

Social discontent

The extreme nature of the inflation and the unemployment growth of the 1970s, with all their unfairness, did much to break up the optimistic consensus that had more or less lasted through the 1960s, and now some of the clashes between groups became more militant. The conflict between the producer bureaucracy and individualism intensified. Economic growth, the new affluence and the new freedoms of course continued, but now in an atmosphere of uncertainty and sometimes tension.

This was particularly so in the area of work. The Labour government brought in much new legislation to repair the damage of the miners' strikes, without greatly appeasing the unions. They also continued the vain attempt to control wages directly with norms and pay limits, and ultimately the realities of life took over. By 1976 prime minister Callaghan had formally abandoned full employment as an achievable national policy, and both the TUC and the Labour Party Conference rejected his 5% wages norm of 1978. The scene was set for the 'Winter of Discontent'. Strikes had become set-piece battles for principles against government policies. In 1977 there had been a firemen's strike for a 30% pay increase, in which troops had been brought in. Then in the winter of 1978/9 there were strikes against the 5% pay norm by lorry drivers, water workers, hospital and municipal workers, often with mass secondary picketing. The corporatist attempt to settle issues between government and the TUC simply could not cope with individuals' and groups' wants; and there had been little attempt to deal with the real issues of industrial restructuring, training and productivity. The new Conservative government of 1979 started rather hesitantly in facing all these problems. Though the rhetoric emphasised control over inflation and public spending, via monetary squeezes and reforming the 'supply side', most of the early efforts went into applying a traditional Stop stage, which caused a severe recession, and then recovering from it.

Not surprisingly in these circumstances, the excitement of the social change of the 1960s became somewhat muted. But it certainly did not go into reverse, and society gradually continued to fragment. Participation, involvement, consumer protest and action all became a bit more serious. The women's movement became more active, the number of divorces rose and the proportion of children born outside marriage went up to 15%. Youth culture changed rather more markedly from the 1960s, when the revolt was against the traditionalism and complacency of British society. Now it seemed more to be attacking the weaknesses and unfairness of the capitalist system. Both skinheads and punks represented a new aggression and outrage against unemployment, which particularly affected young people.

By 1982 there were more hopeful signs for marketing services companies. During the second recession expenditures on advertising and market research rose, even though company profits fell. It seemed that marketing companies had learned from their experience in the mid-1970s that it could be a mistake to cut all their marketing effort in a recession. Nevertheless the period as a whole had been pretty grim.

Learning the hard way

The tough times made research agency managements more commercially aware. It came slowly, and unevenly; with changes like this it is never possible to fix on a date when they happen. But gradually, over the 1970s and 1980s, research agencies began to turn themselves into businesses, with proper profit targets, fee structures and cost controls. Research executives, once dismissed as 'rarely the most financially acute of men', became the managers of growing and successful businesses, which were well placed to take advantage of the upturn which was to come.

One of the areas looked at was the research product – what exactly was it they were selling. Managements took on board the notion that it would help them, as it obviously helped their clients, if they could *package* services such as advertisement testing or brand awareness tracking and promote them as distinctive *brands*. It was not simply a matter of making data, collected once, work harder: this principle gave the continuous services their edge, and the same idea underpinned omnibus surveys and services like BMRB's Target Group Index. It also simplified the marketing of the service; it reduced the executive hours spent in winning new business, and made the selling task easier by producing more ammunition in the form of earlier success stories, normative data, etc.

Eileen Cole (Chairman of the Society during 1977-79) discussed the importance of branded research services in an ESOMAR paper entitled 'Taking Stock: Our Present and Our Future':

> Branding here involves all the characteristics of branding elsewhere in industry. The selection of a market opportunity and a target group; the specific design of work to fit a market gap; the selection and protection of a brand name; the development of supporting advertising; a brand launch; systematic selling activity, all these are involved. So too is the periodic revision of the design – the modification of the brand – to fit the changing market.

Many did not succeed in achieving this ideal, but some did, most notably perhaps the agency Millward Brown, which grew from a standing start in the early 1970s into a multi-million pound international company, entirely on the back of a skilfully-branded tracking service. The success of Millward Brown International reflects in almost every particular the specification outlined by Eileen Cole. It is not a coincidence that the two founders of the agency came from direct experience of marketing on the client side, and knew the 'language' that their clients spoke and understood their preoccupations; this was rarely the case with their competitors.

The recession in the 1970s coincided with a swing of emphasis among advertising agencies away from quantified measures of advertising effectiveness, especially at the testing stage, towards qualitative techniques which, in many cases, they operated in-house. The shift had started earlier, in the mid 1960s, but it was during the 1970s that it reached its peak. These years were also the high point of the rather sterile debate about the values of qualitative versus quantitative research, in which each side kept trying to put the other down, which we deal with later in the appropriate chapters, and which happily now appears to have come to an end.

In 1978 the Society introduced its Interviewer Card Scheme, the objective of which was to give every interviewer a card stating that they were an accredited interviewer employed by an organisation with methods of training and operation which the Society had approved following a regular inspection. This scheme is difficult to operate in practice and has always attracted controversy, but its main purpose is to guarantee to clients that they are buying good quality work, and at the same time reassure respondents that they are engaged in a respectable market research interview.

International research

The 1970s also saw the first serious growth in international research. It had, of course, already been there for some years. A number of research companies had links with agencies or subsidiaries in Europe, and some had local departments to specialise in international business, such as BMRB's foundation of EMRB as a separate division in 1969. Research International had earlier been founded by Unilever to ensure that they would have their own access to high quality research in all their main markets; this was why RI had offices in some (in those days) unlikely sounding places, such as Kenya and Finland. However, it was between 1970 and 1980 that companies such as Market Behaviour Limited began to see a huge growth in international business, especially in developing countries, following the needs of international clients such as Unilever or Beecham: West Africa (Nigeria, the Ivory Coast, Cameroun, Sierra Leone, Liberia), the Middle East (Lebanon, Jordan, Egypt, Bahrain, Kuwait, Saudi Arabia), India, Sri Lanka and the West Indies.

International in this context meant especially research commissioned from a UK company, with fieldwork to be done in one or several overseas countries and, in part, subcontracted to local agencies. Sometimes there would be a network of tied companies all belonging to the same parent, and the entire job would be passed around in parcels; but the other method developed in Britain as 'multi-national research' involved the British sub-contracting agency buying fieldwork only, from any agency of its choice, and maintaining control throughout on all other aspects of the job including the analysis and presentation, which would be done in the UK. The British company would thus take over from the client the entire burden of ensuring that the research was done economically and efficiently; executives who knew the countries concerned would be responsible for ensuring that translations were accurate, that data were comparable, and that national differences would not be misinterpreted.

This style of multi-national research has been, and remains, the corner-stone of British international research business, and the main reason for the UK's pre-eminence in this sector. Most global companies are English-speaking, and find it easier to deal with a single operator in the same language. American agencies might have filled the same role, but it is a curious fact that the US research industry, advanced though it undoubtedly is in many respects, has tended to be inward-looking and to concentrate on covering the different markets within their own vast territory. Until the 1990s, few American research agencies had ever shown an interest in directly subcontracting research work outside the USA except, to some extent, in Central and South America. As a result, American multi-nationals saw Britain as the natural 'gateway to Europe' (or even farther afield), and enabled British agencies to build up their unique reputation as international research coordinators.

Research commissioned outwards from the UK in this way far exceeded, for a long time, research commissioned inwards (ie from overseas agencies to be done in the UK), and it has been a major means of keeping research agencies afloat in times of recession at home, including the most recent one in 1990-92.

All recessions eventually come to an end, however unlikely it seems at the time. When this happened in 1982, it ushered in a new Go phase which was somewhat different from the previous post-war norm.

PHASE 4: Experiments with Enterprise and the New Uncertainty, 1983 to Date.

Thatcherism – 1982-89

The new Conservative government in 1979 finally ended the consensus in British politics. There was still agreement on the nature of the problems, but not on the solutions. Mrs Thatcher, tough and confrontational, dominated in a way that no other post-war prime minister had, and her plan was to create an enterprise economy. Individualism was championed against the producer bureaucracy, tax cuts and self-reliance against public spending and the nanny state. Vested interests were challenged: at various times, those of trade unions, the law, the church, the social services, 'scroungers', teachers, universities, doctors, the NHS and the European Commission.

After the 1980-1 recession the new rhetoric was translated into action. Exchange controls were abolished in 1980 and 'Big Bang' deregulated City institutions in 1986. Take-overs and financial conglomerates boomed. The new commercial freedom for banks, building societies and insurance companies led to intense competition to lend to consumers, causing a huge expansion of consumer credit. Between 1983 and 1991 some 16 state-owned companies were privatised, and over £50bn was raised. Market forces were brought into the area of housing too. The government encouraged private ownership and private renting, and gave new rights to council tenants. By 1995 over a million and a half council and new town homes had been bought by their tenants, and over two-thirds of homes were owner-occupied.

The most striking achievement was curbing the trade unions. The closed shop and secondary picketing were banned, and secret ballots before official strikes were imposed. The new laws were soon put to the test by the National Union of Mineworkers and the printing unions, and there were violent pitched battles between massed flying pickets and massed police. Ultimately the authorities won; the NUM was a spent force and the unions were forced to accept new technology in newspaper production. From 1986 onwards the number of strikes and working days lost ran at a lower level than at any time over the past 20 years.

The 'new radical economics' did seem to be working. The UK got a high share of the inward investment into Europe and grew faster than most major industrial competitors. The rise in real earnings was the fastest on record. For seven years real personal disposable incomes grew, averaging about +4%, though the gap between the richest and poorest families grew markedly.

These years were exciting and generally popular. More people had their own houses, which were proving a wonderful investment, as house prices doubled in five years. They became more confident as consumers, readier to experiment and trust their own judgement. The new freedoms of the 1960s, which had wilted a little in the 1970s, now emerged again in an even more individualistic world of designer everything. There was no need any more to apologise for success or for making money. Social mobility seemed to have arrived at last. Youth culture became more fragmented and more grown-up, in particular embracing the new world of home computers.

British companies too rediscovered a zeal for success, and recognised that international competition was here to stay. There was a new business professionalism. Productivity grew faster than in previous decades, and faster than the OECD average: by the mid-1990s three-quarters of the productivity gap with France and Germany had been closed. New technology gradually became a more important factor, especially for offices, banks, the media, retailers, financial and other services. There was a growing recognition of the crucial importance of brands, and in particular of company brands. In an era of rapid technological leapfrog, people were choosing brands not only for their functional values but also on their assessment of the company management's and staff's skills, behaviour and culture. The long-promised service economy was arriving.

Market research comes of age

As already indicated, this has been a period of spectacular growth for research, with only a temporary dip during the 1991-2 recession years. By 1984, membership of the Society had reached 4,300; by 1985, 4,800; by 1995, about 6,000, excluding interviewer members.

Many of the market research businesses now came of age (as interpreted in the entrepreneurial spirit of the time). Some sought and obtained stock-exchange listings and went public. Others were bought up into mega-conglomerates such as Martin Sorrell's WPP Group, which swallowed Research International, BMRB and Millward Brown, as well as the advertising agencies JWT and Ogilvy & Mather. The trend continued towards polarisation between large composite agencies with the power to invest in new technologies and smaller groups offering specialist services (qualitative, fieldwork, data processing etc.) The businesses that were squeezed were the small to medium general ad hoc agencies without a special branded service to offer or the clout to invest in developing one. As Tim Bowles remarked:

... even where a company does not possess branded research services, the establishment of distinctive expertise in specialist markets such as motoring, finance and pharmaceuticals does seem to have distinct advantages over being seen simply as a general research agency.

'Issues Facing the UK Research Industry',
MRS Conference keynote speech, 1991

In July 1989, when the period of massive growth (unknown to the participants) was about to end, a joint conference was held in Boston under the auspices of the Market Research Society and the Advertising Research Foundation, which brought together a number of leading UK and US researchers to share their views. The proceedings of the conference, published by the MRS Journal in October the same year, provide an excellent bird's eye view of what had been happening and how things appeared at the time. The opening speaker was John Goodyear, Chairman of the MBL Group, a noted entrepreneur and a consistent advocate of the importance of running market research companies as profitable businesses without compromising on standards. His paper includes a number of interesting statistics. For example, the following table from it shows the ownership and revenues of the top eight British research supply groupings:

AMSO Companies	Owned by	Group Revenues, 1988
Audience Selection AGB RSGB	Robert Maxwell (Pergamon AGB)	£36.6 million
Nielsen	Dun & Bradstreet	£26.2 million
Research International RI Specialist Units	WPP	£17 million

Continued overleaf...

AMSO Companies	Owned by	Group Revenues, 1988
Taylor Nelson MAS	Motivaction (27%) MAI (23%)	£16.4 million
NOP Survey Research Associates	MAI	£13.4 million
Millward Brown	WPP	£13.3 million
MIL Group	independent (later acquired by MAI)	£12.5 million
BMRB Mass-Observation	WPP	£11.8 million

Thus, if we exclude MAI, a total of £105 million of revenue, a third of the estimated total, was accounted for by just three organisations. The pattern has radically changed since then, of course: for example, AGB's UK operations were bought by Taylor Nelson after the death of Robert Maxwell. There will be more combining and splitting of conglomerate groups, but the principle remains: market research agencies are considered proper candidates for large-scale corporate ownership.

The uncertain nineties

In 1990 the bubble burst. Monetary targets were abandoned, the balance of payments deficit soared, interest rates went up to 15%, inflation was back over 10%. A new Stop phase came in, with a recession in 1991 and 1992. Companies made a virtue of leanness, and unemployment, which had fallen since 1986, started rising again. The pound came under attack and was forced to leave the Exchange Rate Mechanism, with an effective devaluation of 20%. House prices fell, creating 'negative equity'. Taxes were raised. It was not until 1994 that the peak year of GDP, 1990, was overtaken. By 1995 the economy was more or less back on the trend line, with low interest rates, low inflation and falling unemployment, but the shock had been considerable.

Once the myth of a permanent boom had been destroyed, many uncertainties emerged. Could the UK ever compete internationally, if it only survived through constant devaluations? Would there be any real benefits from closer integration in the EC? Would 'full' employment ever return? Since the nature of work had changed, with companies making much more use of outworkers, sub-contractors and freelancers, could anyone ever feel confident again of having a regular income? Had the balance between fairness and efficiency swung too far towards money-saving and profits? Were private monopolies any better than public, and would they compromise safety? Were market forces a sensible model for professional, social, educational and artistic endeavours? One-third of children were now born outside marriage, one in six households was headed by a lone mother and between a third and a half of secondary schoolchildren had tried 'recreational' drugs: had the new individualism gone too far? Was it tolerable or even safe to have a large and growing underclass, with an increasing gap between them and the richest families? Was the British education system suitable for the modern world? Could the NHS cope with the increasingly expensive demands being put on it? Could the state continue to provide properly for people's old age?

As economic growth returned, the anxieties quietened down, but there was little left of the exuberance of the mid-1980s. It seemed that a new political consensus was emerging, based on some of the old values of fairness, but recognising that only a successful enterprise economy could provide them. The basic themes of the new individualism, the buyer's market, the service economy, the development of information technology and the proliferation of media seemed set to continue. Throughout this phase they had provided an excellent environment for market research, as long as it improved its own skills to deal with the increasing complexity of life. The proven values of market research to government and businesses, as the surrounding uncertainties have grown, seem likely to be in even greater demand.

Current trends

A number of other trends, which are still continuing, can be summarised for the last dozen years. One is the continuing spread of market research outwards from its original fmcg (fast moving consumer goods) core, to take in new areas of business (finance, medicine, business-to-business, etc.) which have come to it more slowly. Another is the continuing spread of international research in the wake of 'global marketing' and the EC single market: increasingly, as long predicted by John Goodyear, this is involving the emerging 'tiger' economies of the Far East, where a number of British companies, including his own, have active links and subsidiaries.

An unwelcome trend, which has come over here from the USA, is unattractively named 'downsizing'. Companies have severely cut back, if not abolished, their own research departments. This is partly justifiable by the fact that handling data is not as labour-intensive as it was, but the main reason is the pressure to become 'leaner and fitter'. There is thus an increase of dependence on agencies for research, and an increase in unemployed researchers who, if they are good, set up as independent consultants. But there are also fewer people in client companies who understand what research is about, and this puts an increasing pressure on the research suppliers to become interpreters and advisers, not merely sellers of a product.

In some respects, market research has become steadily more difficult. People now lead less structured lives; actually contacting a specific target sample is more difficult than it used to be. People are more wary of strangers; there are more and more places where interviewers cannot be expected to go, especially after dark. Dawn Mitchell has contrasted the present situation with the mid-1950s, when doors were always open:

> Not so today, when we are suffering from falling response rates, through fear of crime, selling under the guise of research, and generally less confidence in the value and confidentiality of surveys, and the sheer difficulty of finding people at home during social hours... Statistics [from the NRS] show that in 1954 a far higher proportion of interviews were conducted in the evenings 40 years ago, when it was socially acceptable for a lone woman to walk in darkened streets on her own.
>
> In those halcyon days fifty percent of interviews were achieved on the first call: there was less out-of-home entertainment, the shops closed early and the evening meal, eaten early, was a family event. Even so the NRS interviewers were making six calls to achieve their response rate, 85% in those days, just over 60% nowadays after eight+ calls, even more on some re-issues. The effort which goes into obtaining a successful interview was always great, but in 1955, half of the response on a pre-selected survey did come from the first call.
>
> *Dawn Mitchell, 'Forty Years On',*
> *AMSO Conference Paper, 1995*

These are world-wide problems, not merely in Britain. They throw more weight on other data sources such as respondent panels, and previously compiled databases, which are increasingly becoming the province of researchers. EPOS scanners, which we shall discuss in Chapter 4, have provided a new source of data swamping marketing companies and requiring expert help for their digestion.

Technological developments are now making major impact on market research, in several ways. On the data collection side, telephone research has become an accepted method for many types of research since, in the early 1980s, telephone possession reached 90% of the population. To date, it accounts for some 18.5% of all interviewing (AMSO 1995 figures). Most telephone interviewing is done with the help of computers, through the system known as CATI (Computer Assisted Telephone Interviewing). With CATI, interviewers telephone from a central location, where they can be directly supervised, working with a computer into which the questionnaire has been pre-programmed: the next question is flashed on the screen according to the previous answer, enabling much more complex question sequences to be used than an interviewer could work out herself, and the replies can be entered immediately into the data bank for analysis. This greatly increases both the speed and the accuracy of the results. Experiments in automatic speech recognition by computers are under way: if these are successful, it will be another breakthrough, making it possible to conduct more complex and qualitative studies over the telephone.

Much interviewing is not suitable for the telephone, especially when questionnaires are long or things have to be shown to respondents; but the development of portable lap-top computers has introduced a new computer-aided system, CAPI (P for Personal). This involves a large up-front investment, to equip a whole field force with lap-tops, but the investment becomes easier as the hardware becomes cheaper. CAPI is now routine on a number of omnibus services and on the National Readership Survey.

Data processing and analysis have become steadily faster. There is increasing power to manipulate and model data, and it can now be delivered to a client to work at on his own PC: the specialist bureau is a convenience, but is no longer so vital. This again throws the onus on the research supplier to become an interpreter and not merely a reporter of information. There are still some things the computer cannot do well, such as the ability to process voices or understand the meaning of English sentences from unstructured interviewing, but these are being worked on. When they are achieved, there will be another leap forward in potential productivity.

We shall return in our final chapter to the challenges posed by these developments in technology. They have made data provision and manipulation almost painless; but, at the same time, they have raised hard questions about data sources. When massive databases can be held and accessed easily on-line, and made to yield usable information, does it matter (from the point of view of the user) that the database itself may not be a very good sample of the population which, by conventional means, is getting harder and harder to reach? Difficult questions about research quality follow in the train of this new technology. There are also difficulties which concern the funding of what has now become, in many areas, a capital-intensive, as well as highly competitive, industry. As Tim Bowles said in a keynote speech at the 1991 Conference, "investment in research is now risk investment in the true sense of the word".

Bowles, in the same speech, stressed the increasing drive towards branded services, which he saw as a way in which agencies can afford to keep their most talented executives whilst remaining competitive on price. The business success stories of the 1980s had been "drawn more from ad hoc research companies which have developed branded research services, often on a shoe string, to meet specific client needs", than on the new generation of expensive technology-driven databases. Clients have never been clearly aware of the technical details involved in carrying out a research project, any more than when they employ an accountant or visit the doctor; they buy from individuals whom they trust, and take the research skills for granted. "The added value from the client's point of view arises from the interpretation of the data and from the help which this interpretation gives in making business and marketing decisions". The key to success, as with any professional service, stems from the ability of the researcher and the relationship he or she is able to form with the client. In Bowles's view, this relationship is (or should be) enhanced rather than diminished by the growth of branded services.

3

Research and the
Public Sector

It is hard to realise now to what extent public policy before the war depended on guesswork about the public's behaviour and attitudes. Today's complex and individualistic society would be chaotic if government were to operate with the same degree of ignorance.

It was only the wartime adaptation of market research methods to the social area that enabled Britain, with surprisingly few false starts, to develop an effective welfare system and a modern society.

A *Times* leader on July 25th, 1945, after the election of the new Labour administration, said:

> No single duty imposed on the new Government is more urgent or important than the collection and dissemination of the facts on which public policy must be based... Policy in the future must rest more than ever on the widest and freest interchange of information between the Government and the community.

Referring to several of the post-war reconstruction issues then under debate, the leader continued:

> In every instance the argument has been conducted without the indispensable minimum of up-to-date factual knowledge.

The AMSO figures for the 1995 year suggest that some 13% of turnover came from government and public bodies, public services and utilities. On an estimated total base of over £600 million, this would suggest over £78 million for 'social research'. But this is almost certainly a large underestimate, since it only covers work which is placed out with commercial agencies. The bulk of the work done for 'government' is handled by the Social Survey Division of the Office of Population Censuses and Surveys (OPCS), which grew out of what used to be known as the Government Social Survey. A substantial amount of what does go out to tender is handled by Social and Community Planning Research (SCPR), an independent, non-profit institute specialising in social surveys, which now has a £10 million turnover, but is not covered in the industry estimates. These two sources between them add many millions of pounds to the total spend on 'social research', since every major government department carries a substantial and regular investment in research.

An indication of the huge range of interests which 'social research' includes can be gleaned from the following list, taken from the contents page of SCPR's 1993-4 list of publications:

British General Election Survey series

British Social Attitudes Survey series

England and Wales Youth Cohort Studies

National Food Survey (continuous)

Workplace Industrial Relations Survey series

Training, Employment and the Workplace

Health and Welfare (subdivided into Health, Social Services, Social Security and Income Support)

Housing and the Environment

Education and the Arts

Politics and Local Government

Law, Crime and the Police

Transport, Planning and Public Involvement
The Voluntary Sector, Leisure and Family Life
Consumer Services
Ethnic Groups

The Government Social Survey

The adoption and acceptance of survey methods by government was kick-started by the war, and this is the appropriate place to start. The birth and first forty years of the Government Social Survey (GSS) have been chronicled by Louis Moss, its first Director and one of the founding fathers and early chairmen of the Market Research Society ('The Government Social Survey', HMSO 1991).

Commercial companies had started to do social research in a small way before the end of the 1930s. Mark Abrams recalls, from his time at LPE, doing a survey of housing conditions in North London for the Gas, Light and Coke Company; he comments that it was almost unique, since very little was known about housing conditions at the time. Abrams also mentions the first census of distribution (in six towns) for the Board of Trade, the first town planning survey in 1938 (in Birmingham, for Cadbury's Bournville Village), and a study of working class diets and food consumption habits in 1938-9 which was a preparation for the possibility of wartime rationing and later grew into the National Food Survey.

There was also the much better known foundation of Mass-Observation by Tom Harrison, Charles Madge and (briefly) Humphrey Jennings in 1937, which introduced the idea of using anthropological methods of observation to the study of human behaviour in Britain. Madge and Harrison were colourful characters, both university dropouts: Madge was a poet and journalist; Harrison had been on a number of scientific expeditions and, after his colleagues returned home from the last one, stayed on, went native and lived for a year with the cannibal and strongly anti-white natives of Malekula in the Western Pacific, where he discovered that "cannibals were at least as civilised and pleasant as Old Harrovians".

The idea of subjecting the population of Britain to 'anthropological study' originally came from worries among the intelligentsia about the 'primitive' or 'irrational' way the public seemed to respond to events. The immediate stimulus was the reaction to the abdication of Edward VIII, which "had brought to the attention of intellectuals the extraordinary hold which the monarchy still had over the British popular imagination". Underlying this was the deeper worry about Hitler's rise to power; it seemed that a new 'barbarism' was sweeping Europe; could anything be done to check it? Madge wrote a letter to the *New Statesman* (2nd January 1937), presenting the idea that British society could only be understood if studied in a roundabout way – it was so 'ultra repressed' (in a Freudian sense) that 'clues' could only be hit upon in this form – and calling for 'mass observations' to create 'mass science'. Harrison responded to this letter, and Mass-Observation was born.

The idea was to use untrained observers to keep one-day diaries, called Day Surveys, covering in detail everything they did on a specific day. They would act as subjective cameras, 'each with his or her own distortion', recording 'not what society is like but what it looks like to them'. The reports sent in by the panel of Observers began to be published during 1937-39 and attracted attention from the press. Everybody, on 18th June 1938, in a friendly article entitled They May Be Watching You, said:

> Mass-Observation sets out to be a new science; or, rather, a new method of finding out scientific truths. The originators of it reasoned that if a body of information were available as to why we do or say certain things, how we behave in special sets of circumstances, this would help us to know ourselves and other people better.

... The machinery for an analysis of motives, feelings and behaviour may become of inestimable service to us, living as we do in an age when, while the mechanical sciences have advanced tremendously, the social sciences have lagged far behind.

This was all of a piece with the writings of George Orwell and the documentary movement in films: the cameras, or people acting as cameras, would show what was 'really there'.

Of course, a system as voluminous and undirected as this could not possibly last. The results were socially biased, lacking in rigour, and becoming unmanageable to analyse and publish. The war gave Mass-Observation a new lease of life, 'a sharpness of focus it had been lacking'. The diaries returned by the panel Observers became a source of information on national morale, not only civilian but in the forces, since a number of called-up Observers continued to report. This continued through to 1946, and some of the reports at that time give an insight into the reasons for the Labour post-war victory. It was not until 1949 that Tom Harrison (having failed to settle in England and become curator of the Sarawak Museum) finally relinquished his rights in the company and it turned into a normal market research agency, Mass-Observation Ltd, which remained in business for the next thirty years before being bought by the JWT Group in 1979 (it eventually merged with BMRB in 1991).

Mass Observation was a colourful interlude, outside the main stream of development of market research, but it had an important effect. It brought the concept of detailed qualitative observation as a valuable thing to do in its own right, something that could provide insights into human motives and behaviour which statistical descriptions would tend to miss. And some of the Observers went on to become leading market researchers, such as Mollie Tarrant and Len England (who became managing director of Mass-Observation Ltd before founding his own agency, England Grosse, and became Chairman of the Market Research Society in the 1961-62 year). Such people were a leaven in what might otherwise have easily been a total commitment to statistical quantification, since they never lost their belief in the qualitative insight, and their presence was undoubtedly a factor in the evolution of a respectable qualitative research industry in Britain, avoiding the excesses of the wilder 'motivationists' (as we shall see later). Other social researchers such as William Belson, in his studies of the effects of television violence on children, have inherited some of the same influence.

Louis Moss comments that, until the war, "very little official use was made of surveys based on adequate samples despite the accumulating social and economic problems of the years between the wars". The pressure of war provided the necessary will. Moss quotes Lord Woolton as saying, in his presidential address to the Royal Statistical Society in 1945, that "those who found themselves in 1939 responsible for the conduct of the country in the rapidly changing conditions of war – when facts were more important than precedents – had very little to help them". The first use of survey methods seems to have been by the Ministry of Information, particularly as a means of monitoring morale; but the morale studies became the object of a newspaper campaign which attacked the MOI's home intelligence activities (why is not clear). Duff Cooper, the Minister, was singled out for criticism, and the survey interviewers were pilloried as Cooper's Snoopers. This reaction alarmed the MOI, which decided to cease sponsoring morale studies.

At the same time, other government departments were demanding a better quality of information apart from questions of morale, and a group of academics from the LSE were invited to set up an organisation on market research lines. This became the Wartime Social Survey (WTSS), and took over the (non-morale) survey work which the MOI had been doing. Louis Moss became the first Superintendent (later Director) of WTSS, reporting to Dr Stephen Taylor (later to become a Minister), head of the Home Intelligence Unit of the MOI. WTSS started work with 50 interviewers by the end of 1941, undertaking work for several government departments, especially the Board of Trade, the Ministry of Food (concerned with consumer needs and shortages), and the Ministry of Labour.

From the beginning, there was a sensitivity that the surveys should be publicly acceptable. This was not merely in response to the Cooper's Snoopers campaign, which was countered easily by evidence that most people interviewed were 'interested and co-operative' (73%, according to an analysis of questions asked on a number of the surveys about what the respondents had thought). In 1942, WTSS was examined by a parliamentary Select Committee. The report noted that the original intention was that the work of the unit should be "on the same lines as various Market Research organisations". The committee found that there was "little evidence of objection on the part of the public to being interviewed". However, it confirmed the view that morale should not be a subject of the surveys. "Enquiries should be factual and used to guide a Ministry on some particular policy... occasionally a questionnaire must contain a question or two the answers to which entail an expression of opinion."

The Times of 28th March, 1942, gave the report a warm welcome:

> The development of a national social survey machine was one of the most interesting wartime social innovations... an active and practical research body the justification of which is pragmatic... it would appear necessary to bring to the notice of potential users the facility for investigation which the Survey provided.

The Times went on:

> Research on this scale is something new in sociology. It is concrete evidence of the advance of democracy... a new and quantitative bridge between the central Government departments and the people of the country.

Through the rest of the war, WTSS continued under the mantle of Dr Taylor and the MOI to carry out surveys for government 'customers'. As Moss makes clear, it was not plain sailing; the unit had to struggle under tight expenditure controls and cutbacks, as wartime pressures on resources increased. In 1943, WTSS undertook a 'survey of sickness' which turned out to be of crucial importance for its future life; it was the first continuous survey, and associated the Social Survey with the discussions which followed the Beveridge Report in 1942 and led to the eventual National Health Service. Without this survey, the needed for the effective planning of the NHS would not have been available.

By the end of 1944, Louis Moss reported to the Scientific Advisory Committee that over 100 separate surveys had been done by the unit, with samples ranging from 500 to 5,000, of which 28% had been concerned with Board of Trade interests, 25% with food and nutrition, and 18% related to various publicity and information activities.

Not all government wartime work was done by WTSS. Some was contracted out to the commercial field, especially BMRB, the main independent research company then existing. John Downham, in his history of BMRB International, remarks that without government survey contracts "BMRB could not have survived". These surveys included surveys on food consumption, including the Points Survey which apparently ran until 1948, and the regular monitoring of readership of the Ministry of Food's Food Facts propaganda bulletins, which suggested how people could make best use of their rations. There was also a regular panel monitoring purchases and ownership of clothing and the use of clothing coupons.

After the war ended, the Attlee government dissolved the MOI and formed the new Central Office of Information. The Social Survey (no longer 'wartime') came under the COI in 1946 and remained there until 1967, when it became a separate department (the Government Social Survey Department), under the direct control of the Treasury. Three years later, in 1970, it was to be merged with the General Register Office into the newly founded OPCS (Office of Population Censuses and Surveys), making a partnership between the two main information tools, the census and the survey, which was felt to be natural and complementary. This gradual transformation of the Survey from an adjunct to 'information' into a separate government department in its own right is as good an indication as any of the continued value which the Survey's 'clients', in other departments, attached to its product. The merger during 1995 of OPCS and the Central Statistical Office, which used to have a separate 'watching brief' over the surveys commissioned by government departments so as to avoid duplication and waste, completes this process of rationalisation; it is too early to tell what effects it will have on the supply and commissioning of government survey work.

The Rise of Government Research

From the post-war period, social research was set to grow, in step with the recovery of the economy and the establishment of the Welfare State. Growth was not uninterrupted: economic crises, recessions and tight budgets caused fluctuations. But there is a constant underlying thread, described by Roger Jowell as the 'almost linear' growth in survey work for government departments, mainly through the GSS and, after 1969, SCPR (Social and Community Planning Research).

SCPR was set up by its founders (Roger Jowell and Gerald Hoinville) as a charity, so as to be able to take advantage of available research grants. They are the only other organisation which offers exclusively social survey facilities, and, being free of commercial constraints, the only one considered, by departmental statisticians, to be in a position to carry out government surveys to the level of detail and accuracy required. Almost all government department work, including all the major continuous surveys, is conducted by the GSS and

SCPR; relatively little goes elsewhere. Only some five or six commercial research companies are regarded as serious competitors for such research; most others, even those who are members of AMSO, get relatively little involved. In the early to mid-1980s there was an apparent exception to this, when a series of large Housing Condition Surveys and later the Labour Force Survey were put out to tender and successfully bid for by a consortium of companies (which separately did not have the resources to cope with the scale of fieldwork required without unacceptable strain on the rest of their business); but, according to Roger Jowell, this was an aberration, "a minute in time".

The growth of the Social Survey (and SCPR) is landmarked by the establishment of the 'flagship' continuous surveys. The National Food Survey continued on from the war, being taken over by GSS in 1953. The Family Expenditure Survey took final form in 1957, the International Passenger Survey in 1961, the National Travel Survey in 1964 (now with SCPR), the General Household Survey in 1970, the annual Labour Force Survey (replacing less frequent ones) in 1983. These are massive surveys, with sample sizes annually in tens of thousands. But they are only examples of the range of coverage of the Social Survey (and not counting those, like the Home Office's British Crime Survey, which have been with SCPR since their inception). Louis Moss says that, between 1945-6 and 1981-2, the Survey Vote rose in real terms by 580%.

It has undoubtedly increased at a similar if not greater rate since. In the early days of the Thatcher government, the Rayner and Merchant reviews were thought likely to result in severe reductions in the work of the Social Survey Division of OPCS. What happened was a change in the *method*, so that client departments became paying customers and were encouraged to put work out to tender when appropriate to the private sector; but there was virtually no change in the amount of work done. In Roger Jowell's opinion, the cost-cutting efforts of the Thatcher years were 'utterly unnoticeable' in the overall trend.

SCPR had thought government work might dry up, under pressure from a political culture which saw social research as an expression of socialism, and made plans to strengthen grant-sourced projects instead, but "we were wrong – Margaret Thatcher's government spent as much on research as the Labour government which preceded her and the Major government which succeeded her." Rayner proved a footnote, no more. More significantly, during the 1990-1992 recession, SCPR's income from government projects increased at a rate "far in excess of previous years", and in the four years since 1992 it has doubled: "spending and spending unabated".

What explains this robust survival of government-funded research against every assault of economic crisis and political ideology? A large part of the explanation lies in the fact that, in spite of what the papers sometimes say, we have a relatively open democracy. What Jowell calls 'the tyranny of Question Time' (or of the select committee) means that ministers must have trustworthy information on call at all times. Moreover, such information has to be of unchallengeable quality. Ministers and departments dare not get involved in a service which is not effectively bullet-proof. If public survey information is obtained by methods which can be shown up to be 'imperfect', nobody believes it, and the minister relying on it can be tripped up. A good example is the use of quota sampling methods, which can be labelled as 'imperfect' in this sense because they lack a theoretical foundation in academic statistical theory, even though they have been proved, empirically, to be both accurate and cost-effective and are now adopted in almost all commercial surveys.

This is not peculiar to Britain. Throughout Europe and the USA, according to Jowell, "the best quality research is done by governments – not by academe, but by governments"; especially in democracies, where there is always an opposition to challenge the basis of government-produced information. Governments alone have both the need and the ability, when pushed, to find the money. Professor (Sir Claus) Moser, who was appointed in 1967 to head the Central Statistical Office, saw it as the aim of government statistics that "nobody worries about their veracity, they can only argue about their implications"; opposition and government alike should be able to accept that the figures are true, beyond question.

In May 1946, Political and Economic Planning, in a broadsheet titled The Social Use of Sample Surveys, said:

> It has become absolutely vital that the state should have an accurate knowledge of the ways of thought and action and of the environment of the people for whom laws or services are intended... the facts set out should be enough to prove beyond question that the social survey is an essential tool in social policy, and indeed in government policy.

One might add that this pressure for better information as a ground for policy decisions does not only come from within government. An increasingly sophisticated electorate, fed by a wider diversity of news sources, demands it. Pressure groups draw on independent research whenever possible to strengthen their case. In this environment, it is not surprising that government departments are reluctant to make serious moves without conducting their own, unbiased research first.

The continuing demand for sound information produced a concern for high quality, coupled with inventiveness, which fed through into the industry as a whole and has been of immeasurable benefit to it. Sample design is an example. According to Moss, random or probability sampling was used on almost all work done by the Social Survey from 1949 onwards. Random sampling is theoretically preferable to other methods because it is based on known probabilities of selection, and has an obvious appeal when the main requirement is to describe the population accurately; as Moser and Kalton put it: "Although skilful quota sampling can succeed in practice, it is not suitable for surveys in which it is important that the results are derived from theoretically safe methods. Only random sampling fulfils this requirement". But 'pure' random sampling is intolerably expensive (imagine the cost of sending an interviewer to visit the only person you happen to have picked in St Ives, Portmeirion or Thurso).

Percy Gray and Tom Corlett, at the Social Survey, developed practical methods of random sampling which the Survey could use cost-effectively. They described these methods in a classic paper to the Royal Statistical Society in 1950 ('Sampling for the Social Survey', Journal of the RSS, Series A, Vol CXIII, Part II), and in other papers. Their ingenious approach to the problem – first selecting areas (such as wards or polling districts from the Electoral Register), and then selecting individuals by probability methods only within those areas; stratification methods to ensure that the areas properly represented the country; the first look at the problem of non-response bias – became the foundation for general practice throughout the industry.

The paper was very well received at the RSS. Frank Yates, an eminent statistician, said that it presented for the first time the formulae giving the sampling error of two-stage random sampling with probability proportional to size, and also introduced practical methods for achieving samples on this basis. The description of these methods and of the available registers had made random sampling a more accessible method for serious researchers. Gray and Corlett pioneered other advantageous methods, for example the use of postal interviews for scattered populations.

The sampling methods developed at the Social Survey fed into the private sector wherever random sampling was done (for example the National Readership Survey, for which Tom Corlett became responsible after he left the Social Survey to join BMRB). But their importance was far wider, because they were used to improve the quality of non-random, or quota, samples. Most commercial research does not require the breadth and depth of description which is sought after by the public sector, and does not justify the cost of strict random selection. But the main cost advantage is obtained at the final stage, at which interviewers are given freedom to find respondents, provided they follow certain rules, rather than being allocated specific names to contact. Up to that stage, the selection of sampling areas can be done by the same methods as for random samples, and with the same degree of accuracy and coverage. This gave commercial companies, using frames like the Electoral Register, the advantage of considerable cost saving with relatively little loss of precision. The resulting samples, although strictly 'quota' and therefore not provable in current statistical theory, have been shown (by their results) to be accurate and consistent enough for most practical commercial use.

The sampling methods which the Social Survey pioneered have continued to be used ever since, improved from time to time by innovations such as the Marchant-Blyth method of selecting self-weighting samples of household inhabitants from the Electoral Register, and by developments in the sampling frames available, especially the now universal replacement of the Electoral Register by the Postcode Address File and the growth of geodemographic classification of areas based on the Census.

Both the Social Survey and its complement, SCPR, have continued to invest significantly in survey methodology. Bob Barnes, the current Director of the Social Survey Division, wrote in 1992:

> The Social Survey has throughout its existence aimed to carry out survey work to high technical standards. For example, although quota sampling methods were used in some of the very early studies, the superiority of random probability sampling was recognised and soon became used almost exclusively. Also, high quality fieldwork and data collection have characterised the work since the start. Response rates are just one, though perhaps the most visible and easily measured, manifestation of this and, in the early years, response rates of over 95% were achieved in surveys of the general population.

Most Social Survey interviews are still carried out face-to-face. Barnes suggests one reason why; interviewers can be faced with tasks which are well beyond the requirements of most commercial surveys:

> Apart from the conventional asking of questions and recording of answers using paper and pencil methods, the interviewer's task may include, for example: using a computer during the interview; taking physical measurements of people; taking urine sample; pulse and blood pressure readings; obtaining saliva specimens for laboratory analysis to show biochemical evidence about exposure to cigarette smoke; and coding data in the field, such as occupation and industry descriptions.

The Joint Centre for Survey Methods, formerly a unit housed within OPCS and jointly supported by OPCS, SCPR, the LSE and BMRB, now works entirely within SCPR, and concentrates on methodological questions; it is the nearest we have in this country to an academic chair of survey research methods, apart from the Chair of Marketing Research at the City University (an MRS foundation). The 1993-1994 publications list of SCPR on 'survey methods' includes, between 1986 and 1993, 9 papers on sampling, 5 on questionnaire design, 10 on face-to-face interviewing, 4 on telephone interviewing, 4 on self-completion surveys, 4 on panel surveys, 4 on researching special populations, and one paper on 'statistical ethics', as well as several papers from earlier years, and 22 newsletters which report the proceedings of seminars held by the Joint Centre for Survey Methods in the years between 1980 and 1993 (these seminars are grant-aided by the ESRC and each one is on a major methodological theme).

The Rise of 'Social Research' in General

It is not only central government which has found itself under pressure to develop social research; all sorts of other institutions have also done so: local government, public utilities, research councils, academic departments, the arts, charitable institutions – the list is endless.

Roger Jowell distinguishes a number of 'landmarks' in the progress of social research in Britain. The first two are the confluence of the establishment of the Government Social Survey in response to wartime needs, already discussed, and the availability of certain key researchers who had learnt the techniques before the war, were in contact with American developments, and returned to commercial life with an even broader appreciation of what well-conducted research could achieve as a result of their wartime service. Perhaps the best known and most innovative of these men was Mark Abrams. Even before the war, while at the London Press Exchange, Abrams had done, among other things, one of the early readership surveys (IIPA, 1937), the first group discussions, and (as already noted) the survey of working class diets which later developed into the National Food Survey. During the war, Abrams worked in psychological warfare, during which he used surveys to find out how civilians were reacting to heavy German bombing of various industrial cities. In an interview in 1978, he said:

> The conclusion I arrived at... was that if you bomb civilians who think they are making an important contribution to their country's victory you'll get nowhere; you'll kill some of them; the others will go away for a few nights but then they will come back and work harder. If you bomb a civilian body which thinks it's making no contribution to the war, they will clear away in three nights, but it will make no difference to the nation's ability to fight the war, because they were not contributing anyway. This proved true in Korea and it proved true in Vietnam; I think in every major conflict where someone has attempted to bomb the civilian population that has held true. It was not a particularly popular finding as far as British Bomber Command were concerned (they wanted to use their bombs).

Abrams also developed content analysis on German propaganda in order to determine the directives behind it; changes in the frequency of points made in the propaganda led to inferences about changes in policy.

Abrams returned to LPE after the war and founded Research Services Ltd in 1946. In the same interview, he attributes the acceptance of survey research methods in Britain to a long tradition:

> Whereas other countries, when it came to the study of society, produced eminent sociologists like Durkheim and Weber and so on, we never produced a single sociologist who is a theorist. But what we did produce were people like Bowley, who did a survey of poverty in four towns; Booth, of course, and Rowntree; this was the speciality of British social studies... On balance, I think we probably got the better of the bargain. To know a lot about the factual information about society is as important as having theories about them. One has to bear in mind that there was a well established awareness among the British elite (if one can use that sort of word) – civil servants, managing directors – an awareness of this particular technique of studying society, and that helped. I think this explains why so much more of it was done in this country than was done in Germany, France or any of the continental countries.

The third landmark period was the development of the whole market research industry, as commerce took off again after the ending of post-war restrictions. This commercial work adopted as far as it could the standards that were being set in the Government Social Survey. The foundation of the Market Research Society in 1946 by a group of professionals most of whom shared an LSE education and who included social researchers like Mark Abrams and Louis Moss was a sign of the prevailing mood; if research was to be accepted, comparable standards would have to be set. The commercial firms in existence at the time, notably BMRB and RSL, received a share of the social research commissioned by government as well as from other sources.

During this time the so-called 'Colin Hurry affair' provided a salutary object lesson in the importance of keeping the public confidence in research intact, and not allowing it to be hi-jacked for political ends. Colin Hurry was a PR man who persuaded the steel industry to do a massive survey on attitudes to steel re-nationalisation, at the time a major issue in dispute between the parties. David Pickard was the MRS Chairman at the time (1958-9), and takes up the story:

> BMRB were commissioned to do the job, and a sample of 1,000,000 was proposed (BMRB can't have believed their luck!). With 248,000 interviews already completed, the Press got hold of it and then the Labour Party. Morgan Phillips, the Party Secretary, made highly publicised statements to the effect that clearly the steelmasters and other capitalists would be given the names of anyone who was in favour of nationalisation, and everyone knew what would happen then, didn't they? A nice juicy story, but one with horrid implications for the market research industry.
>
> As it happened, this blew up the day before our Annual Lunch, when we had abruptly to put in an extra table to accommodate an army of journalists. The Council held an emergency meeting just beforehand and I made a statement at the lunch. "Morgan Phillips", I said, "was acting irresponsibly because there was no way in which Hurry, or anyone else, could get access to the names of informants. In pursuance of a political objective, he was making statements with untrue, damaging implications". "He was", I said, "acting like a small boy – give him a stone and he looks round for windows to break". The remark did not go unreported.
>
> Arriving back at my office at about 4pm, I received a phone call from a highly incensed Morgan Phillips. I was holding him up to public ridicule and unless I withdrew my remarks categorically and publicly he proposed to sue me for slander. I expressed polite scepticism as to whether ridiculing a politician was an indictable offence. However, we agreed to meet, and I went straight round to his office together with Brian Copland, who was handling PR for the

Society at that time. Phillips huffed and puffed a bit, but I proposed a deal. I would withdraw my statement about his irresponsibility provided he accepted publicly that there was no possibility of any respectable market research agency handing over informants' names. He agreed. We drafted a joint press release then and there and we all went round the corner for a pint.

This was, I think, a moment of genuine risk for the market research business. In the event, no informant hostility was later reported; indeed, a statement by a well-known personality accepting that we placed a high value on informant anonymity probably did us good. It is worth adding that it was a great comfort to me over a very harassing three days (my phone never stopped ringing) to know that there was solid evidence in the Society's files of an intense concern with standards and ethics to back me up if the going got tough.

In the event, BMRB, realising that the project was in danger of developing into a propaganda exercise, withdrew.

Jowell's fourth landmark period was the development of the Local Authority market for research in the late 1950s/early 1960s, led by the London County Council (later Greater London Council) and fuelled after the Labour government was returned in 1964. Much of this work went to private companies, especially MORI (and still does). Local Authorities came to value the greater accuracy with which research could inform them about what residents really thought about their services (complaints received being notoriously misleading). The effectiveness of Council communications with the community could be measured, and it could be seen as a fairer and more effective way of consulting people about future plans, an antidote to pressure groups.

For instance, it was not until 1988 that Warwickshire District Council did its first piece of consumer research, to look at its service to council tenants. Members of the Housing Department had always felt that they gave an excellent service, and were glad to find that the overall level of satisfaction was the best recorded by MORI up to then. But they were quite surprised to discover that a high proportion of tenants were dissatisfied with their heating, with the lack of consultation over repairs and improvements, the slow speed of repair work and, most of all, how badly they were kept informed about housing services. The Council quickly set up an action plan, with much consultation, meetings, a Repair (Dis)Satisfaction Card, a Tenants' Handbook and a Newsletter. Two years later a follow-up survey showed marked improvements in attitudes. All concerned now realised that consumer research was not a luxury, but an essential part of giving good service (source: *Research Works*, 1991 – papers from the AMSO Research Effectiveness Awards).

The fifth landmark was the establishment of the research councils, particularly the Social Science Research Council (SSRC), later merged into the Economic and Social Research Council (ESRC), as major sources of funding for social research projects. The SSRC was active by the 1960s, providing a major impetus to academic research into social subjects, much of which involved survey work. SCPR, in 1969, was founded as a charitable institution partly in order to take advantage of these grants. The ESRC continues to be important for academic and other institutes which do social research, together with such bodies as the Rowntree Trust, the Nuffield Foundation and the Sainsbury Trust, supplemented increasingly by work commissioned via grants from the European Community. SCPR, for example, currently have two research centre grants with funding for ten years. According to Cooke and Whitaker (MRS Conference paper, 1996) the ESRC invest "several million pounds" each year in academic research projects.

The sixth landmark, in the mid-1970s, was the sudden demise of Local Authority work from the levels it had reached the decade before. This was the time of financial stringency after the oil price squeeze, when Anthony Crosland said, "the party's over" and Denis Healey went 'cap in hand' to the IMF. During that recession, social research done by agencies outside central government was severely depleted. SCPR were compelled to institute the only redundancies in their history, and to look for other, grant-funded work. During these years, the Social Research Association was formed, as a forum to bring together researchers in different organisations, commercial, academic and otherwise, with an interest in social research.

There followed a period of consolidation, and then came the Thatcher government. There was consternation; the New Conservatives, including many in the Cabinet, were known to be hostile to social research, regarding it as a cloak for socialism. However, it was the collapse that never happened.

Before the 1980s, surveys carried out by the Social Survey Division of OPCS (as the Government Social Survey had become) were financed out of the annual vote to the division from central exchequer funds. Customer departments did not themselves have to find the money. Sir Derek Rayner, in his review of the Government Statistical Service (1980), recommended that, in future, ad hoc surveys should be paid for by the departments which commissioned them, and should be contracted out to the private sector where there was a cost advantage. A repayment system was proposed later in the Merchant Review of the Commissioning of Ad Hoc Surveys. All this only applied to ad hoc surveys: the continuous surveys being done by SSD were not yet affected.

There was prolonged debate about these proposals. On the one hand, introducing 'market forces' might lead to better value for money, but on the other there were fears that "the pressure of competition would force the quality of work to deteriorate" and that SSD might lose its recognised reputation for survey expertise. A further review, the Machinery of Government Review of 1986, reaffirmed that the Social Survey function should remain with OPCS, thus calming some fears, but also recommended a more rigorous repayment system which would cover all surveys, including continuous ones. This gave greater flexibility to SSD in budgeting for changing levels of work, allowed SSD to tender competitively for government contracts, and required it to give quotations and charge for services (including its consultancy work as well as the conduct of surveys) in a more 'commercial' manner.

There were also serious attempts made to compare the performance of SSD and the private sector, so as to assess what government work could safely be contracted out, as was done, for example, with the Labour Force Survey of 1983 and the National Travel Survey before it became continuous in 1988. According to Bob Barnes, the quality of SSD work showed up well in the comparison. The new OPCS Omnibus Survey, which started in October 1990, set a target response rate of 75% "... which compares with response rates of about 50% for commercial omnibus surveys using probability samples", and exceeded this target in each of its first six months. Barnes adds in fairness, however, that "to balance the picture... high quality sometimes conflicts with high speed and low cost, and... it has not always been possible to deliver outputs as quickly or cheaply as survey customers would like".

The important point is that the change to a more 'commercial' and competitive system, after a brief period of uncertainty, "did not realise the fears of those who had felt threatened". Since 1984 the demand for SSD's services has remained strong, and several factors have led to growth. Although some cuts were made following Rayner (e.g. by reducing the General Household Survey sample by 14%), a huge expansion of the Labour Force Survey in 1983/4 raised the continuous survey component of SSD's work from 50% to 75%. It has since increased again, with the start of the new Omnibus Survey and another major increase in the Labour Force Survey in 1991/2 (60,000 households per quarter); this survey now provides a major source of data on both employed and unemployed for the Employment Department, measured according to international guidelines. At the same time, the ad hoc component of SSD's work remained steady.

We are now in Jowell's final landmark period, in which every department of state has at least one 'flagship' survey, plus a number of others. A huge infrastructure depends on these surveys and 'feeds off' them; they seem to be related to a department's prestige. The only department which does not have its flagship survey in the Treasury. Most of these surveys are published through HMSO and accessible to the public.

A good example of a continuous departmental survey is the British Crime Survey, carried out at regular intervals since 1982 and now subcontracted to SCPR. Its origins have been described by Pat Mayhew and Mike Hough of the Home Office Research and Planning Unit, in an article first published in 1991 and reprinted in the JMRS in January 1992. According to them, a nationwide survey on crime and victimisation had been "considered throughout the mid-1970s", whilst a number of specific studies were done (e.g. in Sheffield and Manchester), but this was ruled out at the time "mainly on cost grounds, but also because of anxieties about the political snares which survey estimates of unrecorded crime might create".

The case for a survey:

> ... rested largely on the value to policy-makers of having at least a rough guide of the extent and shape of the problem which the criminal justice system was intended to tackle: police statistics of recorded crime were adequate as a measure of police workload, but – because of unreported and unrecorded offences – deficient as an index of crime.

A crime survey would offer a more comprehensive picture of the crime problem. It could also serve as an antidote to what were believed to be public misperceptions about crime levels, trends and risks.

> A survey-based index of crime would demonstrate the possibility that the index of crime based on offences recorded by the police might be subject to 'statistical inflation' by virtue of changing reporting and recording practices.

It was expected to "demonstrate the comparatively low risks of serious crime, and puncture inaccurate stereotypes of crime victims"; it would thus "help create a more balanced climate of opinion" about law and order. Comparison between the surveys and police records has amply justified this objective.

For example, the BCS has shown up significant divergences from police files in the crime trends between 1982 and 1988: a lower overall rate of increase, much lower increases in vandalism, woundings and thefts from cars, but much higher increases in bicycle thefts and residential burglaries, as shown in the following comparison. The table on the following page shows increases in notifiable offences, as shown respectively in police records and the BCS, between 1981 and 1987.

Once such differences are laid bare, one can find reasons for them: changing patterns of insurance, for instance, may be one reason encouraging the reporting of some types of crime more than others, and besides, it is easier to report to the police when most people have a telephone. The surveys have also made possible an objective analysis of the true risks of crime – what localities and what types of person are most at risk – which have been extensively modelled. Surveys such as this assist Home Office policy-makers by assisting them to define the problems which have to be tackled, and by providing a continuous policy data-base, "a continual flow of information on disparate topics". That is their main function, but in addition they serve (or should serve) as a corrective to mistaken public views. The authors are equivocal about this aspect: "How successful", they say, " it has been in changing lay perceptions is hard to assess".

Trends in Crime 1981-1987: A Comparison Between BCS Estimates and Notifiable Offences Recorded by the Police

	Percentage Change 1981-1987	
	Police	BCS
Vandalism	52	9
Theft of motor vehicle	17	36
Theft from motor vehicle	74	63
Bicycle theft	5	80

Residential burglary
   Attempts and no loss
   With loss
	38
	46
	36
		59
		78
		39

Robbery	62	9
Wounding Wounding & robbery	40 44	12 11
All offences	41	30

Source: *1982 and 1988 (core sample) BCS. Quoted by Pat Mayhew and Mike Hough: 'The British Crime Survey: the First Ten Years', JMRS, Vol 34 no 1, January 1992.*

The British Crime Survey is thus an illustration of the value of well-conducted survey research for counteracting public misconceptions, which are often based on other less controlled sources of information which, however suitable for the purposes for which they were devised, can be flawed for objective, unbiased description of the true state of affairs. Another example is the differences which sometimes show in the employment (and unemployment) statistics between the Labour Force Survey on the one hand (in which individuals in households are correctly sampled) and the data from employment offices, which depend on who is signing on the dole. The reconciliation of competing sets of figures, with well-conducted research as the benchmark for interpreting differences, is still very inadequately done, and must be one of the major tasks for researchers in the future. It is not a matter of exalting one set of figures and throwing out all the others, necessarily, so much as comparing them properly and understanding the reasons why they are different, and (most important) getting this understanding itself more widely understood. At a time when the very nature of 'work' is changing fast, only the intelligent use of objective research can give government and the general public a proper picture of the whole truth about employment.

The publication *Social Trends*, which started in 1971, is one approach and a valuable one to the business of publicising information drawn from government and other surveys. By focusing in turn on the issues which generally interest people – demographic changes (what is happening to marriage and divorce, how many children are being born out of wedlock), employment trends, the state of medical and dental care, household size (are there more lone parents? Are 'families' disappearing?), and so on – and presenting the survey-based facts, correctly but in a selective and palatable way, so that they tell the story, this publication contributes much to people's education if they will only read it. Through publications of this kind, research may have a very beneficial effect on democracy. We need more of them.

The Census

It would be wrong to leave the government research scene without taking a look at the decennial Census, for which the 'other half' of OPCS is responsible. It has been of major importance for the development of all research in this country, not merely for government. The population figures provided every ten years and updated in annual projections are the background information needed for structuring and weighting survey samples; the quality of the sample depends on the security of the census base. The Census is thus *the* ultimate benchmark data source: "the 'bedrock' upon which most other social and market research is founded" (*An Introductory Guide to the 1991 Census*, ed. Barry Leventhal et al.). Technical developments in the Census have been responsible for major improvements in survey procedure, especially since the 1981 and 1991 Censuses: the geodemographic clustering systems derived from Census Small Area Statistics, which give an unrivalled basis for sample stratification; the Postcode Address File; the marketing of Census data on tape for customers to use themselves on their computers.

Britain has been exceptionally well served by its Census, which has been repeated every tenth year since the first in 1801 (except 1941): there have thus now been nineteen full censuses. There was an additional mid-term sample census in 1966, but this has not been repeated. OPCS is responsible for the Census in England and Wales only, co-ordinating with the General Register Office for Scotland (GRO(S)), and the Census Office in Northern Ireland.

The Census is a compulsory survey of the whole population, providing a snapshot, taken on a single day, which can be examined at many geographical levels, down to blocks of streets that form neighbourhoods. A wide range of information is collected, about households and individuals. The coverage of the Census is both consistent, because every household answers a similar set of questions at the same time, and comprehensive, because the enumeration achieves a response rate which no other survey can approach. The operation of the Census is governed by the Census Act 1920; for each specific census, Parliamentary approval must be specifically obtained. To ensure public co-operation, very strict rules and safeguards govern confidentiality of the information provided, so that no individual households or persons can ever be identified in the results.

OPCS produce tabulated statistics for all sorts of geographical areas in which users may be interested (counties, Health Authority areas, parliamentary constituencies, postcode areas etc.), and most of them are available also on tape or CD-ROM. But perhaps the most valuable for researchers have been the SAS (or Small Area Statistics), which were an innovation in the 1981 Census and have proved extremely popular. The SAS provide statistical tables for the very smallest geographical areas available, the EDs or Census Enumeration Districts (on average, EDs consist of 200 households, although there are wide variations; for confidentiality, there are certain restrictions on SAS for the smallest EDs). OPCS also produce maps at ED level, and (from 1991 for the first time) a directory listing postcodes in every ED.

The SAS have been the basis for a computerised instrument which has been of major benefit to the research industry. It carries the rather unwieldy name of 'geodemographics'. In the decade since 1981, the market for geodemographic services has grown to a size estimated at approximately £25 million in 1992, and still expanding at a minimum of 20% per annum.

Geodemographics has been loosely defined as 'the analysis of people by where they live', or 'locality marketing'. The technique was first developed for social research purposes during the 1970s, by Richard Webber, who at the time was working at the Centre for Environmental Studies investigating measures of deprivation in Liverpool. Webber used cluster analysis methods on data from the 1966 mid-term Census to build a classification at ward level which identified different types of deprived area; the wards were described in terms of *combinations* of Census-based variables relating to types of housing, employment levels, age and social grade of the population, etc.

BMRB were the first company to see the commercial potential of these methods. Ken Baker, the statistician there at the time, experimented with Webber's classification, using it to code the sampling points for the Target Group Index (BMRB's single-source multi-product and media survey, described later in our chapter on media research). Baker found that the Census-based codes were highly discriminatory; for example, they could distinguish between readers of the *Guardian* and the *Daily Telegraph* far better than traditional indicators such as social grade, age or education.

In 1979, this experience with the TGI was published in a paper at the Market Research Society Conference. In the same year, CACI Ltd, a company which had been running a computer-based geographical mapping system used mainly by the retail industry, recruited Richard Webber to develop his system for them. The system was re-run at ED level, named ACORN (A Classification Of Residential Neighbourhoods), and began to take off. ACORN was useful both for analysing survey data, as a demographic variable, and as a stratifier (a very good one) when selecting primary sampling areas. Its potential value when targeting specific populations, especially via direct marketing, mailing or product sampling schemes, posters etc., was obvious. It was quickly linked not only to the TGI but to the National Readership Survey, most of the AGB consumer panels, and (importantly) to the Electoral Roll, by then computerised.

Fresh classifications were done on the new (1981) Census. Competitors emerged for ACORN, and there are now several other major suppliers, often linked into other data sources, and with subtly different classifications of the neighbourhood 'types'. Such suppliers are 'Census Agencies', acquiring the relevant Census material from OPCS and building it into their own marketable systems.

Geodemographics is not unique to Britain; the Americans were developing their own zip-code classification system (Claritas' PRIZM), based on Bureau of the Census data, during the late 1970s. But the speed with which it has developed, in both countries, is a tribute to the sophistication of the Census base from which it is derived, as well as the commercial acumen shown (again in both countries) by OPCS and the Bureau, which one would not always expect to find in civil service departments.

Apart from geodemographics, the Census now provides a wide range of commercially valuable products linking geographical information with other data sources, which are used by marketers and retailers to add precision to their efforts. Direct marketing and database users are increasingly beneficiaries. Market research has benefited from improved sample selection and analysis, for example the provision of postcoded addresses from the Postcode Address File (which has now superseded the Electoral Register for most sampling applications). Increasingly, such services are being provided in such a way that users can operate on their own systems, using bespoke software.

Political Research: The Polls and Other Animals

Besides the uses of research for government administration and other social purposes, we must look at research in the political arena: a smaller spend in total but a much higher profile.

There is more to research in politics than is usually realised. Everyone knows about opinion polls; fewer will be aware of the private research on political issues which is regularly done by the main parties; fewer still are likely to know much about the serious contribution which research has made to the study of British elections and our understanding of the political process.

Opinion Polling

The polls hang like a sword of Damocles over the research industry. Although they occupy only some 1.5% of total research turnover, they are the most public face of the business – indeed, for many, the *only* face they ever see. And they are highly vulnerable. The 'prediction' they provide before an election is tested by the event as no other research results are, and if they 'get it wrong', the whole country knows it in next morning's newspaper. The research industry has always been extremely sensitive to the damage this could do to the public acceptability of research (although there is little evidence of such errors having ever had any serious effect on clients' research budgets), and when problems have arisen, the Market Research Society has swung into action to investigate and explain them. Another result of this sensitivity is that the companies who do opinion polling, who have remained relatively few in number, have over the years reviewed, refined and perfected their procedures to an extent few other parts of the business can match.

Opinion polling started, like most research innovations, in America; the first 'straw poll' by journalists on the eve of an election is attributed to a Pennsylvanian paper in 1824 ('straw poll' is derived from 'a straw in the wind', i.e. a hint of things to come). The doyen during the 1930s was Dr George Gallup of the Gallup Poll. In 1938, the Gallup Poll was brought to England and started, with the support of the *News Chronicle*, by Dr Henry Durant, another of the LSE alumni who was later to become one of the founding fathers and an early chairman of the Market Research Society. The *News Chronicle* asked Durant to forecast the West Fulham bye-election:

Edith Summerskill was Labour candidate. It was a
Conservative seat and she upset the Conservative, as I had
forecast, and by a miracle I got it on the nose within 1%;
beginner's luck.

Henry Durant, interviewed in 1979

After that, the new Gallup (under the name: The British
Institute for Public Opinion) continued to publish election
forecasts, getting them right in almost every case; the contract
with the *News Chronicle* continued for 23 years until the paper
disappeared. On Wednesday, October 19th, 1938 (a fortnight
after Munich), the Chronicle published the exclusive first
results of a nationwide survey conducted by the British
Institute of Public Opinion: 57% of the public said they were
satisfied with Mr Chamberlain as Prime Minister, 43% said
they were not, a quarter of whom had been supporters of the
National Government at the last election. The *News Chronicle*
went on to say:

> Believing that an accurate assessment of public opinion is
> of the first importance to the people of this country, the
> *News Chronicle* has commissioned the British Institute of
> Public Opinion to take a series of surveys in Great Britain.
> The technique used is that of the Sampling Referendum
> which has proved highly successful in the United States. It
> was devised by Dr George Gallup, founder and director of
> the American Institute of Public Opinion and its British
> counterpart.

Durant continues:

When the general Election came, in May 1945, Gallup
showed that Attlee was going to win with the Labour Party.
Nobody believed us, including all the *News Chronicle*
people. There was only one, I learned later, who believed
Churchill would lose: the Duke of Devonshire. And he
believed it for very personal reasons. His son, later killed in
the war, had in '44 stood in a bye-election, as Independent
in Chatsworth constituency, and lost. Devonshire correctly
argued, "If my son, standing in my own bailiwick, can't win
the seat, then the Conservative party is going to lose."

The Gallup Poll did not stay alone for long. By the 1950 election the *Daily Express* and *Daily Mail* had both entered the field; the *Express* continued running its own polls into the 60s (although there were some doubts in the market research world as to exactly how they did them), and Associated Newspapers founded NOP (National Opinion Polls) in 1957, which thereafter polled regularly for the *Mail*. Other organisations came and sometimes went. Marplan was founded in 1959, ORC in 1968, MORI in 1969, ICM (following Marplan's demise) in 1990. RSL, under Mark Abrams, made a brief entry with the *Daily Graphic* at the 1951 election, which folded with the paper; they entered the market again twice (with two different papers) in 1964 and 1966, and with the *Observer* in 1979. By the mid-1960s the quality newspapers had taken up associations with polling companies, and the 1966 election set the pattern which has persisted ever since of (give or take) about six polls published across the main national newspapers. *Business Decisions* entered briefly for the *Observer* in the two 1974 elections, but did not reappear.

There have always been mixed feelings about the polls. Durant, referring to the 1945 election, comments that polls were 'very much disliked' at that time; the Gallup success in predicting that election was a startling confirmation that sample surveys were capable of accurate work and helped everyone in research. Morgan Phillips, General Secretary of the Labour Party, is quoted as warning against "a new technique of propaganda, the publication of polls". This is of a piece with Michael Foot's later comment, writing in the *Evening Standard* (1973): "I have always regarded public opinion polls, audience ratings and a sizeable chunk of what passes under the name of market research as tosh and dangerous tosh at that" (but it is not recorded that he ever discontinued his party's private polling).

The suggestion that polls are dangerous because they 'influence' people in their voting, in a possibly wrong direction, continues to surface from time to time, sometimes with suggestions that they should be banned or at least suppressed from publication before elections. The Speaker's Conference recommended in 1967 that polls should be banned in the immediate period before polling day, and a Private Member's Bill was introduced to the same end in the mid-1970s. Bob Worcester tells how a senior Labour NEC member expressed to him a desire to ban polls for the fortnight before an election, explaining "it is sometimes necessary to be anti-democratic in order to save democracy" (adding that of course they would continue to do their private polls).

A quite different concern was voiced by another MP, this time a Conservative, Christopher Hollis, at a debate at a Market Research Society lunch in 1948. Hollis was worried about a recent opinion poll about capital punishment. He had no doubt that the poll had been carried out with 'complete integrity', but whether the result had been fortunate was, he thought, much more doubtful:

> Here was a question that was fundamentally psychiatric, and it was unfortunate that perfectly honest public opinion should be given in this very definite statistical form. The information given was dangerous, not because it was wrong, but because it was right.

Hollis went on:

> The politician lives with his ear far too close to the ground... We are less likely to get good government if he is so mathematically certain of the short-term opinion of his constituents. If you were crooks or charlatans, I should not worry in the least. It is because you are so honest and conscientious that I am afraid you are enemies of democracy.

Another speaker in the same debate, the Labour politician Dr Stephen Taylor, noted "the failure of opinion polls to differentiate between informed and uninformed public opinion".

The counter-argument against those who would ban polling before elections is easy to deploy. Bob Worcester, who since his foundation of MORI in 1969 has become by far the best known public exponent of the polls, puts it well in his book *British Public Opinion: a guide to the history and methodology of public opinion polling* (1991). The polls are information, of better quality than most. If they were suddenly removed, there would still be information, but of worse quality. The public would still seek to know what is happening, and there would be no lack of contenders with their own persuasive agendas to fill the gaps for them. Political parties "would do even more polling than they do now, and leak it even worse than they do now". Underlying this fear of the polls' 'influence', as well as the attitudes expressed by Hollis, one can discern a contempt for the ability of voters to make up their minds for themselves; better for them to remain in ignorance, so that they can continue to be led.

To quote Worcester:

> The banning of publication of polls has been widely condemned and yet some countries do ban their publication and in other countries there are periodic attempts by well-meaning or publicity-seeking politicians to enact legislation restricting them. It is up to editors and journalists, public opinion researchers and interested members of the public to be alert to these misguided efforts, to join together to defeat these attempts to limit press freedom and to use their ability to follow good practice in the conduct and presentation of polls to remove from their opponents any ammunition that they may derive from examples of bad practice.

Worcester is unrepentant about the possibility that polls may influence voting behaviour. They do, and it is a good thing. The evidence is that in general elections such effects are small and largely self-cancelling; they have more effect in by-elections, where people wish to make a protest against the ruling government. People will be influenced by whatever is available: how can it improve matters to increase their ignorance?

Because the polls are so public, there is heightened concern about their accuracy. They must be squeaky clean. The supporting newspapers, of course, will still publish them and, indeed, will get extra editorial mileage out of variation between polls or a maverick result, because the entertainment value is part of the attraction. But no poll could afford to be consistently wrong, and if it happens widely, as it did in the 1970 and 1992 elections, a frisson of fear goes through the whole research community in case there should be a damaging rub-off on *all* research.

Dulce et decorum est pro patria Robert Worcester

Polling organisations have therefore been meticulous in checking and refining all aspects of their operation – sampling, weighting, questionnaire design, field organisation etc. – so as to eliminate as far as possible any bias in the response, or at least identify and aim off for it where elimination is impossible. According to Bob Worcester, over the 13 general elections since the war up to 1987, polls have performed, on average, as would be expected from the science of sampling. Of the 55 election forecasts over this time, a quarter were able to estimate the Labour and Conservative share of the vote to within plus or minus 1%, and over 60% to within plus or minus 2%. This is an impressive enough performance. Just as importantly, polling organisations have been as careful as possible in their relationships with their sponsoring newspapers to ensure that these make clear to their readers the nature of the questions and sampling on which the results are based, the limitations and caveats required, so as to avoid misinterpretation. A particularly important aspect of this is the question of how far polls can *predict* election results. It is constantly reiterated that polls can only be a 'snapshot' of what people were thinking at the time the polls were taken, and that opinions can change at the margin very quickly as an election campaign progresses, so that only the most last-minute polls can really be taken to 'predict', and then with a pinch of salt. 'Prediction' of election results, it must always be remembered, involves predicting two quite different things: the share of the vote, which as Worcester says is usually very accurate, at least on the eve of the election, and the share of seats (i.e., which party will win power), with which the papers are generally more concerned, and which involves some extra calculations.

There have been only two serious stumbles where the polls have got the election result wrong. The first was in 1970, when all the polls except one 'predicted' a Labour victory with leads of between 2% and 9%, and the Heath government scraped in with a Conservative lead of 2.4%. This has been referred to as Britain's 1948, a reference to the disaster in the USA when all the polls forecast that Dewey, not Truman, would win the presidential election. The second was in the 1992 election, when four polls on the eve of polling suggested a marginal Labour lead, but the actual Conservative lead was 7.6%. This was the greatest gap since polls began. In both cases, the Market Research Society mounted an intensive investigation, with support from the polling organisations concerned (e.g. with programmes of repeat interviews with respondents to assess the extent of late swings). These investigations have made clear the difficulty of achieving precision in this field. Late changes of mind, response biases, and a slightly lower willingness among Conservative supporters to reveal their loyalties, all proved to have some influence in 1992. David Butler, in his summary of the report of the investigation, said that it was not possible to assign a weight to the importance of these factors, and there were other minor influences. He recommended attention to these three main sources of error: one would be easy to avoid in future, one would be harder, and the third (late swing) might well be beyond solution. Butler comments: "the standards of accuracy which are demanded from pre-election polls – and which the pollsters seem forced implicitly to accept – are far more stringent than those applied to any other form of survey research." He also says, importantly: "we do not believe that deliberate lying to pollsters occurred to any significant extent."

Private Political Research

Bob Worcester regards the 1960s as the period when polling came of age. New companies entered the field, together with the quality press, and television as well as newspapers started to take the polls seriously. Private polls were regularly commissioned by the political parties and by other pressure groups.

Both main parties started to flirt with survey research during the 1950s, but did not at first do much with it. By the mid-60s, the Conservative party were undertaking substantial private research; they became the first major client of the Opinion Research Centre (ORC), founded in 1968, and for some years ran a panel of voters through BMRB to measure changes in attitudes within the same individuals.

Mark Abrams, Chairman of RSL, began work for the Labour party during the 50s with some small-scale enquiries. One of the things he did, at the time when Enoch Powell was making his speeches about immigration, was to show respondents seven of Powell's statements, without attribution, and ask for their views and then their party support. A majority of Labour supporters turned out to be in agreement with

Powell. The reaction of the then General Secretary of the Labour party, Len Williams, was: "Damned waste of money; I could have told you that without a survey".

Nye Bevan opposed the use of polls; after his death, and other changes in organisation, Mark Abrams began to get larger commissions. A more substantial survey in marginal constituencies was done in 1962, and panels of voters revisited at intervals during 1963 and 1964. These surveys showed that the views of the electorate were not at all what had been assumed. It was not true, as Wilson had thought, that at least half the population were solidly Labour; only two thirds were loyal supporters of either of the main parties; class was far from perfectly correlated with that support; there were uncommitted voters of both sides; and most people were only vaguely interested in politics, if at all. By 1964, the Labour party was using its own surveys effectively to improve advertising and party broadcasts, and target relevant voters better. Previously, as Abrams commented in an article about this time, Labour (unlike the Conservatives) had had no communications machinery which could have made effective use of survey findings.

Bob Worcester quotes a comment from Austin Mitchell, a former politics lecturer and Nuffield Fellow and later a Labour MP, about the 1979 election:

> More modern parties see the need for objective information of the type forthcoming from surveys of opinion. In 1978 such surveys provided early warnings of the changing predilections of the skilled worker, of the growing feeling for a 1978 election, of Labour's weak points. They can also provide much information about specific groups, and reactions to policies, individual issues and even the party generally. Yet polling needs to be done regularly to warn of trends and to allow the party to develop the skills and the habits of dealing with the information. This does not mean adopting the Tory approach of formulating policies just because they are popular, though in a democracy popularity

has to be a major argument in favour of a policy and certainly not one against it. Rather the information is used as a chart of the territory through which the party has to trek. Polls bring knowledge of which subjects to tackle head on, which to strike, which issues to push home and which to avoid, which policies will sell and which won't. Labour is as much in the merchandising business as the makers [of] biological Ariel. There is little point in confusing bad merchandising with high principle.

It is interesting to compare Austin Mitchell's image of research being used to chart the way through unknown territory with the British Crime Survey discussed earlier, and its use as a data-base for policy-makers and a corrective for popular misconceptions about crime. The common ground is the danger of going wrong: without a good map, we lose our way.

The parties have continued to rely on research, between as well as during elections. Labour moved to MORI in 1969, while the Tories continued with ORC.

Election Studies

Besides their immediate interest for politicians and publishers, the polls have fed the academic world. There is now a well-developed discipline of psephology, based on the painstaking accretion of knowledge over the years. Every British election since 1950 has been studied, and an analytical book written about it. The leading figure has been Dr David Butler of Nuffield College, known to the television audience as the man who invented 'swing', the measurement which excites our commentators on election nights. Swing is calculated by subtracting, say, the Conservative lead at one point in time from another, earlier, point in time and dividing by two; a swing of 2% suggests that two people in a hundred have moved from one party to another. It can neatly be calculated for all sorts of interesting sub-groups: geographical regions, marginal constituencies, etc.

The British General Election Survey series was originated by David Butler and Donald Stokes, and constitutes the longest academic series of nationally representative probability sample surveys in the country. Its broad aim is "to explore the changing determinants of electoral behaviour in contemporary Britain". These surveys have taken place immediately after every general election since 1964, giving a total of nine so far, plus two intervening surveys. SCPR has been co-responsible for five of these, two in 1974 and the three since 1983 carried out jointly by SCPR and Nuffield College, Oxford. As a result of this collaboration, and to establish a base for work on election studies, SCPR and Nuffield College established JUSST (the Joint Unit for the Study of Social Trends), later awarded ESRC status, and funded by the ESRC and, more recently, other sources including the Sainsbury Family Charitable Trusts. Data from the post-election studies are deposited with the ESRC Data Archive, so that they are available to future scholars (the Archive was originally set up by the SSRC in the 1960s, and contains a number of surveys from the private as well as the public sector which have been donated for academic use).

The BGES surveys have now become quite elaborate affairs, involving telephone surveys with panels of respondents both before and after the election day, including samples who had been interviewed after the previous election, and a face-to-face survey with a fresh sample.

Measuring Reactions to Policies and Events

Opinion polls do not merely refer to elections and political parties: they are used to monitor public opinion on important events and issues of the day. Unquestionably, their publication does not simply trace opinion, but can help to direct and strengthen government policy. Bob Worcester gives a convincing account of this happening during the Falklands conflict:

The public mood towards the handling of the Falklands War – coming as it did totally out of the blue – was initially one of cautious, wait-and-see support for the government As the crisis developed, however, the level of satisfaction with the way the government handled the situation improved steadily – from 60% approval in early April to 84% in late May...

Initially there was some doubt in the British public's mind about the importance of retaining British sovereignty over the Falklands if it resulted in the loss of British servicemen's lives (44% believed it important enough, 49% disagreed)There was even less enthusiasm if carrying the war to the Falklands caused the loss of Falkland Islanders' lives...

As the crisis developed and the island of South Georgia was taken without loss of life, the answers to the conditional question turned from negative to positive, with 51% in agreement that the loss of servicemen's lives could be justified in the 20-21 April survey to 58% in the 23-24 April survey, then down slightly to 53% early in May after the first loss of life, and finally to 62% at the end of May.

The dip in early May coincided with the sinkings of the Belgrano and the Sheffield:

An examination of the findings showed that the downturn in confidence was occasioned by the sudden loss of life, i.e. with the sinking of the General Belgrano, rather than the loss of British lives specifically. With the death toll rising into the hundreds, the late May findings showed that although nearly two-thirds of those questioned believed retaining sovereignty was justification enough for the loss of lives, 34% disagreed. This issue of 'proportionality' remained the hardest for polling questions to elucidate.

In contrast, the proportion who said they 'cared very much' about the sovereignty issue remained remarkably constant throughout the whole conflict.

By mid-May, when all the negotiation attempts had clearly failed, a clear majority (59%) were in favour of a full-scale invasion of the Falklands. After the landing, when British losses became serious, "some observers expected public support to begin to dwindle. In fact, the opposite occurred". Worcester comments that this response was similar to what happened in Suez, when support for the Eden government and for Eden himself remained high even though "opinion was eventually equivocal" about the expedition itself.

These regular polls must at least have given comfort to the government that their actions had popular support. They may be contrasted with the claim made by Tony Benn in the House of Commons during the early days of the crisis that "Public opinion in Britain is swinging massively against the war", based on several hundred letters which he said had been sent to him. If public opinion is not monitored accurately, with representative sampling and careful and sensitive questioning, one is not left with a vacuum; one gets distorted and misleading impressions, based on biased reports and the differential energies of pressure groups. There can be no argument which is the more dangerous for a democratic system.

However, the Falklands example illustrates another important point that can be too easily forgotten. People's understanding of an issue is often, understandably, vague, especially if it seems to involve a distant future which is remote from their daily lives. Responses can be volatile and insecure, and very much affected by the precise question asked. As the issue becomes more immediate and is regularly discussed in the media, views consolidate, although question wording can still affect the 'answer'.

In 1975, before the referendum on whether Britain should stay in the EC, NOP asked five different question wordings on five matched samples. The results varied widely, from majorities for staying in ranging from 0.2% to 18.2%; the experiment was published in the *Daily Mail* (Feb 24th, 1975) under the headline 'The Market: it's not what they ask, but how they ask it'. It was hypothesised that one reason for this divergence was that the situation was not close enough to people, the actual voting still being some way off. At a time when referenda are again in the air, on an even more abstruse subject (a single currency), there are two important lessons to be drawn: first, the subject needs to be approached from several angles (just one question almost certainly will not do), and secondly, measurements need to be repeated continuously. It would be most unwise for a government to rely on a single question, obtained at one point in time, as a basis for assessing the 'true' public reaction to an important political decision.

4

From Sales to Marketing

As we have seen, most of the basic market research techniques still in use today were already in place before the start of the war. During the wartime and post-war periods of shortage, when commercial activity slumped, they were refined and polished by Government use. But the real flowering of modern market research in Britain began in the late forties-early fifties, when the economy escaped from its post-war straitjacket and started to expand. It is at this point that market research begins to be pulled together into a *commercial* discipline, thanks largely to the twenty-three founders of the Market Research Society.

The expansion was consumer-led. People on a wide scale were feeling better, with money to spend. This was a new phenomenon, not merely since the war but looking back to the depression years in the early thirties. This 'consumer-centredness' was at the heart of the growth of new patterns of retailing and the emergence of 'marketing', both as a concept and a company function, of which market research was an integral part.

Before this period, one did not talk about 'marketing' but about 'selling'. Consumer goods companies were essentially divided into Production and Sales, with R & D as a tool or adjunct of the former and advertising of the latter. The producer was in control. If he had a good product which met people's needs, and a sales force which could give him distribution over the country, he would be hard for a would-be rival to challenge. As Harry Henry put it, consumers

> ... were obliged, to a great or less extent, to take what industry produced, within the limits of a rigidly circumscribed buying power. And at the same time cumbersome and difficult-to-change manufacturing processes, frequently shrouded in secrecy, very much restricted the flexibility of action open to an industrialist.

The sales force was also a vital asset, when supermarkets were unknown, and the local shopkeeper relied on the regular visit from the rep for his district to renew orders and keep abreast of things. Companies like Reckitt and Colman grew powerful by buying up unique inventions such as Dettol, Steradent and Harpic (all developed originally by small businesses) in order to give them distribution through their immense sales force. The sales director of Reckitts in the fifties used to tell the story of his early days as a young rep, of how the Area Manager would once a year make a royal progress around his district, in his top hat and his Rolls, always stopping outside the shop so that the shopkeeper came out to him.

Bill Wilson, a founder member of the MRS and later Chairman, described his days with Heinz during the early 1950s:

> Heinz didn't have a marketing department at that time. They had, in fact, a very big sales force of about 700 salesmen and they had four specialist managers; one was the merchandising manager, who developed point of sale material; two were advertising managers, one of whom concentrated on posters and one press and magazines – we're talking pre-TV. These were specialist functions and there was no marketing as such.

Alistair Sedgwick, in a paper written in 1956, when he was Advertising director of Gillette Industries Ltd, described the first introduction of market research at Gillette immediately after the war:

We took the decision, which at that time seemed most daring, of forming our own market research department. I well remember those early days. To say that our market research manager and all he practised was held in high suspicion by many of our executives is a gross understatement. I think that at the beginning most of our people considered that he practised some form of black art; that in place of a desk in his office he had a cauldron and that most of his days were spent in concocting some devilish brew out of which, from time to time, a genie would appear and announce that Blue Gillette held eighty per cent of the market.

This attitude slowly changed in the fifties and sixties. From being at the bottom of the pecking order (having to take what was provided), the consumer moved to the top, and the distribution system, with the greater choice it could provide, changed to accommodate him. And with consumer power came the rise in importance of the marketer, as companies invested in building up the long-term franchises for their brands.

Research lubricated this change. It was research which taught the manufacturer how many *young* people had false teeth (a surprisingly large percentage); what housewives really did with Dettol (most of it was used in the bath); how many times a week people cleaned their shoes, or baked their own cakes; how often they shopped (often daily, then), and what they put in their shopping basket; how many families had refrigerators, television, phones, cars or holidays, and how quickly this changed (in the mid-1950s, less than 15% of families owned a car and 7% a fridge); how many (or rather, how few in those days, compared to today) owned their own home, or had a cheque account, or owned shares, or ate foreign food. Research in 1948 told Alistair Sedgewick at Gillette that, in Italy, less than one man in ten shaved every day (compared with more than six out of ten in Britain). Research found that Johnson's Baby Powder was just as likely to be used by grown-ups as babies. Research charted the demise of the 'great British breakfast', and discovered that cornflakes could make quite a good evening meal. Research results were fed through into strategic development and tactical marketing plans, and when R & D had designed the formulation and packaging thought most likely to appeal, research would be used again to test it, so as to get the whole mix of product, pack and price 'right' at an acceptable cost. A large proportion of company research budgets during the 1950s, and even earlier in pre-war days, was devoted to the trial of product variants.

The switch in emphasis from the needs of production/ distribution to brand building imposed a new structure on companies:

> Marketing was a new profession – one with terrific potential for career advancement, in that the disciplines of managing the profitability of brand portfolios were an excellent training ground for a career in general management. Brand building was everything; markets were growing and private label negligible. Very many of the leading brands today trace their heritage to these decades (the 50s and 60s).
>
> *Mike Penford: 'Continuous research - Art Nielsen to AD 2000',*
> *JMRS, January 1994*

Measuring Purchases

The need to obtain reliable estimates of sales at the retailer end – what actually goes over the counter – was an early stimulus to research. A.C.Nielsen, who pioneered the methodology in 1933, introduced it to Britain in 1939, in his first overseas subsidiary, in response to interest shown by manufacturers in the food and drug fields. Nielsen became, and remains today, the doyen of retail research, in spite of being joined by a number of competitors over the years.

There were three main reasons why manufacturers needed to know what happened to their product when it reached the retailer. One, obviously, was to understand what the competition was doing. Another was timing; relying on ex-factory sales alone could be very misleading if, for example, stock was failing to move out of the wholesalers. But a third factor, of great importance when these systems were set up, was distribution. When most sales were through small independents (supermarkets did not start appearing until the mid-fifties), keeping track of distribution was a key sales management function. Even more important than volume distribution was the distribution in value terms: ensuring that one maintained a presence in those stores which had the potential to deliver the most sales for the least relative cost.

Maintaining this distribution on a regular basis was the function of the sales force. Why not rely on salesmen's reports? Because they were not objective. A salesman's job was to get into a selling relationship with the retailer; he must take a position, be an advocate, be prejudiced. This was incompatible with detached observation. And, even if this were not so, he would not have the time. The only facts a salesman could report would be those a retailer told him, and they would bear little relation to the truth. Moreover, each salesman could only see a small part of the picture, that in which he himself operated, and organising salesmen's reports into a coherent whole would be a very difficult task even if individually they could be believed.

The retail audit, as Nielsen developed it, was designed to give managers an objective overview of sales off-take, goods in stock, and distribution, within different types of retailer (small independent, large independent, cash & carry, multiple branch etc.) and different regions. It was seen essentially as a sales management aid, to spot areas of weakness (e.g. stock shortages) so that action could be taken to remedy them, and to reassure that one was standing proud against one's competitors. The data were obtained from a panel of stores, sampled so as to underpin their objectivity (but a source of weakness if a major chain refused to play, as happened from the outset with Boots).

A Nielsen audit would be bought for a product field. It reported every two months according to a fixed formula. At the beginning and end of the two months, Nielsen auditors visited the store and physically counted all the relevant stock; they also counted all deliveries to the store during the intervening period, adding up delivery notes, invoices, cash & carry records, etc. The stock and distribution figures were provided by the stock counts, and consumer sales by the simple formula: stock at beginning plus deliveries minus stock at end. Other useful data, such as selling prices and other promotions, could be collected at the same time. 'Sterling sales' and 'sterling distribution' would be calculated as well as volume sales and distribution, enabling the client to assess more accurately where his and his competitors' revenue was coming from, and whether, for example, expenditure of effort to cover the bottom 5% of stores where he might lack distribution would really justify the cost of the extra sales he was likely to achieve.

Although the main focus for retail audits has remained the fmcg markets through grocers and chemists, audit panels employing similar principles of measurement have been set up in several other types of outlet: newsagents and tobacconists, pubs and off-licences, prescription medicines (counting doctors' prescriptions). Besides the strategic monitoring of distribution channels, there are valuable tactical uses. Audits can provide actionable data on the results of, say, a price change, a promotion or a package change before a long history has built up, and they have often been incorporated into local market tests. Sometimes for this purpose special panels are set up, with retailer co-operation, in test areas and compared with stores in other (control) areas.

As marketing became dominant in companies during the fifties and sixties, the retail audit often turned into a weapon in the internal dogfight between marketing and sales. Many of those old enough will recognise from personal experience this account by Mike Penford of AGB:

Marketers were fascinated by the audit's ability to measure their market and shares, the results of their marketing efforts and the opportunity to criticise the sales effort behind the brand. Indeed, throughout this era and for many years further, a partnership would be formed between the Marketing Director and the Nielsen Account Director in attacks on a company's sales force. The Account Director would gleefully point to out-of-stock and low stock figures – his cries of 'extremely high' and 'disappointing' translated by his marketing ally as 'unacceptable' and 'appalling' to the squirming sales force. The Nielsen Account Directors of this period, apart from having an ability to spot high levels of stock and choose a good claret, certainly knew their paymaster.

Penford, 1994 (Ibid.)

Mike Penford in this quotation illustrates a danger that research still faces even in a more sophisticated marketing climate: that of being seen purely as a tactical device. The problem does not apply exclusively to retail audit data. There is a tendency for some marketing men to demand research which can be 'directly applied' to decision making, or 'action-oriented' (another favourite term). Useful though this may be, too great a concentration of it can result in the research being misunderstood, and the risk of losing sight of the important strategic revelations it might contain.

The practice of retail auditing remained with little change until the early eighties. However, audits reduced in importance, as the gradual concentration of retailer power swung the emphasis away from questions of distribution and stock pressure to the tactical demands of merchandising, competitive pricing and promotions. The pressure grew for more sensitive analysis (now possible with computer programs which could easily disaggregate and re-shuffle the database), and faster reporting times; the traditional bi-monthly report fitted less and less well with the reaction speeds now being required.

The change in the balance of power between manufacturer and retailer related to another important development: the growth in continuous consumer panels, which gradually assumed greater importance as retailer concentration grew. Use of consumer panels in any country strongly correlates with the concentration curve of retailers. The main reason for this is the need for manufacturers to monitor brands' performance within key named accounts.

Traditional retail audits have always been hampered by the reluctance (frequently, downright refusal) of retailers to co-operate if their own information is separated out. When most of the market is in scattered independents and small multiples, this does not matter so much; but as concentration grows, it becomes vital. The 'retail share of trade' in the grocery or chemist market is an important part of the currency required for negotiation between manufacturer and retailer. The competitive promotional situation today in Tesco, say, will be utterly different from that in Sainsbury during the same period, and aggregating them together removes all practical actionable meaning.

Consumer panels escape from this restriction, since households on the panel can give information about where they make their purchases, and the panel operator, unlike the retail audit company, is free to report this information, since he does not depend on the retailer's permission for access to the data. According to Tim Bowles, now European managing director of IRI but formerly with AGB, the named account problem was a major reason why AGB's TCA consumer panel was able to survive against Nielsen in the sixties: Nielsen was bound, under the terms on which it obtained the data, not to report on individual named accounts; AGB, obtaining data from its own consumer panels, had no such limitation.

Thus, by the end of the seventies, it looked as though retail auditing had sunk to the position of a rather boring regular information supply: necessary to keep track of certain aspects of sales efficiency, but providing little of the impetus to marketing.

EPOS

Then, in the early eighties, a new technology appeared which was to revolutionise retail auditing. This was Electronic Point-of Sale (EPOS for short). EPOS enables the price of each item sold to be checked as it is bought, at the check-out, and recorded on a computer at that point. It can be done by manual entry, but the real revolution came with the invention of the bar-code. This is a unique code printed on the package, which simply has to be passed over a magic eye at the check-out to be recorded instantly.

The bar-code which the laser reads is a system of black and white lines which is unique for each product and the same wherever the product is sold within the country. Standardisation of this coding system is obviously crucial to its success. In North America, where the technology began, the system used is a 12-digit code known as the Universal Product Code (so that scanners in America are always called UPC Scanners); we have a different one, the EAN (European Article Number), which has 13 digits and is used throughout Europe, Asia and Australasia.

That will be £1.75 for the groceries and £250 for the EPOS data

EPOS has an obvious value to the retailer, if he is a major multiple like Sainsbury or Tesco. He can get an instant record of exactly what is moving off his shelves, and such information can be centrally collated every day with on-line transmission. For the audit researcher, it made the expensive personal bi-monthly check redundant; the same detail, and more, could be obtained on a daily basis if required, and reported at far greater frequency. No longer would clients have to wait two months for the next Nielsen report. Weekly reporting has now become commonplace.

Moreover, the sales measurement is now direct, and no longer a calculated estimate from stocks and deliveries. There is a sense of immediacy: the closest possible contact with each actual purchase event. Such data can be disaggregated and summed into varying periods as smoothly as the available software will allow. Because the data appear on a weekly basis, they can be fitted with marketing activities which can also change week by week, and provide many more data points from which to model sales volatility, price elasticities and promotional effects. As Mike Penford explains, the traditional monthly or bi-monthly audit led to 'numbers in a box': "my brand share is 26.7% this period, compared with 25.2% for the same period a year ago". These data, as he says, are fine, but limited to strategic monitoring and loosely calculated effects of marketing activities. Now it can all be tightened up, and effects related directly to (at least some of) their causes.

The traditional audit has not disappeared completely. There are still contexts (e.g. unusual types of retail outlet) where it is needed. But audits in the main grocer and chemist outlets are now scanner driven. The adoption of bar-coding, under the supervision of ISBA and AURA representing the manufacturers concerned, and the conversion of Nielsen panels to scanner measurement only took a few years and were complete by the mid-eighties in Britain.

The new magic has a price, however. One aspect is that scanning systems produce a much greater flow of data, which on the whole users have not yet found adequate means to cope with. This is not merely the result of weekly collection and reporting. It has coincided with the increasing fragmentation of markets during the eighties, as manufacturers sought to expand by means of line extensions and cross-market fertilisation. These two factors, more frequent counting times additional lines, produced a huge burden on both data producers and users. Penford quotes as an example the number of 'data facts' (i.e., separate numbers) handled by Nielsen in the coffee market, which rose from 23,000 in 1971 to 940,000 in 1991, a 40-fold increase. This problem of data overload is being coped with, gradually, by the development of ever more sophisticated software; the battle between Nielsen and its main rival in this field, IRI (which entered the UK in 1991), is largely fought by means of rival software systems which enable their clients themselves to manipulate and model the data.

"If the average store DID exist, I think this one would be it."

Another trouble, which will not go away, is the named-account problem. Some grocery retailers, as Tim Bowles puts it, are 'still absolutely adamant' that their data will not be released. Sainsbury are perhaps the most important. Kwik Save have never co-operated with any tracking service. In recent years, some retailers (starting with ASDA), recognising the value of their account data, have decided to market it themselves through a broker. This has brought about a new type of company, the data broker, which takes the data from the retailer and sells it on, either to the scanner companies or directly to manufacturers and others who may wish to use it for their own purposes. This brokered data is 'named account', and the appearance of it has made it easier to calculate by elimination the share of those, such as Sainsbury, who do not want to be identified.

Paul Freeman of Kraft Jacobs Suchard (and Chairman of the ISBA Research Group), speaking to the 1995 AMSO annual conference, set out a horror scenario which is all too possible. In a typical product, Tesco and Sainsbury account for 20% of the available market each; Kwik Save, Asda and Safeway have about 10% each, and there are some smaller ones. This in all is only about 60% of the total market, since those retailers who are responsible for the other 40% refuse to collaborate in the measurement. Suppose Gateway, say, withdraws from the general account and goes 'named account' like Safeway and Asda. This then forces a choice on the key accounts like Tesco and Sainsbury. They are too large to 'hide' in the remaining data. If they wish to remain private, which is their right, they can withdraw co-operation. The measurable market would then fall to about 20% of the total, and its value would collapse. Alternatively, they could insist on demanding higher fees for their agreement to stay in.

Sainsbury, indeed, have recently threatened to cease supplying data altogether, since the above was written.

A third major problem is keeping track of new products. Bar-codes are being added at a rate of about 3,000 a week. It is essential, but difficult, to maintain an up-to-date and standardised shopping list. It is even worse in some other countries like France, where it is possible for an abandoned bar-code to be re-used for something else. This, plus the ever-increasing volume of data to be processed, has meant that the scanner companies have had to maintain a clerical capacity, for checking the accuracy of information, no less than they used to need in the days before computers.

Consumer Behaviour

Consumer behaviour measurement has been the backbone of marketing research since its inception. How has it developed and changed over the years?

Pre-war

Although sources are scanty, it is clear that consumer research was an established practice well before the war. It started in America. In the early days, much of it was instigated by publishers or advertising agencies seeking to establish the effectiveness of media advertising. This was the time of Claude Hopkins, who, in his seminal book *Scientific Advertising*, first published in 1923, insisted that advertising can and always should be tested by results; he meant sales increases, but consumer research could add evidence.

Some say that modern marketing research really began in 1911, when Charles Coolidge Parlin, as manager of the commercial division of the advertising department of the Curtis Publishing Company, undertook his famous 'garbage soup audit', in order to persuade the Campbell Soup Company to buy advertising in the *Saturday Evening Post*. Campbell told Parlin that the *Post* was mainly read by working people, who would have little interest in a canned soup; rather than pay the princely sum of 10 cents for a can of soup, they would be making it from scratch, peeling the potatoes and scraping the carrots. Only rich people would pay 10 cents for a can of soup. To demolish this argument, Parlin drew a sample of Philadelphia garbage routes and arranged to have the city dump the contents of each garbage cart in a specified area in a local National Guard armoury he had rented for the purpose. He then counted the number of Campbell soup cans in each pile. He found that the garbage from Philadelphia's Main Line areas contained few cans; the rich people did not use canned soup. They did not make soup from scratch either, but their servants did. The preponderance of cans in the garbage from blue collar areas showed that these were Campbell's customers; probably it was economical for them to heat up the soup and devote the time saved to making a dress, say, and really saving money. Parlin's project is commemorated by a plaque in the National Guard armoury.

The first independent survey organisation was set up in 1919 by Percival White, whose book *Market Analysis: its principles and methods*, first published in 1921, stressed the idea that markets were measurable, and encouraged the use of surveys to research customers, distribution, sales competition, products and the company. The advertising world took up the practice of market surveying. The J.Walter Thompson Company, already an advertising agency with offices in many parts of the world, was one of the principal practitioners (and the first advertising agency to have a research director), and conducted surveys from 1922 onwards in most of these places, including Britain.

Although some authorities have claimed that commercial market research proper did not get under way in Britain until the 1930s, there seems to be good evidence that survey methods were being used during the 1920s for a variety of commercial purposes, using modern (if rudimentary) sampling methods, controlled interviewing procedures and uniform questionnaires. These included investigations into consumer, wholesaler and retailer attitudes and behaviour, retail audit studies, product development, test marketing research, and advertising impact tests. One source alone (the files of the London Press Exchange, courtesy of Leo Burnett Ltd) provided over fifteen commercial survey reports from the 1920s based on nationwide samples. JWT London, by the end of the 1920s, had an impressive list of research clients including Lever Bros, General Motors, Bisto, Coty, Kraft, Quaker, Carreras, Coca-Cola, Gillette, HMV and Pyrex, and many others.

John Downham, in his history of BMRB, gives some details of the first survey in JWT's Record Book: 'Survey

No. 1', dated 1925. This bore the title 'Report of Investigation on Pears Soap Consumer, United Kingdom', and the description of its stated 'purpose' is worth quoting as an indication of the wide range of issues many of these early surveys set out to cover:

> The purpose of this investigation was to find out the kinds of soap used for toilet purposes by men, women and children; whether one soap was used for all toilet purposes or different soaps for different purposes; whether all members of the family used the same brand of soap or not; who bought the soap and how much at a time was bought and how often. We were also interested in discovering whether the housewife had a definite preference for any particular kind of toilet soap, and if so, why she preferred that particular kind; how often on an average the housewife washed her hands, how often she washed her face and how often she bathed; whether she had ever used Pears soap and, if she had used it and given up, why she had done so; and what qualities in a soap she was most particular about.

In the 1930s the practice of research became established, although still led by the advertising industry: relatively few manufacturing companies were confident or forward looking enough to set up their own market research facilities. Mark Abrams recalled in a Newsletter interview in 1978 how he had started in the research department of the London Press Exchange in 1934, and that his favourite work there was doing product tests for Cadburys:

> Since Cadburys were at that time beginning to diversify out of the simple milk bar, it meant that once every two or three weeks there would be a few cases of new sorts of chocolate bars on which we had to carry out tests. This was a godsend in a family when trying to live on £350 a year.

In the same interview Abrams comments that:

> Most of the work in the thirties, the big jobs, were all concerned with getting descriptive accounts of markets: Who does what? Where? How?

It was only later, post war, that the emphasis moved to focusing on the 'why?' of consumer behaviour rather than the 'how?', the subject of our next chapter. Sometimes the new understanding of consumer behaviour uncovered by research could lead to a total, and successful, change in marketing strategy. A classic example of this was Horlicks. When JWT acquired the account at the end of the 20s, Horlicks had been marketed for some years as a nutritious product for growing children and as a mid-morning drink to provide adults with the energy they needed to get through the working day. JWT carried out a survey of the milk food drinks market which showed that, in fact, much of the consumption took place not during the day but late in the evening, at bedtime. This led to the extremely successful 'Night Starvation' campaign of the 1930s and beyond. Harold Stansbury of JWT, speaking to the Market Research Society in 1949, made the point that what had mattered here was the way the research had been *interpreted* at JWT: "The market research did not tell us that sound sleep was people's motive for drinking Horlicks. We told the people that."

Stansbury is a good example of an important strand of thinking which has persisted in market research to this day: the trust in objective and quantified, as opposed to qualitative, measurement, and the insistence that the findings are not in themselves prescriptive but must be built on and interpreted. He is worth quoting at more length to illustrate the point:

> It was JWT's interpretation of information disclosed by market research, not the information itself, and it was the way the information was used to feed the creative imagination, that differentiates JWT's approach to advertising from others.

> The closer it [market research] sticks to quantitative rather than qualitative measurement, the more it can be trusted... The only kind of copy test I have any real confidence in is a properly conducted sales test.

Post-war

Through the 1950s and early 1960s, more and more manufacturing companies became regular users of consumer behaviour research. A clutch of what were to become leading research agencies were founded: Research Services in 1946, Attwood in 1947, Market Investigations in 1956, National Opinion Polls in 1957, Marplan in 1959. And leading manufacturers (Unilever, Reckitts, General Foods, Mars, Nestlé) developed their own research arms, complete with dedicated field forces.

Many of the early post-war surveys helped marketing companies to separate reality and myth in describing regional differences. Comparing North and South, there were some real ones. In the South they preferred to grill meat, grow roses, use china or earthenware teapots, buy indigestion remedies and slimming products; in the north they were more inclined to boil meat, grow vegetables, use metal teapots and buy laxatives. In the South they liked to have separate dining and sitting rooms or 'lounges', while in the North the kitchen was the place where one ate and lived (the 'parlour' being kept for 'best'). Equally, there were many traditional views about the differences which turned out not to be true (source: E. Elliston Allen, *British Tastes*).

It was also a time when professional standards were established and demanded. This was undoubtedly influenced by the fact that so many of the resurgent agencies and research departments post-war were being led by people who had been involved with the Government Social Survey or other government work, a trend that continued until well into the 1950s. These people would have become aware of a higher demand for accuracy than the commercial bottom line of 'good enough to help me make the decision'. They would also have been in touch with the important developments in statistics which took place in the universities during the previous thirty years or so (such as, for example, R.A. Fisher's pioneering work in experimental design, developed for agricultural testing). Statistics became a serious concern, and sampling theory, multivariate analysis, correlation and regression analysis, and hypothesis testing were all developed in the market research context during this period. Leading academic statisticians were retained as advisers (e.g. Professor Maurice Quenouille at BMRB). Dawn Mitchell, in a review paper delivered at the AMSO 1995 conference, commented as follows on the work her agency (RSL) was doing at the time:

> The research that was done 40 years ago was of an exceptionally high quality: great emphasis was laid on the statistical reliability of the data, academics were frequently called in to oversee the sampling processes. Sample sizes were much larger for Fast Moving Consumer Goods surveys than is common today, 3,000 for a chocolate product test, for example. Questionnaires were exceptionally well designed, with virtually no redundancy... Of course, the tedious business of data analysis in those pre-computer days made such self-discipline essential.

Besides ad hoc consumer behaviour and attitude studies, other methods developed during this period.

Consumer panels offered an advantage over retail audit data, as has been mentioned earlier, because they did not depend on retailer permission. But they offered much more than this: the ability to interrelate consumer purchasing patterns with much other data, both about the consumers themselves (their social class, size of family etc.) and attached to each purchase occasion (how many brands were bought, in what quantities, at what prices, and so on). These patterns could be followed through sequential measurements taken from the same people over time. And, if the panel was syndicated (by collecting data across several product categories from the same informants) the collection costs were relatively cheap. For many years there was one supplier, the Attwood

Panel, founded in 1948 by Bedford Attwood, which was based on information collected in a weekly diary and remained for many years the sole pioneer of this type of research. Then, in the early sixties, a new company, AGB, entered the field.

AGB, named from the initials of three of its founders (Audley, Gapper, Brown), was set up to exploit the rapid expansion of television and to win the prestigious TV viewing audit. Its official name, Audits of Great Britain, was chosen because, as Doug Brown put it in a 1980 interview, "we clamped on to the word audits because Arthur Nielsen had given this a tremendous respectability and we didn't see any reason why we shouldn't piggy back on the Nielsen innovations." Brown, like many others who went on to make careers dealing with continuous data, started his research life at Attwoods.

AGB introduced a new service, the Television Consumer Audit (TCA), initially in one television area (the Midlands), later extended as other television companies became interested. The TCA operated a dustbin plus diary system (harking back to Charles Parlin's garbage audit); each panel household was given a dustbin in which to put empty packages, which were removed and counted every week. The service was initially directed to the commercial television companies, who would provide the TCA data free to their advertisers as a means of attracting more advertising revenue. As Doug Brown explains:

> We decided, Bernard Audley and I, that the television companies had reached a point where they could no longer continue to sell by flogging cost per '000... with cost per '000 you are only selling to the advertising agencies, but behind the advertising agencies lies a bunch of men called manufacturers. They don't talk about cost per '000. They talk about thousands of case loads, they talk about tons, they talk about brand share, they talk about product movement, and if you are to continue to get money from them or more money out of them, you have got to learn another language.
>
> *Doug Brown, interviewed in 1980*

AGB ran other specialist panels apart from the TCA, notably the Home Audit for durables and the TCPI (Toiletries and Cosmetics Purchasing Index). The TCA itself became the forefather of Superpanel, which now, consisting of 8,500 homes nationwide and supported by a range of specialist panels, is considered one of the leading consumer panels in Europe. The original TCA 'dustbin' has, of course, long been superseded by more modern technology, including hand-held scanners, with which panel members record the bar-codes of their purchases and from which the data is automatically downloaded to the computer. Other companies also set up syndicated panels in specialist areas: food, baby products, cars etc., some of which continue to run.

Later, in the 1970s, when much tougher economic times were to hit the industry, these continuous services (together with retail audits and BMRB's TGI) were to prove a godsend to those agencies which supplied them; companies which found it easy to drop ad hoc research when under budget pressure tended to be much more reluctant to abandon the continuous monitors on which they relied. As Antony Thorncroft put it, writing in the *Financial Times* about the 1973 MRS Conference:

> It is not hard to discover why AGB and Nielsen dominate the industry. They both specialise in offering continuous services, syndicated under contract.
>
> Once a client is dependent upon your data you are in a powerful position. And the fact that Nielsen can cream off £5,000 per product field means that the amount of research cash available from a company for ad hoc surveys is limited. That is why, although the options seem few, it is worth the effort for research companies to try to build up a continuous audit of any industry.

The existence of continuous records from consumer panels stimulated an interest in ***understanding consumer behaviour***. For the first time, one could follow through the changing patterns of behaviour and choice of individuals. How could these best be described? Were there any common factors? Most importantly, could any general knowledge be derived which would enable us to predict what will happen in the future, a) if nothing changes, b) if we deliberately take some marketing action? In the fifties and sixties there began to be an upsurge of interest in consumer behaviour theory, and many books were published, mostly American. In Britain, Andrew Ehrenberg and his colleagues developed their theory of repeat-buying behaviour in a number of papers, culminating with the first publication of *Repeat Buying* in 1972. It is a truism that the academic community in Britain has, in general, been relatively uninterested in developing market research method and theory, certainly compared with America, but Ehrenberg's work has been a very influential exception.

Ehrenberg's theories are unashamedly empirical, derived from examination of what actually happens as revealed by panel data, taken from purchase records for the same samples of households over long periods of time. They have been tested and found to hold over so wide a variety of products, countries and situations that it is now possible to say with confidence that we understand some of the basic laws which govern consumer purchasing behaviour.

In stable markets, the normal situation is for all brands to be bought at similar frequencies and a similar repurchase rate. What differentiates brands is their 'penetration', the proportion of buyers (of the category) who buy the brand at all. If the penetration is known, one can predict to a close degree of accuracy all the other relevant statistics: its average purchase frequency, its repeat purchase rate, and the proportion of those buyers who will buy any other specific brand.

An important point is that, in most frequently-bought categories, relatively few buyers only buy one brand; consumers may repeatedly buy the same set of brands, but they also like variety. Brands do not cluster in groups among certain people: any brand will be bought in the same relative proportion by buyers of any other brand. This may seem to confirm common sense, but curiously it needed saying; even in the sixties it was still common to find marketing people who thought it was their main task to convert consumers from the competition to Brand A, rather than simply to ensure that Brand A stayed on their shopping list for the category. It was not until people started to look seriously at panel data that they realised that 'conversion' is very rare: advertising is seldom a blinding light on the road to Damascus.

Ehrenberg's findings were not always popular with marketing and advertising people, because they did not explain how to influence the prime factor (how to achieve a satisfactory penetration for the brand in the first place). However, these models have been so widely validated that they define the scope of any future theoretical development: any theory of advertising or marketing which appeared to conflict with them would have to be submitted to very severe scrutiny before it could be accepted. And their power to predict what is expected to happen if there is no change makes them a practical device for testing marketing actions. Since Ehrenberg, there have been many other attempts to build market modelling systems linked with rival testing and measuring systems, with varying success. They fall into two main groups: those, like Ehrenberg, which model the population as a whole (e.g. the population of category buyers), and those which model the choice and decision-making of individuals.

Modelling, of buyer behaviour, of the relationship between behaviour and attitudes, and of the way that markets work, has been a developing interest of researchers since the necessary data became available (e.g. from consumer panels such as those of Attwood and AGB), and especially since computers have made it easier to do. A model, to quote Peter Sampson, can be regarded as: "a simplified, but structural and valid representation of a real-life system or process. Alternatively, we can take a more down-to-earth view and regard a model as a simple way of explaining how something complicated works". As such, they have been used by major advertisers and their agencies as an aid to strategic planning and to forecasting the likely results of marketing activities. One thinks, for example, of the Parfitt-Collins method for predicting repeat-purchase rates from early data for newly-launched products, promulgated in the 1960s and the basis for a range of later new product evaluation systems, and also of the growth during the 1970s and 1980s of econometric methods for assessing the contribution to sales of different elements in the marketing mix.

Much of the original development of these modelling processes, and the software to implement them, has come over from America, where the academic resources devoted to market research have always been very much greater than here. The British contribution has tended to be very pragmatic: models are justified, not by theory, but by how useful they are. Peter Sampson, in his guest editorial to an issue of the *JMRS* devoted to modelling (January 1995), wrote that by the early 1960s the terms 'model' and 'modelling' were commonplace, and that by the early 1970s the research buyer could go shopping for a model and be faced with a considerable choice. But:

> There was a great deal of disappointment... Our industry is a graveyard of models, and yet new ones continue to appear, as is right and proper in a milieu where R&D is, and must be, ongoing. There have been many successful models, typified, for example, by the predictive/Simulated Test Marketing models of the late 1970s/early 1980s. So we know that some models do work.

The British research community, in contrast to some others, tends to avoid writing about its modelling work in complex, equation-filled academic papers. The following little poem by Tom Corlett, in which he commented on an MRS Conference paper in 1964, and which was printed in *Commentary* in the spring of that year, makes some serious points about the problems of computer modelling in an unusually palatable way:

"A Ballade of Multiple Regression"

If you want to deal best with your questions,
    Use multi-regression techniques;
A computer can do in a minute
    What, otherwise done, would take weeks.
For 'predictor selection' procedures
    Will pick just the ones best for you
And provide the best-fitting equation
    – For the data you've fitted it to.

But did you collect the right data?
    Were there 'glaring omissions' in yours?
Have the ones that score highly much meaning?
    Can you tell the effect from the cause?
Are your 'cause' factors ones you can act on?
    If not, you've got more work to do;
Your equation's as good – or as bad – as
    The data you've fitted it to.

But it's worse when new factors have entered
    The field since your survey was made,
Or even the old ones have varied
    Beyond all the bounds you surveyed.
Has your leading competitor faltered?
    Have you got, with old brands, one that's new?
This won't have come in your regression
    Or the data you've fitted it to.

So 'get with' the Efroymson programme,
    And list out your factors with zeal,
With their sesquipedalian labels
    And wonderful client-appeal.
But, brothers, please always remember,
    Be you Marplan, or Schwerin, or who –
Your optimum only is bonum
    For the data you've fitted it to.

Omnibus surveys are another way of obtaining the benefits of syndication. These are surveys on reasonably large samples, run at regular intervals, on which clients can buy space without the cost of setting up a dedicated survey. They are particularly suitable when one needs a quick answer to just one or two questions, provided the sample needed is not a tightly-defined minority. Most major companies have run omnibus surveys from their early years, and still do; they have been among the first services to benefit from advances in data collection such as telephone interviewing and, more recently, CAPI. Some companies run international omnibus services in several languages.

Experiments

Surveys have not been the only way of measuring consumer behaviour. A survey is essentially descriptive: what do people buy? How do they use our products? This is the type of information needed to formulate strategy. But marketing decisions are often of a different, more tactical kind, concerned with the testing of alternatives: *which* of the possible product formulations, tastes or packs should be marketed, which promotional mix is likely to be most effective, what is the best way to word instructions for use, etc. One can only go so far making comparisons in a laboratory; when the products have been fully checked to make sure that they *work*, it is almost always necessary to try them out among target consumers.

Product testing has been an important part of commercial market research since its earliest days, and developed fast during the growth period after the end of rationing.

Traditionally, the design and formulation of products had been driven by the production engineers and R&D, aided (as the mythology would have it) by the Chairman's wife. As market research began to unfold how consumers actually *used* the products, it showed the directions for R & D to take. Companies put more effort into improving products, getting the taste right, making them user-friendly, with packages that poured easily, informative labels and instructions that were easy to follow; and, having listened to the consumer's voice at the design stage, they would test the different R & D offerings among the same consumers to make sure that it all worked properly in real life.

With testing, costly mistakes were avoided. For example, in the 1960s the experts in corned beef knew for certain that the best product came from Latin America. But product tests showed that consumers preferred the less fatty African product, and that was the start of the very successful Fray Bentos Special Lean Cut brand of corned beef.

There were two areas for such testing. The first was concerned with the launch of new products, new brands in existing fields, or new variants of existing brands. The second, no less important for the manufacturer, was the testing of alternative ingredients, new formulations, more economical materials. Between these two the research requirement was quite different. With new introductions, variants and improvements one is looking for approval, an edge in advantage against the competition: one is looking for a *difference*. With re-formulations one is seeking to save costs and is therefore hoping to find *no change*; the aim of the testing is to check whether, if the cheaper ingredient is introduced, consumers will notice the difference and become alienated.

The attention paid to these two types of objective coincided with an increase of interest in the appropriate statistical techniques: tests of significance, hypothesis testing, and the methods of experimental design which statisticians like R.A. Fisher and others had previously developed for agricultural testing. The market research department's responsibility in a company was to advise both marketing and R & D departments on the testing method and sample size necessary to provide a 'safe' answer on whether or not the proposed change should go ahead. At the same time, of course, the testing process would also yield valuable diagnostic information about things that might be wrong or repay attention.

Product tests, especially new product launches, were seldom simple matters: they often involved several different elements which all needed researching separately or together. Is the concept right? Does it work? Is it appealing? What about the packaging and presentation, and any brand associations? How does it stand out against competition? And then, how will consumers find it in use? These required many different research devices: a previous understanding of the market in adequate depth (it is assumed we have this before starting serious work on a new product at all); organoleptic (or, scent and flavour) panels (which manufacturing companies frequently run themselves); tests of the concept, often preceded by extensive qualitative work; hall tests to try out the appeal of various packaging designs, price levels, etc.; last but not least, trials, probably in-home over an extended period, during which users report on their actual experience of the product. These last would often be done using variants in blind packaging as well as named, since it is well known that the brand name and appearance can radically affect the evaluation of a product by consumers.

All of this was seen as a wise precaution, at least, before a manufacturer undertook the investment needed to launch a new product. Research agencies met the need by developing comprehensive testing and modelling systems which would help the client to predict, on as wide a front as possible, the likely success of the new launch. A number of these remain international proprietary research brands.

But it is never quite enough to test something in a laboratory. In real life, there are many other factors outside one's own control which will affect the future sales of a new brand, not least what happens in the store, and how one's competitors react. It became common practice, before undertaking a national launch of a developed new product, to **test market** it in a specific area. This meant that the manufacturer would limit the selling-in and merchandising cost to that area only, supporting it with only local advertising. The test would be run for as long as was needed to assess the product's longer-term success, perhaps for up to a year.

There were many problems with area test marketing. One was the difficulty of finding 'typical' sales areas. Another was the relative ease with which a competitor could mount a spoiling operation in the same area, once he found out that the test market was in prospect (it could hardly be kept secret once selling-in started). Companies developed sophisticated analysis systems which worked on the principle of comparing pre-launch sales in the test area and a control area (as similar as possible), observing what happened during the test in both areas, and calculating the sales growth actually achieved in the test area compared to what *would* have been achieved without the test (by reference to the control). One could thus learn about what the new product was doing, e.g. from where was it taking sales (from competitors or other brands of one's own)?

A key statistic for test marketing was to calculate the level at which the new product will 'settle down'; the common pattern is for the launch effort to stimulate early trial, some of which falls away as trialists fail to repurchase. Models to predict this from test results began to be developed in the sixties.

Test marketing became harder to achieve with the advent of commercial television, which was difficult to use on a limited, regional basis (although some small ITV areas, such as Border, sought business by presenting themselves as unique test marketing areas). More importantly, the concentration of retailing and the emergence of centralised, car-based supermarket shopping changed the whole concept; manufacturers could no longer 'sell in' into a region, but had to negotiate with the all-powerful head office. In addition, the need for greater speed in launching a product, and increased competitiveness leading to more spoiling tactics, contributed to making test marketing unviable. John Davis, who at BMRB in the late 1950s became JWT's expert on test marketing systems, and later ran JWT's modelling department, wrote in *Commentary* in July 1965:

> Test marketing is a complex operation. Its foundation in statistical theory is not particularly sound... In general test markets are under-researched, with far too many organisations content to measure one aspect of the end result through retail audit, and ignoring the possibilities, and the need, to collect other types of data as the test proceeds...

> Even on the present basis, however, test marketing can provide a great deal of knowledge and experience relating to a new product, and it should give at least a clear indication of a plan which is failing to meet its objectives, even if at present it is not possible to produce the precise national forecasts which manufacturers would like.

Research companies filled the gap by other means: simulated shopping environments, or vans which call on the same housewives repeatedly so that both initial trial and the all-important repeat purchase rate can both be measured. Over time, marketing people came to see that the real value of market testing was not so much to 'predict' future sales as to pilot the new product in order to improve quality and performance (much the same movement as has occurred with advertising pre-testing research). A good example of such *pilot marketing* was the regional launch of Mr Kipling Cakes in 1967. With a new marketing concept like this, it was important to know roughly the scale of the business that might ultimately be developed nationally, and consumer panel data and attitude tracking were valuable for that purpose. But it was just as important (in a sense, even more so) to try out the sheer logistics of launching a new range of 24 lines through an untried distribution system. Two minor disasters were thrown up, which could have been very expensive on a large scale: the glue on some of the packs failed at the seams, so that the cakes fell out, and one of the types of cake stuck to the top of the pack when the outer packs were roughly handled. The test enabled these failings to be caught and corrected while still at the pilot stage.

In today's service economy, product tests have tended to become much more complex affairs. For instance, Barclaycard in 1990 wanted to identify the likely effect of introducing a fee, as a means of building profitability in a fiercely competitive market: how many customers might they lose, and which ones? There were many possible options – different sizes and types of fee, possible additional services to soften the blow, compensating declines in interest rate, possible links with other types of card. With the help of research, four different 'packages' were designed for testing. The complexity of the options and the need to go beyond people's initial reactions to the idea of a fee (usually instant rejection) to what they would actually *do* in real life called for a very subtle programme of research. The Qualitative Consultancy and Nielsen Consumer Research carried out several phases of qualitative and quantitative research, ending with in-home interviews using carefully finished promotional material to make the test options as real as possible. The analysis covered initial responses to the brochure and a discussion of the trade-off benefits and costs, with an assessment of people's likely inertia. From all this, Nielsen predicted the number of cards likely to be returned with each package. Putting the chosen option into effect must have been a tense time for Barclaycard, who might well have suffered a marketing disaster. In the event, the research prediction proved remarkably accurate: it had played a crucial part in helping the company to get a new income stream and maintain both its profits and its market leadership (Source: *Research Works*, 1991).

5

Understanding Consumers

It is not enough to know what products people buy and how they act. To appeal effectively to consumers, one must also find out why. The realisation of this need struck manufacturers as soon as they began to take the consumer seriously.

It has probably been in the area of understanding consumers that market research has made its greatest contribution to our social evolution during these fifty years. One only needs to compare the recent failures of the centrally planned economies, which used very little research. Communist states believed that what people wanted were commodities, things that functioned properly, and that a benevolent authority would be the most efficient way of providing them. In the capitalist world, on the other hand, it soon began to be revealed, mainly through the progressive use of market research, that what people actually wanted and bought was much more complex. Competition and new technology were leading to increasing similarity between the goods in any market, as each new invention was copied or substituted by all its rivals. But it became clear that people wanted more than just 'products'; they were looking for some *meaning* in what they bought.

The trend was perhaps most obvious in the designer clothes of the 1980s; but it was equally true of the differences they found between, say, Coke and Pepsi, Persil and Ariel, or

Ford and Renault. Without the constant attempt, mediated through market research, to improve our understanding of what people really wanted and thought, we could never have developed so rapidly the richness and diversity of the life we now enjoy, or the freedom we have to be individuals. This constant attempt to learn what people are really like, rather than accepting hand-me-down stereotypes, has been a difficult and gradual process, often against some opposition; but it has been the keynote theme in our development over the post-war years.

Trusting the People Can Be Hard

In one of the leading textbooks of this new thinking, *Motivation Research* (first published in 1958), Harry Henry wrote:

> Parallel with the development of market research has grown up a gradual realisation that the basic facts of the market situation are usually not, by themselves, sufficient to *explain* that situation, or to indicate the most fruitful lines for production, marketing, and advertising activity. It is essential that these basic facts should be known, but they do not provide the whole answer. Indeed, it may be truly said that, in the fields of marketing and advertising, statistics are like bikinis – they reveal a good deal that is both interesting and instructive, but they usually conceal what is really vital.
>
> And what is vital in the study of a market is to know not only *what* the pattern is, but also *why* – since only with this supplementary knowledge is it possible for an individual manufacturer to be quite sure of being able to change the pattern.
>
> In other words, questions of motive and reason have now become, and are becoming recognised as, of prime importance in any marketing operation. It is not sufficient to know what proportions of the population use particular products, and who those users are: valuable as this

information is, it is only a beginning. What has to be known in addition is what are the motives which lead people to use one product rather than another, to behave in one way rather than another, to choose one brand rather than another. And it is also essential to be able to measure the effectiveness of various methods of affecting those motives, or of acting on them. And this knowledge can only arise from a study of the *reasons* underlying the existing patterns of purchase and usage.

Henry: Motivation Research, p. 11

A similar point was made by Downham and Treasure:

Whilst it is true that it is always desirable to make a better mouse-trap, it is nevertheless the case that the judgement that it *is* a better mouse-trap must to some extent be based on the reactions of the mice as well as on the technical construction of the trap.

*Downham and Treasure: 'Market Research and Consumer
Durables', Incorporated Statistician, December 1956*

Quotations such as this suggest that the concept of 'asking the consumer' did not gain ground without resistance. It is an old adage, after all, that the world will beat a path to your door if you can make a better mouse-trap. There were many (there still are some) who found it emotionally very difficult to subordinate their traditional knowledge or scientific expertise to consumer judgement, and failed in consequence. The prevalence of this obstacle is attested by the frequency with which writers on research at this time kept returning to the point. Here is Harry Henry again, this time in a speech to the British Institute of Management Northern Conference:

The public *does* know what's good, for the plain and simple reason that the public is the sole judge of what goodness is... There are usually a number of very firmly-held traditional conceptions as to what is 'good' and what is 'poor', and it not infrequently happens... that the purchasing public has the poor taste to prefer what is technically regarded as the inferior product.

> For example, in a test carried out as far back as 1952 by the British Baking Industries Research Association, it was found in what is called a 'blind test' that people preferred a cake made with cooking-fat and dried egg to one made with butter and fresh eggs – where they could discriminate at all, which most of them could not!
> *Henry: Two-Way Communication and Market Research, 1959*

The problem never quite goes away. As new areas of business come to realise that they must listen to their consumers (finance, business services etc.), the old obstacle surfaces again. Sir Douglas Wass, interviewed in 1988 during his presidency of the Market Research Society, made this comment:

> Survey research... is recognised to be highly desirable. I believe this is the case certainly when companies are selling at the retail level. But when companies are selling at the wholesale level, as so many companies are in the City, then there is a reluctance to go to formal market research. There is a much greater disposition to say "we know our customers, we talk to them all the time, we know what they think". It's 'do-it-yourself' market research, informal and without the help of professional advisers.

Motivation Research

Harry Henry did not invent the term Motivation Research – as he says in his introduction to the 1988 edition, most of the great figures in American research, including Lazarsfeld, Guttman, Likert, Hovland, Britt and Politz, had been heavily involved in it for many years – but his book comprehensively defined it for a British audience. It is a pity that the term fell into disuse during the next decade, becoming confused with qualitative research, which was starting its growth at the time. Many people undoubtedly think that Motivation Research and Qualitative Research are the same thing, but they are not. Motivation Research is much wider, encompassing all techniques, quantitative as well as qualitative, which bear on the 'why' question. The confusion was particularly unfortunate because, especially during the major growth period for qualitative research in the 1970s and early 1980s, it allowed attention to focus on the methodological differences between qualitative and quantitative instead of their complementary usefulness.

Henry hung the whole development of Motivation Research on a single proposition which formed the title of an earlier paper (ESOMAR, 1953): 'We Cannot Ask 'Why' '. A question of fact can usually be answered accurately by most people, as far as memory allows, but not the reasons for their actions. They usually do not know what their real reasons are. If they do know, they may not be prepared to give them, but fall back on rationalisations or 'acceptable' reasons. Even when they both know and are willing to confess their motives, they are "for the most part quite incapable of assessing the relative importance of the various interlocking motives which normally go to make up a particular behaviour pattern". Motivation Research thus encompasses the whole range of methods by which a true answer to this kind of question can be obtained, *indirectly*. It is "the art of finding out 'why' without actually asking".

Sometimes the required answer can be inferred by detective work from simple analysis and experiment. When a doctor wants to know if his patient has a fever, he doesn't ask him, but measures his temperature and pulse rate. In a product test (this example is quoted in Motivation Research), people were given two packs of biscuits to try and told that one pack was made with butter, the other without. The majority preferred the pack made with butter, and gave their reasons (they were richer, creamier, more tasty etc.). A sizeable minority preferred the one without butter, saying the biscuits were more digestible, less greasy, and other good reasons. The point was that both packs were identical, in both product and pack, and neither contained any butter at all. What the test showed was the *appeal* of the idea of a buttery taste, and that people will actually taste what they think is there.

If all we are concerned about is which colour pack or what ingredients to use, that is enough. But it was soon recognised that we often need to uncover more about the consumer, what he or she thinks and feels, the values that influence choices. For this, techniques began to be borrowed from all sorts of other disciplines in the magpie way characteristic of market research.

Psychology and sociology were early contributors. People like Thurstone and Likert were already working in the 1920s and 30s, developing the scaling techniques associated with their names and used in market research to this day. But by the 1950s a new approach had appeared: the depth interview. This was particularly associated (at least in the public mind) with the name of Dr Ernest Dichter.

Dichter's actual operation in Britain was somewhat less than his reputation; but undoubtedly he was perceived as standing for a tendency which developed during the 1950s for manufacturers and advertising agencies to call in psychologists to provide 'deeper' insights into consumers. At its worst, this sometimes produced laughable results. Henry, in his 1988 introduction, says that:

The reason why motivation research tends to be regarded as being no longer relevant is that most people associate it with the somewhat idiosyncratic practices of Ernest Dichter and his followers (of which it was once said "Very interesting, but why do they call it research?"). Yet the claim that he was both its father and its leading American exponent was never true.

Dichter founded his Institute for Motivational Research at Croton-on-Hudson in 1938. He regarded himself as a 'cultural anthropologist', who probed people's underlying motives and feelings by means of depth interviews and group discussions. He became famous for surprising his clients. For example, the real problem faced by the candy makers was people's guilt feelings about self-indulgence: they were advised to emphasise that candy bars were in bite-size pieces, which would "provide the excuse the consumer needs to buy a bar of candy – after all, I don't have to eat all of it, just a bite and put the rest away". General Mills were advised, in selling their cake-mix packages, to make sure the housewife had something to do, such as add fresh eggs: wives would feel diminished and unhappy unless they were making a contribution (and would rationalise this as suspicion of the product). The reason why loan companies were doing so well, even though the banks offered lower interest rates and were more lenient in accepting applicants, was the banks' stern image of rectitude, which made people feel inferior; if the banks would soften their image, the customer would shift from feeling like "an unreliable adolescent to feeling like a morally righteous adult"; the emotional undertone of the transaction would be changed. And there is his famous advice to the Chrysler Corporation to put convertibles in their show-room windows, because men saw the convertible as a symbolic mistress, something to daydream about – even though, once inside, they would buy the practical four-door sedan "just as he once married a plain girl who, he knew, would make a fine wife and mother."

Sometimes the advice was successful, and consistent with common sense: for example the recommendation to American Airlines to stop emphasising safety (which itself suggested that flying could be dangerous), and concentrate instead on the positive advantages of flying such as its convenience for business travel and the benefit of returning home faster, as well as providing passengers with a 'calm psychological atmosphere'. It was generally agreed that Dichter was a man of often brilliant insight, and that these insights, rather than the research he did to support them, were the true source of his success. There was a strong influence of Freudian psychology (Dichter had studied in Vienna). "The analysis does not stem from the data, but often from the top of the analyst's head, and the practical business action recommended does not stem from the analysis but represents a logical and clever leap on the part of the analyst" (*Motivation Research*, chapter 10).

Dichter was the best known, but there were many others who were consulted at this time and attempted to explain consumer attitudes in terms of psychological theory. They led to the backlash of Vance Packard's *Hidden Persuaders*, published in 1957, which shocked Americans who had been indoctrinated in the post-Korea, McCarthy era with ideas of brainwashing and mind-control conspiracies. Packard used motivation research as his ground for claiming that virtually all advertising had become manipulative, affecting consumers without their knowledge. Packard went much too far in his claims, but helped to tar motivation research with the brush of irrelevance. Henry's book was an attempt to redress this imbalance by demonstrating that, properly understood, Motivation Research was always *practical*, useful if it was done to help solve a marketing problem, and stopping at explanations which were actionable:

> When Motivation Research is used to establish, firmly and unequivocally, that a housewife is more likely to buy a product if it is packaged in a blue wrapper than a red one,

it is doing a useful and worth-while job: when it goes further, to discover that she prefers blue to red because she was frightened by a bull in early childhood, it is simply wasting time and resources.

Henry: Motivation Research, p. 31

Having said that, the range of what *may* be relevant in a particular case is very wide. Peter Chisnall (*Consumer Research*, first published in 1975) distinguished the following areas which a researcher might want to look at:

Personal aspects of behaviour:
- Perception
- Learning processes
- Cognition
- Needs
- Personality and self-concept
- Social learning and environmental influences
- Attitudes

Group aspects of behaviour:
- Culture
- Social class
- Family and group influences

Most research clients, however, tend to converge on just three questions:

- How do people see and respond to the different products (i.e. branding)?
- What 'turns them on' in the first place?
- How do people differ in their needs and responses to our product (i.e. how should we 'segment' potential consumers to identify 'targets')?

Branding and Brand Images

The concept of branding has now become second nature. Everyone now knows that branding happens inside people's heads. Branding is what makes a product more than a mere commodity, to be bought if at all at the cheapest possible price and vulnerable to any economic winds that blow. Brands have values over and above the basic function: they offer familiarity and reassurance, they are recognisable. People feel uncomfortable buying brands no one has heard of. People relate to the brands they buy; they develop distinct personalities; people see in them those values which are important to them, confirmed by their own experience in use, and come to trust the brand and feel warmth towards it. For this they are prepared to pay. Furthermore, it is a mistake to think that branding only applies to grocery products bought every week by women who watch too much television. The values 'added' in the branding process are just as important in 'hard-headed' industrial or financial markets: values such as reliability, after-sales service, speed of delivery, concern for the customer.

Everyone knows this *now*, or at least pays lip-service to it. But back in the 1950s it was not so clear. The growth in the importance of the brand concept has coincided with the growth of competitive marketing and consumers' increasing freedom of choice, and the growing capacity of research techniques to discover what lay behind their choices. It was not until the 1980s that brands received the final accolade of recognition by accountants and identification in the balance sheet.

Before the 1950s, it does not seem that companies thought of researching brand images. Andrew Elliott, one of the MRS 'founding fathers', interviewed in 1981, claimed Imperial Tobacco as one of the pioneers:

> Imperial Tobacco, ahead of many other manufacturers of the time, sensed that the market for smoking... would not automatically last for ever... They were one of the early

pursuers of motivational research. They realised that a purely quantitative assessment of who smoked what, and which brand, was something one was beginning to take for granted... Imperial Tobacco, as it was then called, decided one ought to go a stage further. Here were the makings of *why* do people do things rather than a numerical count.

" If you did use after-shave which one would you use?"

By the end of the 1950s – early 1960s, brand image questions were being used regularly in what came to be called 'usage and attitude' (U & A) surveys, often based on a range of scaling methods derived from psychology. BMRB introduced, on behalf of its parent company JWT, a syndicated brand image measurement survey, the Advertising Planning Index, for which Imperial Tobacco was a primary client. The API was able to attain both regularity and economy of scale by keeping the range of questions asked about any one product category low and simple. The formula adopted was to read out a series of not more than twelve comments or statements representing various aspects of brand image and asking respondents which brands, if any, they associated with each statement. From this one could assess for any brand how far the image idea was associated with it and, in most cases, how positive that was. The selection of image elements was of course key, and for that one depended on qualitative research findings plus the beliefs of the client and the agency. The relative simplicity and speed of this approach, compared to most other scaling methods which, even if more sensitive, were much more cumbersome, led to the API being used as a regular tracking vehicle for some years. The method was adopted by other companies (e.g. Millward Brown), and has only been superseded in recent years by the much greater coverage, sensitivity and speed delivered by modern computer analysis systems and computer-aided interviewing.

As runs of data from the API and similar image studies began to accumulate, the industry began to learn that brand images, attitudes and consumer perceptions were not as straightforward as they seemed. We learned that many 'images', while possibly useful for the strategic positioning of a brand against its competition, were of little use for tactical tracking because they *do not change*. Once a brand has formed its distinctive image, it is very hard to shift it; advertising affects certain measures of awareness and salience in the short term, but seldom makes a dent on the image. We learned that many of the commonest image concepts, in particular those with a strong element of *approval* in them such as 'good/poor value for money', were closely tied to brand usage: those who were buying the brand would associate it with these images, non-buyers would not. This made it essential to analyse image data by usage if we were to understand it at all, and it tied in with Ehrenberg's findings that most other things about a brand are predictable from its penetration (see Chapter 4).

We also learned that the common-sense belief that, 'if only one could change attitudes in a favourable direction, sales would follow' was wrong. The evidence showed that, not only do attitudes not necessarily change before behaviour, but one could just as easily put it the other way round: attitude changes often coincide with or even follow behaviour changes. Marketing people had to accept that marketing was about much more than getting people to start using your brand: it was, at least as much, about reassuring them, once they were already using it, that they were doing the right thing, and building on their satisfied experience. The concept that advertising has a major reassuring and reinforcing function, as opposed to 'conversion', although hardly new (it is foreshadowed in James Webb Young's aim of 'familiarity', which he first developed as a young copywriter in the 1920s), began to take serious hold at this time.

In the 1960s and 1970s, several attempts were made to make sense of attitudes and perceptions and their relation to behaviour. Academic psychologists were much in evidence. Among the best known were Festinger, whose theory of 'Cognitive Dissonance' was invoked to explain the attitudes following behaviour phenomenon (the theory states that we tend to avoid ideas which make us feel uncomfortable, and if we have decided to make a purchase we adjust our minds and feelings to support that decision, so that, for example, someone who has just bought a particular make of car is especially likely to start noticing advertising for that make, and other people driving it), and Fishbein, who proposed a model linking together people's beliefs, how they feel about those beliefs, and social factors in order to explain their actions. Serious attempts were made to develop such models into practical research tools, but they tended to fail because of the difficulty of applying psychological models of the individual to populations surveyed in the aggregate.

At the end of the day, we still cannot generalise about how attitudes and behaviour interact. With Timothy Joyce, who discussed the problem in relation to advertising in an influential paper in 1967, we come down to saying that they each affect the other in a feedback loop of some sort, but we don't exactly know how. But the search for a relationship, while defeated in its own terms, had a valuable by-product. It showed the importance of taking care over the variables we put into quantitative U & A surveys. It showed how easy it is to find oneself measuring response to statements that are of little practical use, if not actually nonsense, and put a premium on the search for more sensitive understanding.

The main problem was (and is still) that uncovering what people really think and feel, even about something so 'unimportant' as a grocery brand, and deciding which aspects matter most, is hard. People have imaginations, and their underlying feelings and perceptions can be fluid and impossible to catch, except by skilful interviewing. Here, for example, are some comments made in interviews in which housewives were asked to imagine certain brands as people: what sort of personalities would they have?

Washing powders

INTERVIEWER: "What kind of a person would you think Fairy Snow would be?"

HOUSEWIFE A: "Well, I think it would be somebody older... somebody whose outlook on life was a little slower, most probably her children would be growing, she would be a married woman again... Generally doing a slower run of life than Mrs Ariel."

INTERVIEWER: "Tell me about Mrs Ariel."

HOUSEWIFE A: "I think she would be the sort of person who has got to have everything done, though very well and very efficiently, to have rather a good social life at the same time. Very sparkling, and would be the sort who would always have a baby-sitter at the ready, to go out in the evening and take good care of herself; and who likes to keep young and follow trends."

INTERVIEWER: "What would Mrs Fairy Snow do in the evenings?"

HOUSEWIFE A: "Well, just sort of sit by the fire and watch television."

Toilet soaps

Lifebuoy

HOUSEWIFE D: "That's an older man, about fifty-ish, somebody whose children are growing up, a very steady job and looking to retirement."

HOUSEWIFE A: "I think the sporty type of man, who is always on the tennis courts."

HOUSEWIFE E: "A male worker in his twenties – dirty job, mining or something."

Camay

HOUSEWIFE F: "Fresh, bright young girl of about eighteen or nineteen, very bright and very clean. She likes to wash her hair at least twice a week – and of course have a bath every day – and looks after herself and her bedroom, very tidy."

INTERVIEWER: "What sort of boyfriends does she have?"

HOUSEWIFE A: "Oh, I should think very go-ahead boyfriends, you know, sort of salesmen and people like this."

HOUSEWIFE E: "She might be a bit like that to everybody and sort of underneath a bit catty perhaps; but she's warm to everyone. But secretly she might be thinking differently about you."

Insights of this kind, elicited by researchers, changed the way in which marketers saw what they were selling. The product still had to do its job: all the functional, rational qualities (whiter than white, kind to hands, kills 99% of all known germs) had to be there, substantiated, or at least not contradicted by experience: but the customers responded better if they were offered something more. If the colour was lacking, they would supply it themselves, and it might not be a colour to the marketer's liking. In an increasingly competitive market-place, this kind of research delving clarified the task for advertising, the packaging, and the other elements in the marketing mix. Intensifying competition required that *your* brand must capture the limelight, be the one your customers would see as warm, friendly, exciting or intriguing: if you did not do this, your rivals would.

Consumer Segmentation

With the desire to understand how consumers see brands went the parallel desire to see how consumers differ. Do brand X buyers have a different set of priorities from buyers of Brand Y, and are they different sorts of people? This kind of enquiry has taken off much more since computers have enabled us to perform clustering and segmentation analyses at speed, but it began to arise in the 1950s and 1960s as a serious marketing interest.

Over the years there has been an evolution in this process of segmentation, which parallels the evolution of advertising, which we trace in the next chapter, towards greater understanding of how consumers respond. It also parallels the change, on which we commented in Chapter 2, from a stratified to a more individualistic and complex society: a change which market research has reflected and mapped and, by educating marketing people, helped to bring about.

At first, segmentation was seen entirely in demographic terms: age, sex and class would be scrutinised in every survey to see if they discriminated between brand users; occasionally other things would be brought in, such as income, education or employment, or presence of children. The assumption was always that people differed, and who you were determined your choices. The next stage, which started to appear in the 1960s on the back of attitude and image research, was to construct psychological variables: people's different 'personalities', or other aspects of their psychology, might be more important for determining what brands they choose and how they use them than mere demographics. This still separates *people* (i.e. assumes that one person can be classified as having a permanent 'personality' which is different from another's), whilst admitting that individuals from the same education level or class, etc., may well resemble members of a different class more closely than they do certain other members from their own group.

Research also revealed, sometimes, that there were dangers in assuming too readily exactly what these labels, whether demographic or 'personality', actually meant. Ideas within these groups have changed in many ways relevant to marketers. For example, the JWT New Housewife survey found in 1964 that 49% of 'young housewives' (engaged or married women aged 16-34) agreed that 'working wives can't really be good mothers'. Nine years later it was down to 28%, and after that it was felt that interviewers could no longer be expected to ask that sort of question.

The final stage has been the realisation that individuals are not constant in themselves, even from hour to hour: they like variety (as was recognised in Chapter 4, when panel data showed that most people like to buy a range of brands in any field), and their choices may vary according to how they happen to be feeling at the time. It therefore became useful to identify, not only different 'modes' or purposes for which the same individual might use different varieties, but the 'moods' or states of mind to which the versions (and the advertising for them) could appeal. This kind of segmentation has been gathering pace since the 1980s (it is impossible to be precise about timings when looking at an evolutionary process).

Wendy Gordon has encapsulated the idea in her telling phrase; 'the me that I am':

> Each person is made up of a number of different people who require a different brand solution in any particular circumstance. Take yoghurt, for example. The 'me-that-I-am' when I buy yoghurt for my toddler is different from the 'me-that-I-am' when I buy one for myself as I start to diet. The 'me-that-I-am' when I buy yoghurt depends on different contexts, moods and conditions, each of which may require a different brand solution...

> At the supermarket I may be representing a number of different 'me's' by simultaneously filling my trolley with Sainsbury Family Shampoo, Silkience Conditioner for permed hair and Wash'n'Go, one for the 'me-that-I-am' when thinking of shampoo for the shower, one for my dry hair and one for the toiletry bag in my locker at the gym. Or on another occasion I may simply be representing one 'me', the one that is completing a major stock-up and is thinking of family needs, hence two or three large bottles of Sainsbury Family Shampoo.

> *Wendy Gordon: 'Retailer Brands', MRS Conference paper, 1994*

Another leading qualitative researcher, Sue Robson, explained "the increasing contribution that qualitative research makes to marketing planning" in these terms:

> When I choose an Audi saloon instead of an equivalently priced Vauxhall, I am buying a particular image that matches my own self-image and self-beliefs in some way. When I buy clothes from Next rather than from Marks and Spencer I am, similarly, making a statement about myself. When I choose a Sainsbury own label alternative to a premium brand I am not just buying on price. The retail store image superimposed on the own label concept fits in with the type of housewife and shopper I like to believe I am. In other words, products and services are no longer ends in themselves... Alongside this, the self-conscious consumer of today is no longer content to be part of a 'mass market'. Mass markets are fragmenting at a fast rate. For example, look at the changing nature of the bread market, at chain store clothing, at savings products, at holidays abroad. The list is endless.

Sue Robson: 'The Qualitative Story', Survey, Spring 1986

These 'stages' in the evolution of segmentation have not replaced each other; it would be truer to say that they interact and overlap. Each layer may be relevant for a particular marketing problem. And old-fashioned demographics were given a new lease of life by the invention of geodemographics (see Chapter 3), which enabled marketers to locate certain types of people because they tended to live in certain identifiable neighbourhoods. This process, which gave a substantial boost to direct marketing, is now being applied to psychological segmentations as well.

Cultural and social differences, personality measurements and self-assessment techniques have all been borrowed from various disciplines, especially psychology, sociology and anthropology, to try to construct ways of classifying consumers which would improve on the old faithfuls of social class, age and sex. One approach which has achieved a degree of cult status is the family of systems known collectively as 'life-style research' or (less mellifluously) 'psychographics'. These involve clustering people into groups according to whether they agree with statements like; 'What I do at work is more important to me than the money I earn' or 'Most women need a career as well as a family'. They are then labelled according to the clusters they fall into with names like 'belongers', 'achievers', 'survivors, 'sustainers' or 'emulators'. Alternatively, the groups are given pen-portrait encapsulations such as, 'Fred, the frustrated factory worker'. There have been a number of these systems, the oldest dating back to the 1960s. In the USA, the Yankelovich Monitor and VALS (Values and Life-styles, developed by the Stanford Research Institute) have been particularly influential. Agencies such as Research Bureau Ltd have produced life-style clusters here, and BMRB's TGI service now carries psychographic classifiers derived from Leo Burnett's American system.

It's up to you... you can have a tailor-made segmentation for ten grand or an off-the-peg for a quarter of the price

Although these classifying systems undoubtedly can give useful insights, none of them has ever been able to oust standard demographics for general use. The main reason is that it is difficult to feel universal confidence in the selection of the questions which form the input to the analysis. They have often seemed to lack real stability. There is always something subjective about them; put another way, there is almost an infinity of possible ways one could select these 'psychological' statements, depending on the point of view from which one starts. None of them therefore stand out as being self-evidently 'right'. It has often made more sense, apparently, to tailor-make one's classification scheme every time in relation to what is relevant to the product.

As computer power developed, the ability grew to model or 'map' a market in several dimensions, so that brand choice, brand images and consumer differences could be understood in the round. This could help a marketer to see more easily which brands were competing most closely, where the gaps might be for possible new developments, what the strengths and weaknesses were of each brand, and which had a general as opposed to a 'niche' appeal. From the mid-1960s onwards, computer programmes began to appear which would take attitude and behaviour data from survey questionnaires and, out of the pattern of correlations, produce such rounded 'pictures' of a total market.

These modelling approaches were (and are) often competitive and controversial. Some attempt to model individual consumers, and how their perceptions relate to their behaviour, while others treat markets as if they were physical or engineering systems. We are a long way yet from a perfect approach (if such a thing could exist). But manufacturers gradually began to have enough confidence in such systems to build them into their own strategic planning and use the power they give to 'simulate' the results of different strategies: what would be likely to happen to the market as a whole if they succeeded in a campaign to strengthen consumers' image of Brand X in respect of attribute Y, with especial reference to sector Z? Increasingly, these days, they are doing it on their own PCs.

But all this underscores even more the need to reassure ourselves constantly that we are measuring the right things. What goes into the measurement matters supremely. Do we really understand what attitudes and perceptions are important in this market? This circles us back to where the input comes from in the first place, qualitative research, and we have now to consider how this discipline has matured over the years.

Qualitative Research Grows Up

Qualitative research covers the family of techniques by which the ideas, perceptions, responses and feelings of respondents can be explored by means of unstructured, conversational methods of interviewing. Most commonly this is done by individual depth interviews or in group discussions ('focus groups' if we are talking American) between a few people. The price for the much greater insight this produces is the limit on the number of people who can be interviewed, since it is individually a far more intensive process: samples are in tens rather than hundreds, and too low for us to make statistical statements about the results.

Qualitative research was, from the start, the main source for the detailed insight and understanding from which the brand image and similar statements measured on quantitative surveys like the API are derived. For a long time, this appeared to be its only function. Qualitative research was seen as a handmaid, and a poorly-paid one at that, of the 'proper' statistical survey. The thirty-odd years between 1960 and 1990 can be seen, among other things, as the time in which qualitative research grew up out of this position of dependence into a management instrument in its own right, with its own professional standards, sought after for different but complementary purposes.

It did not come easily. Throughout this period the research community showed a tendency to divide into two camps, slanging each other at conferences and in the columns of the Market Research Society *Newsletter*, and creating a stultifying fog of mutual suspicion and distrust. This wasted a great deal of time. That we have now come through the fog to a recognition of the value of both approaches owes much to the fact that research buyers were able to ignore this squabbling, saw what was of value to them, and proceeded to do it.

There are three main reasons why qualitative methods were looked on with so much suspicion in the early days. The first was the wartime experience of working for government which so many of the 'founding fathers' shared. Jean Morton-Williams of SCPR, writing in 1977, speculated on the reason why qualitative research was less used in social than in commercial market research:

> The main reason, I think, is that so many people in some areas of public sector research, such as planning or transportation, come to it from other disciplines with a strong quantitative tradition, such as engineering or economics. Their view of the research process is thus essentially quantitative... Even when attitudes are the subject of a social research study, they are often treated mechanistically.

Those who entered or returned to market research after experience with government were likely to bring with them this high regard for statistics. It explains why statistical and sampling errors in quantitative research tend, even today, to receive more attention than non-statistical errors such as poor response or faulty question design. In John Downham's history of BMRB, the following revealing memorandum is reported, dated March 1950:

> Membership of the Royal Statistical Society and the Market Research Society is a personal question to be considered by Research Officers... The Association of Incorporated Statisticians is in rather a different class. This is the recognised professional body concerned with our

occupation... New members of our staff will be expected to publicly demonstrate their professional adequacy by being accepted into the Association as an Incorporated Statistician or a Registered Statistical Assistant.
Downham: BMRB International: the First Sixty Years, 1993

Quite apart from government influences, there was a drive to found the new discipline as a science, and science meant quantified measurement. In September 1982 the MRS *Newsletter*, marking the recent death that summer of Henry Durant, published a reprint from *Nature* of 9th May 1942, reporting a debate at the British Psychological Society between Durant and Tom Harrison of Mass-Observation. Durant supported the motion "that empirical methods in the social sciences should be predominantly quantitative". He argued that organised science in the physical world is based upon measurement, and the more the 'qualitative' sciences (including psycho-analysis and social science) grew, the more they necessarily became like the physical sciences, and the social scientist should try to make them so; "the history of science indicated that progress was most rapid when there was the most vigorous insistence upon exact statistical measurement". In the end, everything became quantitative. Harrison, opposing, welcomed the increase in quantitative methods, but deplored the growth of the idea that only such methods were socially scientific: statistically consistent results could give a false picture, and should be seen in social science as "a check, corrective and extension of the qualitative approach".

These biases towards the statistical and 'scientific' undoubtedly were a strong influence on a new discipline desperate to establish its professional credentials. As Andrew Elliott put it, talking about the new MRS: "It was clear from the word go that if research didn't keep its nose scrupulously clean it wouldn't get off the ground".

A third reason was the disrepute resulting from the excesses of so-called motivation research of the Dichter type, which perhaps reached its apogee when the IPA in the early

1960s solemnly considered (and mercifully rejected) the proposition that hypnotism could be a valid method of research, and the MRS formally banned its use.

For all these reasons, qualitative research on its own was generally distrusted, and only valued as an input to 'proper' measurement. Users mostly sympathised with Harold Stansbury's view expressed in 1952:

> The closer it [market research] sticks to quantitative rather than qualitative measurement, the more it can be trusted... The only kind of copy test I have any real confidence in is a properly conducted sales test.

What began to change these perceptions was the gradual realisation that structured questions did not only depend on good statistics for their value but also had to be meaningful. At their worst, and they were often that, they could be damagingly limiting and distorting in the picture they gave; moreover, they could in the repeated monitoring of attitudes become a tyranny. You could not change details in the questionnaire without losing the valuable comparisons with the past data you had expensively built up; it was therefore possible to enter a sort of research cul-de-sac, because one simply failed to see the other changes that were happening in real life but which the research was not set up to measure. This could be particularly deplorable when these limited, imperfect measures became action standards, so that advertising campaigns, say, were designed not so much to sell the brand as to pass the thresholds imposed by the research.

At the same time as people began to see these defects in quantified questions, they also began to find qualitative work valuable, as well as cheaper, and to take decisions based on it. The use of qualitative research by clients who found that it 'worked' for them in its own right began to take off during the mid-1960s, and continued to grow rapidly during the 1970s. The strictures against assuming that qualitative results could ever represent the real world, because they were not 'statistical', began to lose some of their force. Advertising agencies were particularly vocal during this time in adopting qualitative methods for testing copy, but manufacturers did so too. Mike Vineall was research manager for Guinness in 1977, and wrote in these terms:

> Qualitative research is only part of the market research input. However, it is not a subsidiary part or an inferior part, or merely a preliminary pilot stage of quantified research. It is a form of informational flow from the market that is complementary yet unique, irreplaceable and standing on its own... Major decisions involving millions of pounds rather than thousands are made for markets both here and overseas on the basis of qualitative findings by companies such as Lever Brothers, Cadbury-Schweppes, Rowntrees, Beechams and Guinness, to name but a few.

A point echoed by Peter Cooper, founder director of the qualitative agency CRAM:

> Many marketing companies have over time accumulated considerable data on their markets, and this leads to greater confidence nowadays in using it as a method. Users judge that the benefits of qualitative research outweigh reservations about sample size or the absence of statistics.

Vineall makes the point that the *use* of information by companies, even that from quantified sources, is itself essentially 'qualitative' in nature:

> The most elegant quantitative study must ultimately be reduced to qualitative terms to become part of the array of considerations influencing a decision.

To understand one's brand, one relies on concepts which can only be expressed in qualitative terms:

> To give one example I deal with all the time. What does 'Irishness' in relation to Guinness mean to a German beer drinker? This is such a complex and subtle problem that only a qualitative treatment can cope. One needs a 'feel' of what is right and what is wrong in this respect.

John Goodyear, who in 1965 founded Market Behaviour Limited, a qualitative research company which remains at the centre of the world-wide and very successful MBL Group, expressed the new value being attributed to the approach in these terms (writing in the same year, 1977):

> Just as marketing has changed and management has become concerned with a wider range of problems over the last ten or fifteen years, so the scope and application of qualitative research has changed in turn.
>
> Marketing has become more and more concerned with brands and less concerned with products in general; more concerned with brand imagery and personality and with targeting a brand at a sector of the market and less with aiming at the market in total; more concerned with the life-style than just the income of the target market; more concerned with life-cycle stage than simply with age of respondent.

And elsewhere in the same article:

> The qualitative researcher... is being asked to provide the marketing, advertising or management team with an *understanding* of behaviour, an *insight* into what is happening in the market, and an *evaluation* of people's reactions.
>
> The qualitative researcher will not be asked to find out how many families eat breakfast, and of those that do have breakfast how many eat a cooked breakfast, how many have breakfast cereals, etc. The qualitative researcher will be asked to provide information about *what breakfast as a meal means to people*; how they *feel* at that point in their day; what they *believe* they are deriving for themselves, or giving to others, by serving different items; and so on...
>
> He is being asked to provide interpretation, understanding and insight.

With this acceptance came professional discipline. AQRP (the Association of Qualitative Research Practitioners) was formed in 1982, with the aim of providing a forum for qualitative researchers and "promoting confidence in qualitative research within the rest of the survey research industry" (Leslie Collins, first secretary of AQRP, January 1982). It produced, as soon as possible, a Code of Conduct covering technical and ethical standards.

Qualitative researchers were (and still are) sensitive to the charges brought against them by the quantitative tradition: subjectivity, lack of a statistical base. It was all too easy to find examples of badly done qualitative research, scrappily reported, in which the group moderator or analyst failed to study the data thoroughly or, worse, imposed his own preconceptions, and 'found' what he wanted to find. Qualitative research, according to Mary Goodyear, "seems to have received less than its fair share of appreciation and review":

> ... First, it was dismissed as 'not serious': it lacked scientific rigour; it tended to be based on very small samples; its interview form made it non-replicable, and it was labelled 'subjective' since it quite evidently benefited from the past experience, insight and creative/intuitive skills of the researcher.
>
> Second, it wasn't properly understood: its practitioners and protagonists failed to provide any comprehensive categorisation or description of the many different qualitative approaches and techniques, leading its detractors to perceive it as a large, undifferentiated and imprecise area of research.
>
> *Mary Goodyear, in 'A Handbook of Market Research Techniques', Chapter 14, 1990*

On the contrary, qualitative research at its best is very careful about sampling: the persons selected for interview or discussion must precisely fit the specification required. A project on credit cards, for example, may demand a sample which reflects:

> ... not only ownership/non-ownership of such cards, but also the ways in which, frequency with which and degree to which such cards are used, as well as length of credit

period... single or multi-card ownership, and such more commonplace constraints as sex, life-cycle stage.
John Goodyear

Sometimes, qualitative samples or numbers of groups *are* large, fully big enough to apply statistics; 30 groups, i.e. 240 respondents if there are 8 in each group, are now commonplace, and projects involving 50-60 groups occur from time to time. Multi-country qualitative projects with four to six groups per country, multiplied across 12 or more different countries, are regularly commissioned. Recruiters are carefully trained. The normal practice is to try to ensure that no-one attends a group who has been to one before, although there is a respectable school of thought in the business that too much fuss is made about this, and that there are benefits in 'training' and re-using panels of group discussants.

Techniques used in qualitative research have multiplied, including many varieties of indirect and non-verbal probing. There is always, however, a premium on the objectivity and professionalism of the analyst, and his ability to interpret fairly and accurately. It has become common practice for clients to want to see for themselves the actual groups in progress, rather than simply relying on reports, and there are a number of suppliers of studio facilities in which, by means of one-way mirrors, clients can observe groups in progress without being seen (ethics require, however, that those taking part should be informed beforehand that this observation is taking place).

The long dispute between the qualitative and quantitative traditions in research (John Downham has compared it to the Wars of Religion) was debilitating for the industry. But it had one benefit: it forced supporters of each approach to take note of where they were weak and do something about it. The best quantitative researchers realised that survey questionnaires were often ill-designed, ambiguous and meaningless to respondents. More attention was paid to just how attitudinal questions in surveys should be asked, even though there remained (and still remain) plenty of bad examples. Technological advances, such as computer-aided interviewing, have eased the problem by making it more possible for questions to be directed only to those respondents for whom they are appropriate, and improving the recording and analysis of open-ended questions (those which respondents answer in their own words). On the other side, qualitative researchers (at any rate, those who are respected) have embraced the need for rigour and professionalism in the design, execution, and interpretation of their studies.

Although there is still tension between the two schools, it is (at its best) a creative one. Leading researchers often have experience in both disciplines, and many research companies offer both kinds of service and have learned to use them as complementary instruments. We have come a long way from the old sharp divide between 'scientific' quantitative and 'insightful' qualitative research, and closer to John Downham's call (expressed in a letter to John Treasure, 1986) for "a more effective, and possibly new, synthesis of the different approaches implied by these terms."

6

Research and Communication

Most people, if they were asked to name the features which especially distinguished the last fifty years from earlier times, would probably put the explosion in 'communications' high on their list. As we have moved from a more structured to a more individualistic society and from a product-based to a consumer-centred, service economy, more and more has had to be spent on communication, by government, by marketing companies, and by all kinds of other institutions. It has become increasingly important to get one's communications right.

It is also increasingly difficult. People easily tend to think they are good at communicating, but frequently they deceive themselves. There are now many more channels of communication, a much wider and more educated audience, and a very much greater competition of would-be communicators jostling to be heard than ever before. But the more they multiply, the greater becomes the selectivity of the hearer; it is harder for each individual message to get through. In such a context, effective research becomes not merely desirable, but an essential guide through the minefield; at the same time, the process of research is more complex, harder to interpret and requiring greater sophistication than ever.

Market research has played a major part in developing our understanding of this horrendously difficult area: how communications work, how to plan them and how to evaluate them. The post-war story is one of constant claim, counter-claim, argument, experiment and creative tension between advertisers (both commercial and 'social'), advertising agencies and researchers. It is also a story of real compromise and progress emerging from this hubbub, so that we now have a very much better understanding than we did fifty years ago – although the understanding is far from complete, and the experiments go on.

The Emergence of Communication Research

Communication and market research have always been closely linked. It was advertising agencies who first introduced market research methods into the UK from America, where they were was already established by the 1920s. By that decade, Daniel Starch had established his recognition method for measuring the readership of advertisements, and a range of methods were being recorded in the literature: consumer juries to test advertising appeals, tests for headlines, sizes, positions and type size of ads, brand association and recall tests, and so on. There was also a strong tradition of mail-order advertising, which lent itself to 'scientific measurement' of the relative pull of alternative advertising copy. Claude Hopkins stressed the value to copywriters like himself of actually talking to customers, and using coupon returns to assess sales effectiveness.

J Walter Thompson is credited with first bringing these methods to Britain. From 1925 to 1931, JWT London was managed by Sam Meek, an American who believed in the fundamental importance of research in the development of effective advertising. Harold Stansbury, also an American, who was a copywriter at the time and later became Copy Director of JWT London, wrote:

> Market research was already familiar to the people employed by JWT. The Company in America had been

using it for some years... But even as late as 1924, market research was little known in England and practised almost not at all. JWT did stand out like a sore thumb, it is true, and its door-to-door investigating provided agency men with many a merry quip. But even then JWT's faith was not a blind faith. It was JWT's interpretation of information disclosed by market research, not the information itself, and it was the way the interpretation was used to feed the creative imagination, that differentiates JWT's approach to advertising from others.

BMRB was set up by JWT London in 1933 to take over these activities, and in the same period other advertising agencies, most notably the London Press Exchange, were becoming involved in research. John Downham comments that "most of the UK research carried out up to and during the 1930s was still handled by the advertising agencies." (*BMRB International: the First Sixty Years*).

Stansbury's remark about the interpretation of research "feeding the creative imagination" marks a new development. Advertising agencies came to see that research could be about more than understanding a market, fundamental though this was in setting advertising objectives. They began to see a value from research in developing the content of their advertisements, and finally (with some reluctance) applying quality controls and evaluating their performance. Although display advertising remained at the heart of it, the same principles extended to all the other means by which communication is attempted: packaging, logos and colours, station liveries, designs and layouts of stores; product sampling, in-store merchandising displays, direct mailing, special promotions and price reductions, catalogues; and, increasingly, as consumers have become more demanding, service aspects; the way queries and complaints are dealt with, delivery times, after sales service, the perceived availability of maintenance and repair facilities, the quality and presentation of instruction leaflets, and so on. Research has come to be used in the design, testing and evaluation of all these means of communication. And not only for commercial objectives: research has come to be used extensively by government to improve communication, from big-spending public interest campaigns down to the design of such things as tax return forms or advice leaflets on how to claim benefits.

Post-War Development

After the wartime interlude, advertising grew with the economy, though with some fluctuation, since it was affected not only by consumers' expenditure but by company profits. As the graph below shows, advertising expenditure has generally increased in real terms during these years.

Figure 3: Advertising and Research Spend Growth Rates

Indexed to 1973 = 100   **Constant (1990) prices**

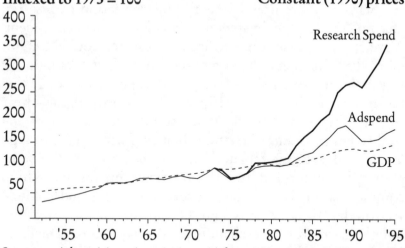

Sources: *Advertising Association, 'Advertising Statistics Yearbook';*
AMSO; OECD STATISTICS – Paris.

The graph shows advertising expenditure, excluding direct mail, at constant (1990) prices between 1952 and 1993. Direct mail was not properly measurable until 1980; it adds approximately 10% to these figures.

We can look at this growth in advertising spend, and the parallel involvement of market research, by referring back to the four phases of development as discussed in Chapter 2.

PHASE 1: 1945-57

This period encompassed the shortages which followed the war (including rationing of newsprint), the gradual recovery and erosion of the seller's market, the growth of competition with the rise of disposable incomes, and the introduction of marketing in response to the realisation of consumer power. During this time, advertising expenditure grew rapidly, from more or less a standing start. Only at the end of this period did the equation abruptly change with the arrival of commercial television.

Interest in 'advertising research' was generally somewhat muted, and most of what was done was a continuation of the pre-war methods imported from the US. The change came with the new marketing departments, which took over responsibility for advertising. There would be at least an advertising manager, possibly (as in Reckitt & Sons at the time) an advertising director with his own department. Many long-standing and fruitful relationships with agencies had already been formed during the 1920s and 1930s, by companies such as Rowntrees, Reckitts, Kelloggs, Unilever or Cadburys; these were consolidated and others created during this period. The advertising manager or director would relate to his opposite number in the agency, the account director and (later, when this animal had been invented) the account planner.

There were, as there had always been, two main thrusts to advertising research: one concerned with the development of the advertising (What do we want it to do? How do we design it to that end?), and the other with evaluation (Is it achieving what we wanted? Are we getting our money's worth?). As marketing became an established discipline, it became clearer that these questions could not be answered purely in terms of sales and purchasing behaviour. It was necessary to understand what went on in people's heads: awareness, attitudes, beliefs and feelings, because those are what the advertising works on. As discussed in chapter 5, this was the time of Dichter and the psychologists, the intemperate attack on them by Vance Packard, and their gradual replacement by more down-to-earth approaches to motivation research. Advertisers and their agencies had begun to see that research had a vital role in getting the 'framework' for the advertising right.

But people began to understand that the same applied also to the second prong, evaluation. Most marketing activity is designed to affect sales and purchasing behaviour; they are the desired end product. But it is impossible to evaluate most advertising in terms of sales or purchasing shifts alone (the exceptions are those types of direct response advertising which can be directly measured by the take-up of a coupon or invitation to phone). People learnt that, even if they were lucky enough to observe a movement in sales which they could safely attribute to the advertising, it only represented a part of the total, and an unknowable part; there was another, invisible effect on those who may have responded to the advertising but had no cause to change their behaviour at the time, although they might well do so later. Also, many other factors could intervene to influence a sale. Advertising cannot be compelling. People choose to attend to it or not; it is not a mechanical process.

Moreover, even if it could be deduced that sales had been influenced, this was not enough to explain how. To understand why advertising achieves success, or doesn't, and find ways of improving it, understanding consumers' response became, increasingly, unavoidable.

PHASE 2: 1958-73

During this second phase, advertising growth continued, but at a slower rate. More striking were the fluctuations in response to Stop-Go policies and variations in company profits. Expenditure reached a peak in the 1973 Barber boom, before the sharp drop into the 1974-5 recession.

As marketing came of age, there was a flowering of interest in communications research as a means of helping advertising to work better. There were many attempts to devise improved (research-based) methods of setting advertising strategy, and of integrating the consumer's voice into creative work. One of the principal influences behind this ferment of innovation was the emergence, from the late 1960s onwards, of account planning departments in advertising agencies, one of whose main responsibilities was the setting of advertising objectives and the evaluation of the work against them.

By the beginning of the 1970s, account planners were deeply involved in strategic planning, being responsible for co-ordinating all the relevant information about the brand: client's and own research, econometric and forecasting models, and everything else needed to develop both strategy and tactics. For some clients, the account planners virtually took over the research function, as far as it related to advertising. The account planning system developed in different ways, from being mainly concerned with strategic positioning in JWT to detailed involvement with creative design in BMP. But account planning departments had one thing in common: they encouraged fresh thinking about how advertising would work and helped to swing their clients' attention away from reliance on crude and simplistic measures. This was particularly clearly seen in the arguments which began to rage in the 1960s about advertising 'testing'.

Testing Copy

There was always an awareness of the benefit of testing advertising before too much was invested in it. Claude Hopkins advocated that it should always be done. But what he meant was that an ad should be inserted in one issue of a magazine, perhaps in one part of the country, and checked for pulling power in terms of applications for the product. Direct mailing has always been able to assess response in this way. But the type of advertising which was now appearing in the press, and still more on television, did not lend itself to this at all easily. It cost too much, was too difficult to organise, and too difficult to interpret the results. Clients did (and sometimes still do) test finished executions on air, perhaps with different weights in different parts of the country; but interpretation can be difficult for reasons beyond the advertiser's control (including spoiling tactics by competitors), and in any case the gamble has by then been taken and the money spent.

There was therefore a strong interest in trying to develop methods of pre-testing advertisements which could be used before the launch of the campaign, if possible before the money was spent on the final execution. There were two main objectives: to find out how viewers respond to the ad, and to try to predict what it would do for increasing sales when rolled out 'for real'. The only way the second of these objectives could be achieved was to construct some measure of change during the test which could 'stand for' real-life persuasion: e.g., some sort of choice question in which propensity to choose the brand advertised before the ads were shown could be compared with a similar question afterwards. A notorious example of this genre, the Schwerin Theatre Test, became popular for a brief period in the early 1960s. It was roundly criticised by other researchers on various methodological grounds and went out of business after a few years, but improved versions of the technique were later to reappear and are still quite widely used (but more in other countries than in Britain).

The appeal of such testing techniques was attractive to marketing departments, and it was to them that research entrepreneurs like Horace Schwerin made their pitch. Advertising agencies held back from the beginning. The agencies especially disliked the tendency to reduce the 'test' criteria to a single branded measure, no matter what it was (a before-after persuasion shift, an awareness or 'impact' measure, or whatever). They were worried by the idea of having to design advertising to beat some 'norm' which might well not be relevant. Consumer responses were much more complex than that, and the agencies preferred to rely on qualitative methods and listen to real consumers.

The problem in regarding pre-test results as any sort of 'prediction' was, of course, that the tests were inevitably artificial. Respondents would be removed for a period to a hall or theatre, and invited to look at advertisements in a structured programme which bore little resemblance to normal viewing; all the other factors which could affect their responses and decisions in the real world were left out. It was therefore very difficult to see, either logically or intuitively, how pre-test results could predict what would happen. But it took time before the users of pre-tests began to understand this point (and indeed, it is still unfortunately the case that some clients hope to use pre-tests to predict market performance).

What pre-testing can do, much more usefully, is give one the best possible idea, or reassurance, in advance that, if everything else works out favourably, this ad will perform well in the sense of achieving the response intended. All advertising if it is to be any good must be directed to some objective, and we test it to satisfy ourselves that it is likely to achieve that objective. But more than this is needed: one wants to know why or how, and how the ad can be improved. Thus, the aspect of pre-testing which is of most use to advertisers and agencies is their capacity for *diagnosis*: investigating the nature of viewers' response, and its strengths and weaknesses. The account planning groups in advertising agencies were increasingly influential, from the 1960s onwards, in forcing attention away from the predictive, normative interpretation of pre-tests to their value as diagnostic tools; in the early 1970s, Alan Hedges' book *Testing to Destruction* gave a considerable stimulus to this change of view. The agencies' eventual support for pre-testing, understood in this more sophisticated way, has enabled it to adapt and survive, to the point where, out of twenty-eight research agencies offering pre-testing services in Britain today (according to the *Admap* guide as at December 1995), all but one or two offer a full range of diagnostic methods, and claim to look at advertisements from many different angles to understand how people are affected by them.

The early 1960s, at the end of this first post-war period of growth, saw a substantial growth of investment in pre-testing methods. At least one agency, LPE, ran a special department whose sole purpose was to make television commercials to test. And major advertisers, such as Procter & Gamble or some of the Unilever companies, adopted standardised methods through which they would require that their advertisements were passed. At this time, too, methods of testing *perception* were developed, which were used not only for advertising but for package designs, magazine covers etc. Electronic hardware was developed, often with techniques imported from America or from other countries: eye-movement cameras, psychogalvanometers, tachistoscopes. These could study, for example, how people looked at a page and what they 'saw' first; how easily and quickly they could recognise a brand name or a design in a natural setting or on a supermarket shelf; what parts of a commercial they responded to most warmly. Specialist companies appeared offering some of these techniques. Some of these early pieces of equipment were short-lived, but a number of the methods have continued, at least in principle, and been superseded now by much more sophisticated electronics. These perceptual measurements would not often be used in isolation; they would be accompanied by diagnostic questions to find out *how* the ad was being perceived and *why* viewers were responding in such a way (since without this the perceptual measures themselves would usually be uninterpretable).

The Consumer in Control

In the mid 1960s, there was more attempt to understand the complexity of consumer behaviour, following the work of

Andrew Ehrenberg with consumer panel data. It began to be realised that people could not be simply classified as buyers of X or Y (indeed, few buy or consider one brand only), and that most advertising would be influential among people who were *already* buying the brand. J Walter Thompson funded a single-source experimental consumer panel, as part of the development work organised by Timothy Joyce for the TGI (Target Group Index); in this panel, housewives recorded over thirteen weeks not only their purchases of many products, but also their television viewing and press reading, which could be translated into OTS (Opportunities To See advertisements). From this came the first analysis in the world which directly related the receipt of advertising to purchase probability, and proved that such a relationship could be observed: some part at least of an advertisement's effect (if it works at all) is immediate and shows up in a shift in behaviour. The papers by Colin McDonald describing these findings had a considerable influence on media planning debates, especially in the United States, but it is only since 1990 that it has been possible to repeat the same type of analysis on a larger scale (with the work of John Philip Jones using Nielsen Household Panel data). This recent analysis has confirmed the potential value of such operations, and single-source panel data are now being produced on a regular basis in Germany (and have started in one TV area in the UK).

Along with the complexity of human behaviour came new ideas on the complexity of people's mental and emotional response to advertising: how it *really* works. Without some sort of agreement about this, it would never be possible to set the right objectives and criteria for demonstrating achievement. It gradually started to be understood that consumers are not passive recipients of advertising, and that therefore advertising effects could not be modelled as if they were a mechanical process.

In the early 1960s, the 'passive consumer' view was still predominant. The conceptual model was what has since been called 'persuasion' or 'hierarchy of effects'. This implies a sequence of stages, in which the task of advertising is first to communicate something to consumers; secondly, when they are aware of it they can be persuaded to like it; finally, once convinced, they are moved to act accordingly.

The idea of the sequence has taken a number of forms. The best known version was put forward in a book by Russell Colley: *Defining Advertising Goals for Measured Advertising Results* (hence the acronym DAGMAR), published in 1961. This stated that an advertisement must carry the prospective customer through four levels of understanding: awareness – comprehension – conviction – action. But there have been a number of other names for the same general process.

Simon Broadbent has set the appeal of this model firmly in the context of the scepticism which followed the advent of television, the rise of the retailer and the decline of direct response, when it appeared impossible to measure advertising effectiveness in terms of the end result on sales:

> Advertising did not always produce immediate results, for reasons which were obscure, and its practitioners retreated. The low point was in 1961 with the publication of DAGMAR: *Defining Advertising Goals for Measured Advertising Results.*
>
> Rather than encouraging agreement to defining goals as a first step, and measuring appropriate results as a second, DAGMAR led people to find out first what could be measured easily and then to set it as a goal. Communication became advertising's objective. DAGMAR was an apparent success (translated into nine languages, and in its ninth printing in 1986) because it let advertising off the hook. The intermediate goal was no longer directly related to financial contributions... Furthermore, it was often just assumed that the intermediate effect *was* positively related to sales, which is not always the case.
>
> Broadbent: *The Advertising Budget, p. 9*

It also seemed intuitively logical: one must after all know about something in order to want it, and want it in order to buy it, but this does not work the other way round (we can be aware and not want, etc.). Combining this intuitive appeal with the practical benefit of measuring things like awareness (which is easy, and responsive to advertising) rather than sales (which is difficult), the attraction for advertisers was obvious. And there were always *some* advertising contexts for which these models *did* make sense. When people are thinking about a new product which they have not used before, or a serious purchase such as a new car or an insurance policy, they might well go through the mental processes described, perhaps in quite an elaborate way. "They imply a rational consumer weighing up the arguments... the object of advertising is seen as being to present persuasive arguments." (Timothy Joyce: *What do we know about how advertising works?*, 1967)

But, from the later 1960s onwards, and increasingly, 'hierarchy of effects' models began to attract criticism. This criticism was based on two main arguments. The first was that very many, probably most, purchasing situations simply do not involve this stylised rational decision making; especially, it does not apply to things which are bought repetitively out of habit. There is empirical evidence to show that the sequential logic breaks down: attitudes follow behaviour rather than preceding it; people try things out and *then* decide whether they like them; people are affected by emotions and moods at least as much as reason. The second was that the sequential model seems to imply a passive consumer, who is moved from one stage of thinking to the next in a uniform way: "a *tabula rasa* on which messages are printed" (Lannon and Cooper, *Humanistic Advertising*, 1983).

The alternative view, which has gained ground from the later 1960s onwards, states that, so far from responding passively, those who receive advertising are *actively in control, and pick and choose what they will attend to.* By the 1980s, this way of seeing things had very largely displaced the other, at least among those who were directly concerned with advertising. It had many attractive implications:

- It fits what we know about purchasing behaviour on a much wider scale, including low-involvement, habitual purchasing where there is no sense in 'a sequence of causal steps'.
- Advertisement impressions have no value in themselves; they only acquire a value if the recipient chooses to give them one by paying attention (otherwise they are simply screened out).
- To sort out the few advertisements of interest to them, people use their power of selective perception.
- Nobody can be forced to buy a product he does not want, or to change his beliefs and opinions against his will, or to pay attention to advertising which is not of interest to him. This puts a premium on the need to *target* advertising, with targets defined not so much in terms of characteristics (e.g. demographic or psychographic types, although these can have some relevance) as of interests or moods. The advertiser will be most effective if he can find the 'right way to speak to' those who are prone to be interested in what he has to say.
- If people respond to advertising in this selective way, it follows that they also respond to other influences, such as price or promotions, in a similar way. This reinforces the view that it is unhelpful to regard them as independent variables each with its own 'value'; on the contrary, we must expect them to reinforce each other when the marketing programme is working well.

This person-centred view is fruitful, credible and attractive. For most advertising and research practitioners these days, the vision of 'people doing things with advertising' has displaced, in most contexts, the vision of 'advertising doing things to people'. Jeremy Bullmore sums up the position thus:

The critics of advertising know that consumers can be *made* to consume in ever increasing quantities. Advertisers *want* consumers to consume in ever increasing quantities. Agencies do their best to *persuade* consumers to consume in ever increasing quantities. And yet, only too often, they don't.

The blame, then, lies inescapably at the feet of the consumer. I'm afraid it has to be said: the consumer of today is quite frequently guilty of gross irresponsibility. "Look here," I sometimes feel like saying to them, "you're a consumer, aren't you? Then why the hell aren't you out there consuming?"

Jeremy Bullmore: Behind the Scenes in Advertising

It would be a mistake, however, to think that this battle has been completely won. There is still a tension (though on the whole a constructive one) between these opposing viewpoints.

The attitude of mind which could be described as 'the myth of the passive consumer' is still buried deep in traditional language about advertising, when people talk of making an *impact* (like a steel ball striking a wall), or people receiving *impressions* (like wax), or messages being *hammered home* (like nails). These are all unconscious metaphors of advertising *doing things to* people. The same tendency is reflected in the 'military' metaphors so often used in advertising language ('targets', 'campaigns' and so on). It is closely related to desire for simple causal inferences: we desperately want to be able to say what *causes* sales, and slip naturally from that into asking what 'causes' people to act or take a decision.

Another implicit reason for the long persistence of the 'passive consumer' is that it suggests uniformity – people or groups all responding the same way to a stimulus – and uniformity is a *simplifying* factor. The picture of a whole population understanding and accepting one's message in essentially the same way is easy to grasp, and therefore attractive. To suggest that, in reality, there is a huge diversity of ways in which people will understand or fail to understand what one is trying to say can be confusing and unsettling.

A third and more sinister reason has been well noted by Jeremy Bullmore. If consumers are passive, it is a short step to seeing them as *manipulable*, and thus excellent ammunition for the generation brought up on Vance Packard's *Hidden Persuaders*. As Bullmore says:

> Television advertising began to have an extremely adverse effect on the reputation of advertising as a trade – at any rate among the chattering classes. Television advertising possessed two characteristics which the middle classes found intolerable. First, it was intrusive – which is to say that it was noticed. And, secondly, it worked. Here was clear evidence that vulnerable and unsophisticated people – in other words, the sort of people who would watch television – were being manipulated, almost certainly subliminally, by sociology graduates who had been brainwashed by capitalism.

Those who wish to take a political position opposed to advertising undoubtedly find it helpful to their argument if they can portray consumers as 'passive'.

Advertising Tracking

For all the above reasons, the new thinking took time to work through the system. Advertisers still wanted and responded to replicable measures of effectiveness which could be repeated over time.

Evaluation of advertising effectiveness continued to be difficult. The brand image and scaled attitude measures developed by the early 1960s such as the API, although they discriminated well between brands, were not on the whole found to be very responsive to advertising. They had to start with being regularly monitored; but, once it was realised how slow they were to move, the measurements were often reduced to occasional (probably annual) dipsticks. The same applied to awareness measures applied to brands: once in the consumer's consciousness, they tended to stay there come what may.

Against this background a new tracking system appeared which took as its main measurement, not awareness of the brand, but awareness of the *advertising*. This was introduced in 1973 by two researchers, Maurice Millward and Gordon Brown, who were unusual in that both of them had previously been working, not in research agencies, but in the marketing department of a major fmcg advertiser (General Foods), and (it could be argued) understood the language and concerns of the client better than most. For many in the research business it was anathema to suggest that memory of the advertising was a valid measure of effectiveness; surely the brand was what mattered? But the Millward Brown logic was that advertising awareness can at least be shown to respond to advertising expenditure, rather better than anything else, and therefore can provide evidence that something has happened, there has been an impact on consumers.

The clients bought it. From this beginning, Millward Brown grew rapidly and became what it is today, a multi-million pound international company. Their ability to offer a measurement of response which was sensitive to advertising expenditure changes, at an acceptable price (most studies were syndicated to begin with), was attractive to advertisers. They capitalised on this success by building a data bank of evidence, so that they could describe and model the conditions under which these responses vary. This database of past measurements largely made them untouchable by competitors. As Tim Bowles wryly put it: "we stood by and let them do it". It has also enabled them to become leading theorists of how advertising works (for example, the importance of creating an advertising story in such a way that it enhances the brand, so that, when it is remembered later, e.g. in a buying situation, the brand connection is what is brought to mind).

PHASE 3: 1974-82

A period of retrenchment now began for most marketing activities and for many marketing people. Advertising expenditure dropped rapidly in real terms in the first recession (1973 to 1975). Although it held up in the second recession, spending in 1982 was at a level no higher in real terms than 1973's, while there was very high media inflation.

The Qualitative Swing

Research, with its close connections with advertising, was bound to be affected. All kinds of research suffered. As Antony Thorncroft wrote in the *Financial Times* in March 1970 (reporting on the MRS Conference): "It cannot be denied... that market research in the UK is slanted too heavily towards media and advertising".

Companies offering continuous research services, like BMRB's Target Group Index, were relatively secure; but in a time of squeeze, the ad hoc advertising research budget was usually the first item of expenditure to be dropped. The experiments in communication which had flowered in the 1960s, both those paid for by advertisers and those done in-house by agencies, were dropped from budgets.

Increasingly, advertising agencies began to invest in qualitative research. Sometimes this would be controlled from within the agency, as with the 'Creative Workshop' concept (small samples with semi-structured interviews) used for developing executions, which was borrowed by JWT London in the late 1960s after being pioneered by Leo Burnett in Chicago. The agencies' disenchantment with quantified measures of advertising effectiveness combined with the lack of funds to make these (often small-scale) qualitative studies more attractive.

Advertising pre-testing and development, during the 1970s, became the principal battleground for the continuing fight between 'the nose-counters and the head-shrinkers'. For developing and improving advertising, it was the insights that mattered, and enabled the creative people to feel closer to consumers. A creative is interested in understanding a person whom he can talk to, rather than a population average. At its most extreme, in agencies like Boase Massimi Pollitt, it became the practice for the senior account planners to become directly involved in running and moderating the experimental group discussions.

Undoubtedly, at its best, this process produced some very successful advertising. However, critics could point to cases where it was badly done: where an agency team would skim the research results for arguments favourable to their point of view, without any evidence of deep or objective analysis. There could still be worries about whether the research done on a few hand-picked people was relevant to the real market 'out there'. Research agencies offering quantitative pre-testing systems were kept going largely by advertisers who still wanted confirmation that their agency's ideas were in the right area; in many cases, pre-tests were commissioned precisely because the agency was not fully trusted by the client.

It is a paradox that this adoption of qualitative research methods within agencies, whilst it attracted contempt from many traditional researchers, in fact marks the acceptance of the idea of research for the first time by the creative teams who had always shunned it. They now had a research which they could control and which would answer *their* questions, rather than those which other people said were good for them. They had always objected to research which set what seemed unreasonable and irrelevant targets to meet, and they continued to do so; agencies were for a long time vocal in protesting against the Millward Brown Advertising Awareness Index, for instance. Research attracted increasing contempt from agency users for being more concerned to measure what could be easily measured rather than answering the difficult (but important) questions. But now they could be enthusiastic about the 'new research' which was directly helping them. David Bernstein, a noted creative director, wrote: "I'm in print saying that research can be the best thing that ever happened to a creative department" (*Admap*, 1975).

Accountability and Modelling

The accelerated reliance by agencies on qualitative research was partly fuelled by the withdrawal by many, if not most, of their clients from concern with the question of how their advertising was working. The increasing power of the retailers, exacerbated during recession, led advertisers to rely more than ever before on price-cutting and promotions; a brand manager's main concern became how to maintain share, in the short term, and avoid de-listing. Advertising principles and the fundamentals of branding for the longer term became more remote, something which could be put off to better times. Many clients appeared to take little interest in monitoring their advertising. 'Accountability' started to become a watchword, as finance directors moved increasingly into positions of power and to demand that advertising expenditure should be shown to 'pay its way' like everything else. Money was not available for developing new ideas in communications research, and the effervescence of the 1960s subsided rapidly.

'Accountability' became part of the political culture, and agencies could not help paying attention. Having once resisted it, they began to argue persuasively for it; "if you can't beat them, join them". It was again the agencies who led the way, during the 1970s and into the 1980s, in developing the use of econometric modelling for helping to understand what was influencing markets; one may instance, for example, Tom Corlett, Jeremy Elliott and Laurence Hagan at JWT, Simon Broadbent at Leo Burnett, Andrew Roberts at Masius. The agencies saw their own survival in establishing a sound accountability, and by arguing for it, they sought to influence the way it was done, so that the 'accountability' process would be helpful to the craft of marketing and not destructive. By the time the industry entered the most recent downturn in 1989-1990, 'accountability' had become a key factor in retaining, or winning, the business. This would hardly have been possible if both sides had not by then acquired an idea of 'accountability' as something which could actually be achieved.

PHASE 4: 1983-To Date

The recovery from the 1981-2 recession was very quick. Advertising expenditure grew at an exceptionally fast (and, as it turned out, unsustainable) rate, leading to a massive drop in the 1990-1 recession and a slow return to the trend line. Research, however, did not suffer in the same way as advertising during this latest recession, unlike the dark days of the 1970s. The speed of growth, the new burst of individualism followed by the new disillusion, the fragmentation of media and the development of new electronic databases have all been factors in making communications research even harder, and even more important.

In this period, advertising research could be said to have grown up. The embattled divide between the exponents of qualitative and quantitative methods softened. Clients became able to value the creative contribution and the part played by qualitative techniques in facilitating it. And even the creative people in agencies acquired a better appreciation of why their clients wanted evidence that the wonderful idea was really going to work.

A number of trends, which had started long before, came to fruition in the 1980s and 1990s. The most important of these, perhaps, was the realisation that the evaluation of an advertisement, or an advertising campaign, is a complex business requiring the simultaneous study of many different measures and factors; it is not satisfactory ever to rely on a single yardstick, whether it be ad awareness, brand awareness, brand image or purchasing behaviour. But, if all the relevant information is studied in a rigorous and sensitive way, it is possible to obtain a very clear idea of how well the campaign is working. The credit for this improved understanding belongs largely to the foundation of the IPA's Advertising Effectiveness Awards.

The IPA Advertising Effectiveness Awards

The principal difficulty in evaluating advertising is that it is so varied. We know that quite a lot of advertising does not work at all, or not very well, and there is no guarantee that any two advertising campaigns which *do* work will do so in the same way, or be measurable by the same measures. We can almost guarantee the opposite.

This can lead to the destructive view that one can never establish advertising's effect, and it is therefore a waste of time to try. Fortunately most major advertisers and their agencies have not fallen into this trap. But the process of learning how to measure advertising effect has to be inductive; it is much more like natural history than physics. One has to examine thousands of different species (examples of different products) before one can elicit any general rules, and even then one must expect exceptions.

It was this kind of reasoning that led the Institute of Practitioners in Advertising (IPA) to found the Advertising Effectiveness Awards in 1980. They have been repeated every two years since then, and the tenth volume is due in 1996. The eight published volumes now contain over 160 case histories judged 'successful'; in addition, all the entries to the Awards, some 600 in total, can be studied via the IPA's Advertising Effectiveness Data Bank.

The Awards were set up in 1980 with the following objectives:

1. To generate a collection of case histories which demonstrate that, properly used, advertising can make a measurable contribution to business success.

2. To encourage advertising agencies (and their clients) to develop ever-improving standards of advertising evaluation (and, in the process, a better understanding of the ways in which advertising works).

They were largely the brainchild of Simon Broadbent of Leo Burnett, who, with his succession of books on how to set the advertising budget, has been an influential propagator of the view that advertising is a vital business investment, that research can be used to draw intelligent conclusions about its effectiveness, but that there are no simple-minded rules of thumb. Broadbent is a firm opponent of 'one-dimensional assessment of advertising', and the assumption that only what can be easily measured is important.

> The fact that advertising may have effects other than short term on volume is too often overlooked, because such effects are complex and hard to quantify. Today, anything without a number attached is invisible. This book tries to turn the reader to a wider view. When advertising is evaluated, it is important that the job is done properly.
> *Broadbent: The Advertising Budget, 1989, first chapter*

'Effectiveness' from the outset was defined for the Awards as contribution to the business. No measures were to be accepted at face value, unless it could be shown that they were connected to the business objectives. The judges were instructed to be very rigorous, and to be careful particularly not to accept the apparently easy cases, where there seemed to be 'obvious' effects on sales movements, etc. The prizes were to be given as a result of judgement, taking account of the difficulties in each case – never according to rule. Most of the judges came from outside advertising agencies.

The published papers provide a "toolbox of evaluation techniques" (Broadbent). Each case is different, but many of them use a number of methods in common, selecting what was right for their situation. By reading how this was done, in a range of successful cases, you can get ideas about what might work in *your* case, and how you might go about it, and as the cases multiply, some general points begin to emerge. They are classified to cover different areas of interest (established goods and services, new goods and services, special projects including financial, corporate, public information etc.) and, since 1990, they have explicitly included a category to cover long-term effects of advertising for long-running established brands, always the most difficult to demonstrate.

Reading the case histories, for all their variety, one can distinguish three general principles which keep recurring, and which have been of great importance for communications research as it is today. These are:

- Clear, agreed objectives for the campaign.
- A holistic approach to evaluation. Advertising never works on just one level, and in no case is one measure alone ever considered good enough. Research methods all or most of which can be used include: sales (obviously), consumer purchases (from panels or surveys), econometric modelling to identify the effect of advertising spend, tracking to check what the

advertising is communicating, before-after and side-by-side comparison tests, pre-testing before the advertising is launched.

- The checking and discounting of other factors, such as price, distribution, other promotions, seasonal variations, competitive activity; advertising is not accepted as a factor unless all these others, where relevant, are accounted for.

A good example of these principles at work was Bowater-Scott's account, in the 1992 volume, of the long-term success of the Andrex toilet tissue campaigns. Andrex has appeared more than once in the Awards. The advertising consists of making specific points with frequent new creative treatment on the basis of an established, consistent emotive theme (the labrador puppy) which has been there since 1972. This advertising has enabled them, in a very 'functional' market, to maintain a premium price, hold off the threat from own label brands and 'green' products, and defeat a dangerous new launch by the chief rival, Kleenex Velvet. Blind vs. named testing showed the effect of the Andrex brand personality in differentiating it from Kleenex Velvet.

They monitor the progress of the brand with consumer panel data, which enables them to understand the structure of customer loyalty. This and other sources (the TGI) have shown that, as housewives get older, loyalty to the brand increases; as the brand increases share, more consumers use it as their only or major brand. The advertising task is to recruit new (young) users without alienating the large body of current users (and an important part of that, of course, is keeping the quality of the product demonstrably high). Tracking data shows that non-users also hold the brand in high esteem.

Bowater-Scott have continuously (since 1974) used econometric modelling, which has determined that advertising is an important variable. The value of this increases with learning over time. The advertising is found to have a low exposure trigger (2 per month at most) and a low decay rate (about 25% per month). Tests have been done at various intervals, to compare up-weighting or drip vs. burst treatments. The model which fits the data best seems to be a convex response curve, which implies that continuous advertising at a low level (drip) is better than higher but separate bursts.

Other factors (distribution, promotions, product quality and packaging) are eliminated as accounting for the differences attributed to the advertising. Product quality is regularly monitored by attitude survey; and tracking is used to confirm the brand values which the advertising communicates (including the emotive effect of the puppy).

Andrex is a classic example of a long-term, consistent advertising and marketing policy, with clear objectives, continuously assessed and driven by research and market modelling based on it. Without carefully directed market research, on a number of levels, it would not have been possible to design such a policy, let alone maintain it. Many other examples illustrating the use of research to demonstrate advertising value can be found in these volumes of Awards. By no means all of them concern traditional 'basic' household products like Andrex. An analysis of Volume 8, the 1994 Awards, shows that out of the 20 winners, five were about some aspect of 'health' (AIDS, anti-smoking, raising awareness of diabetes, a health club, and getting children to drink milk), two were for pharmaceutical products, one was a Home Office safety campaign (smoke alarms), one financial (the Co-operative Bank), one British Airways, two cars, and two clothing. Only six dealt with traditional fmcg products: three were for beers and two confectionery, the only part of this list which may seem a little unbalanced.

The smoke alarms campaign also featured in the first series of Research Effectiveness Awards, a parallel awards and publications programme founded under the aegis of the Association of Market Survey Organisations (AMSO) at the instigation of its then Chairman, John Goodyear, in 1991. An intensive series of campaigns by the Home Office increased penetration of smoke alarms from 5% to 70% over seven years, and alerted people to the speed with which smoke kills. Qualitative and quantitative research, from several agencies, was used to plan, direct, monitor and evaluate the effects of these campaigns; for example, BJM's study in 1990 pointed out that the first campaign, whilst very effective with families, was failing to communicate to an older age group who were especially vulnerable to house fires, and led to a change of direction in the next campaign. This change "encouraged more people of all age groups to install smoke alarms and thus to save more lives than might otherwise have been the case" (*Research Works*, 1991, p 117).

Consumer-Centred Advertising

Underlying the success of the IPA Awards and their more mature use of research has been the further entrenchment of the perceptions of the 'active consumer', as discussed above: the idea that people select and use advertising, rather than being moved about by it.

If the person-centred view is a more mature and realistic one, it helps to explain the convergence one detects between the different sides in the advertising business, and the common appreciation of all relevant research methods, qualitative or not. Everyone can now see that a simple-minded sales response, or some 'intermediate' surrogate for it, is inadequate as an account of the benefits of advertising, so that there no longer needs to be despair if such a thing cannot be found. As Broadbent puts it:

> ... even in the 1960s good marketing executives realised (as they still do) that such simple communication objectives could not encompass all that advertising had done for great brands... They listed their overall marketing objectives and then made the advertising help to accomplish all of them.

> They did not use one numerical measure alone to determine the advertising budget, any more than they evaluated copy by a single score.
>
> *The Advertising Budget*

This convergence into a more mature view of advertising is continuing to develop in new ways. There has, for example, been an increasing recognition that retaining customers involves more than top-quality product performance. Service is important, and the way the customer is treated. Guarantees, service undertakings, loyalty cards and systems, special promotions, not to mention the much-maligned Consumers' Charter, are all being communicated alongside brand benefits, and utilising both display and direct mail advertising. And as broadcast television begins to fragment, new vehicles for advertising are appearing, enabling specific groups of people to be targeted more accurately. Quite possibly, if such things as interactive shopping via digitised television take off (or direct-response television continues growing at its current speed), we shall be returning to the Claude Hopkins world of direct response measurement, applied now to the screen.

All these developments underline the importance of seeing the communication process as a whole. Advertising, promotions, loyalty bonuses and all the other components have to work in harmony. To ensure that they do so, and make the right impact, good research is needed on all fronts. As David Ogilvy said more than twenty years ago, advertising people who ignore research are as dangerous as generals who ignore decodes of enemy signals. Market research is once again at the centre of the development of these new business skills, with techniques such as service quality assessment and mystery shopping.

★ ★ ★

7

Research and the Media

The rise in advertising expenditure which we looked at in the last chapter, from virtually zero after the war to over £8 billion by the late 1980s, soon started to put increasing pressure on advertisers and media owners. Advertisers needed solid reassurance, with so much at stake, that their advertising money was well spent; for many of them it was the largest element in their annual budget. The media owners, on the other side, were increasingly dependent on advertising revenue, and under pressure to sell their space in a market becoming more competitive as new publications were launched – a problem which intensified abruptly when commercial television, a completely new and very attractive medium, came on the scene. They needed to be able to assure potential advertisers that their particular medium would effectively deliver an audience, i.e. would expose their advertising to large numbers of relevant consumers at the lowest possible cost per head.

But this raised difficult questions. How many people actually looked at the newspaper or magazine containing their ads, and who were they? Even if someone did look at the paper, how sure could one be that they would see the ad? If they did, would they really read it or just give it a glance? Who would be watching the television commercials, in which programmes, at what times of day? And how was it possible to set a value, in money terms, on all these options? Such questions attracted intense discussion and argument, leading to experiments to try to solve the problems and provide measurements on which all sides could agree. As a result of these efforts, it was in the UK, without question, that world-wide standards for media research were set.

Media research (that is, research to establish the size and composition of the *audience* to any medium) has always been, and still remains, one of the main areas of commercial research investment. Indeed, it is probably *the* main one in most countries, including Britain. It has also been a powerful engine driving the development of precision research methodology.

The reason for this is easy to state. Audience research data provide the currency which is needed as a medium of exchange between buyers and sellers of media advertising. The buyers need it to know what they are buying and to evaluate the price; the sellers would not sell without it and, since they depend on selling space, would not survive. Even those without advertising, such as the BBC, must satisfy their masters that they justify their licence fee by competitively delivering audiences, and that they succeed in serving the whole potential audience, the nation. A currency of exchange must be of the highest standard, objective, accurate, above reproach.

On the other hand, measuring audiences accurately is very difficult. What do we mean by an 'audience'? The buyers and sellers must know how many people will have an 'opportunity to see' (OTS for short) an advertisement run in a particular issue of a newspaper or magazine, or in a particular commercial break, etc., and who these people are. Merely knowing the audiences to television channels or newspaper and magazine titles in general terms is not enough, since these audiences can vary greatly between different times of day, preferred programmes, newspaper sections read, and so on. What has to be measured, therefore, is nothing less than the probability of reading or viewing events: the probability with which readers or viewers will receive an OTS for every issue or commercial break which might contain an ad. From such information, agency media departments can build up the schedules to deliver the coverage and frequency patterns they want, and media owners can structure their rate cards.

But reading and viewing events are excruciatingly hard to measure, because they are so fleeting and indeterminate. Even in the short term, human memory is unreliable on such matters as these. Which of us could, if asked, cast our minds back over the past 24 hours (or even the past 6 or 12 hours) and accurately recall how many times we had looked at a particular newspaper, or exactly what times we had watched TV or listened to the radio? The problem of obtaining the best possible measures has focused some of the best brains in research during the past fifty years; the importance of these measures has drawn in the investment required to fund the necessary research vehicles.

Audience research was always the main component of media research; but media owners also needed to know *how* their media were used, the ways their readers or viewers responded to them, their image etc., so that they could both improve them and promote them more effectively against the competition. At this level, the media products could be seen as *brands*, and all the qualitative and quantitative methods of research came into play which have been discussed in the previous chapters.

Early Days

Both in America and in Britain, the media became involved in research from the start. It is recorded that the London Research Bureau conducted a survey in 1924, on behalf of the *Daily Mail*, called 'The Nation's Newspaper', and based on a nation-wide sample of 24,000 respondents. It was said to be the first nation-wide media planning survey anywhere in the world (although this has been disputed). Several other studies during the 1930s are recorded. Mark Abrams at the LPE in the 1930s became much involved with newspaper research, conducting the first Survey of Readership in 1939 for what was then the

IIPA, and surveys for specific titles including *The Times*, *Manchester Guardian*, *News Chronicle* and *Herald*.

Broadcasting was also researched. Robert Silvey, one of the MRS founding fathers, who had founded research at the LPE in 1934, became Director of the BBC's Audience Research Unit (a new post) five years later, and set up the BBC audience research system which was to continue unbroken until 1992. Initially the Gallup organisation was used. Henry Durant recalled:

> We interviewed, on his [Silvey's] behalf, a daily national sample of 800 men and women on their radio listening. Not a day was missed during the four years we did the job. It was then carried out by Silvey's BBC outfit.
>
> It was also Silvey with whom we collaborated in interesting work on the impact of Lord Haw-Haw. He flourished during the phoney war period, till April 1940. How far was he making an impact? In what direction and among what groups? These were the questions which had to be answered. It was a striking lesson that he was most effective when he told truths which had not been released by our government.
>
> *Henry Durant, interviewed in 1979*

Although there was no commercial broadcasting in Britain, there were continental radio stations carrying advertising, notably in Luxembourg and Normandy. Andrew Elliott described how JWT, using BMRB, tried to find out whether radio advertising had a future.

> With other colleagues in the research department, we crawled on our hands and knees up to midnight around housing estates outside Southampton, plugging in test phones on people's premises to find out which station, if any, they were listening to, and what sort of advertising came over.
>
> We were doing either the door knocking or with some ingenious system we persuaded a sample of households to allow us to rig up a very simple wiring system whereby an extension to their radio sets led to somewhere, either to the

backdoor outside the house, to the front door, or the gatepost, and every half hour we crept along with our earphones and plugged in and simply listened, and knew of course what to listen out for: a.) whether the set was on at all in the living room inside the house, and b.) which station people were listening to. That was all recorded. It was a primitive type of research...

It led to all sorts of hilarious incidents. The police arrested several of us. This was the time, about 1938, when there were Irish terrorists operating in this country, trying to blow up things like Hammersmith Bridge, for example, and we researchers creeping around until midnight with wires and headphones seemed of course to be prize objects.

Andrew Elliott, interviewed April 1979

Press Readership Research

At first, press research was concerned with *circulation* rather than readership. The Audit Bureau of Circulations was not founded until 1931, and even then membership was not all that widespread, "so that by no means all the circulation claims made by publishers could be regarded as wholly trustworthy". (Harry Henry: 'The Origin and Birth of the NRS', *Admap*, September 1991). So the 'infant discipline' of market research was brought in to produce more objective circulation estimates. The measurement unit was the copy of the publication, in terms of the home taking it, not the individual reader. Harry Henry refers to several surveys of this type, carried out by the London Research Bureau and other organisations between 1928 and 1936. Their titles sometimes made their purpose clear: for example, 'Press Circulations Analysed', or 'Investigating Press Circulations'.

The Audit Bureau of Circulations, founded under the auspices of the Incorporated Society of British Advertisers (ISBA) and now administered by representatives of all the interested parties, requires publishers to produce sales figures audited to a defined formula, and publishes them at regular intervals. The development of this service has effectively neutralised controversy at the level of copies sold. But it was realised early that circulation alone was an inadequate basis for a media buying currency. Publications vary considerably in the number of readers who typically see each copy, and the type of people these readers are. A circulation survey might be able to produce some crude breakdowns of social class, from the households surveyed, but no information about the sex or age of readers, or their habits of product purchase. A proper estimate of the potential audience to a publication required the measurement of *readership*.

During the 1930s, both JWT and the LPE conducted a number of readership surveys. In one (by JWT in 1938) 17,000 individuals were questioned. Henry comments that:

> ... the methodology whereby 'the JWT investigators stopped men in the street, talked to girls in factories, visited spinsters' whist-drives and bachelors' lodgings' might not today commend itself to media research statisticians.

But the landmark survey was the 'Survey of Press Readership', 1939, conducted by the LPE under Mark Abrams for the IIPA (the Institute of Incorporated Practitioners in Advertising, which dropped the 'incorporated' in 1954 to become the IPA). This survey adopted a number of crucial innovations, which laid the groundwork for the future NRS. According to Henry:

> ... in most key respects, the structure and methodology of the IIPA Survey of Press Readership were largely identical with those of the JICNARS National Readership Survey of 1990.

The survey covered 40,500 interviews in Great Britain and Northern Ireland, plus booster samples in 58 towns, with individuals selected by an elaborate quota system of class within age-group within sex within region. And the technique used was the 'recent reading' method which has remained the standard ever since and is now virtually used world-wide. This is the method which asks whether the title has been read during its publication period (dailies during 'yesterday', weeklies during the preceding week, etc.), on the assumption that the reading of *any* issue of a particular title during its latest 'frequency period' is equivalent to the reading of an *average* issue during the whole of its life.

Henry notes that the 1939 IIPA survey was kept in restricted access, exclusive to those IIPA members who had contributed to its cost, and their clients; publishers were not to be allowed to see it, even if they were clients of agencies who were members of the IIPA: "nobody in those days had got around to describing readership figures as 'common currency' for the buying and selling of advertising space."

After the wartime gap, three new surveys appeared in 1947. Two of them, from Hulton Press and IIPA, used the recent reading method, and both were conducted by Research Services Ltd (the successor of the LPE research department) under Mark Abrams; the third, by Attwood Statistics Ltd, used a different method in which actual copies of each publication were carried by interviewers. This method, later known as 'through the book', has now been generally abandoned everywhere, although it survived for several years in America. It severely limits the potential coverage of a survey (because interviewers cannot carry very many copies), and, by focusing attention on a specific issue, it underestimates the average readership which the recent reading method delivers. This was demonstrated by the Attwood survey of 1947, which considerably underestimated certain longer-life publications compared to the other two.

The Hulton survey results were made freely available to advertisers, agencies and publishers, unlike the other two. It also introduced some refinements: housewife and head-of-household classifications, and certain categories of product usage, which would help in setting meaningful targets for schedules. On this basis, the Hulton Readership Survey provided the most attractive 'common currency' for the buying and selling of advertising space, with an annual survey during each of the following seven years. During this time, the survey had to weather:

> ... the occasional disagreeables (inseparable from readership research at all times and in all countries, as individual publishers complain that they have been unfairly treated) and complications arising from rapid changes in circulations as the supply of newsprint increased and as cover prices were permitted to rise.

At one point, in 1952, the survey revealed such dramatic changes compared to 1951 that a separate survey by a different company (BMRB) using different (probability) sampling methods was undertaken to check them (they appear to have been vindicated).

In 1954 the run of the Hulton Readership Survey was brought to an end by what Harry Henry has described as the IIPA National Readership Survey 'conspiracy'. The story is of interest not only because it changed the development course of the NRS but as a moral tale: a piece of raw political manoeuvring out of which came a genuine advance: the practice of title rotation.

The plot was concocted between Associated Newspapers, the Newspaper Proprietors' Association, Social Surveys Ltd (under Henry Durant), and the top brass of the IIPA (but behind the back of the IIPA research committee, who were not informed). The rival survey introduced some advances which were incorporated in the later NRS, including a probability sample and a booklet of mastheads introduced for the first time as a visual prompt. It also introduced certain check questions after the recent reading question – *where* the publication had been read, and at what time of day, or day of week.

Unfortunately, these check questions were asked for each publication before proceeding to the next one, a method which Henry christened 'conditioning to negative' – a respondent might learn during a long repetitive interview that he could save himself from being asked these extra questions if he claimed *not* to have been a reader. Besides, the titles were not rotated, as later became standard practice: 'for reasons which may be guessed at', they were presented in the same unvarying order – daily newspapers, Sunday newspapers, weekly magazines and monthly magazines.

Harry Henry takes up the story:

> The consequences are not difficult to guess: while, when compared with the Hulton survey of 1954, the IIPA aggregate readerships for dailies were up by 30 per cent and for Sundays by 13 per cent, those for weeklies were 5 per cent down and for monthlies no less than 20 per cent down. And, indeed, experimental work carried out by Research Services in 1955 for the IPA demonstrated that, with this form of questioning, the readerships even of daily newspapers came down to absurdly small figures if those titles were presented last.
>
> The conspirators behind this survey naturally put up a fight, producing their tame psychologist to assert that there was a God-determined natural order in which categories of publications should be asked about, and that was the one they were using. But the argument failed to carry conviction.
>
> *Harry Henry: 'The Origin and Birth of the NRS',*
> *Admap, September 1991*

This was not to be the last time in which newspaper publishers were to feel the need to assert their interest in contradiction of those whose concerns lie more towards magazines; it is a tension which periodically resurfaces, most recently with another proposition to run an alternative survey which was floated in 1991-2. But the principle of rotation was accepted ever after.

A Joint Industry Vehicle

The last Hulton survey took place in 1955, after which it became clear it could not continue (*Picture Post* was already on the rocks). The newly-named IPA then picked up the challenge. The next survey was the 1956 IPA National Readership Survey, financed by publishers but controlled by the IPA (with an Advisory Committee set up by the contributors). The IPA had realised that, if the requirement to keep the results secret from publishers was dropped, the publishers would pick up the bill, or most of it at any rate. The 1956 survey again used mastheads, but adopted rotation and a filter question which ensured that only those titles which had been seen in the last three months would be asked about.

This decision by the main parties – newspaper and magazine publishers – to co-operate on the new National Readership Survey under the banner of the IPA may be seen as a watershed. Energies which would otherwise have been wasted in disputing the merits of different measurements (as continued to happen in America) were focused on forging the NRS into the best possible instrument, which would become a standard on which everyone would agree. The survey has continued, with substantial evolution, every year since 1956. A few years later, in the mid-1960s, control moved from the IPA to JICNARS (the Joint Industry Committee for National Readership Surveys), which consisted of representatives of the publishers (newspaper and magazine), advertising agents and (when they started to appear) media independents, and advertisers, via their respective trade associations. This was one of the early 'JICs', or Joint Industry Committees, which became a model for all other main media. The JIC structure meant that all interested parties would have a say in the funding and development of the surveys. The search for improvement was driven by the JICNARS Technical Committee, to which were recruited, over the years, most of the best research brains employed by publishers and agencies. JICNARS continued, with some variations, until 1992, when it was superseded by a limited company, National Readership Surveys Limited; but the principle that the survey is controlled by all the main interested groups remains unchanged.

The NRS did not always have a smooth progress – that could hardly be expected. There would always be some publisher who thought a particular title of his was being understated. The benefit of the joint system was that, the method not being in dispute, it could usually be shown that such fluctuations were within sampling error. More serious differences occurred on the rare occasions when the survey changed contractor. Although it has been put out to competitive tender on average every three years, the NRS has remained with Research Services except for two periods when it moved to BMRB, from 1959 to 1967 and from 1973 to 1976 (BMRB also had the Hulton survey briefly at the end of its life, in 1954-55). A fresh contractor, even working to the same design, always initially produced a distortion in the figures and needed a settling down period to return to equilibrium. It became the practice always to run surveys by the old and new contractors in parallel for at least six months, to calibrate these discrepancies; whether the cost of this has been a deterrent from changing contractor is not recorded.

Many ideas for improving the survey have been tried, and some rejected. None were ever accepted without extensive pilot testing. Certain landmarks stand out. One was the investigation in depth of the questioning technique by Dr William Belson, published in 1962 under the title 'Studies in Readership'. Belson, who at the time was running the Survey Research Unit at the London School of Economics, was invited in by Harry Henry, then chairman of the Technical Subcommittee, following concern about the instability of some of the survey questions, especially the order effects referred to above. The fundamental difficulty was (and still is) how a readership claim can ever be validated, or (just as important) a claim not to have read. Harry Henry describes the conversation:

> I... flung Dr Belson a challenge based on the fact that his primary discipline is psychology. Here are two women, I postulated, one of whom declares in an IPA interview that she has read a copy of *Good Housekeeping* during the past month, and the other of whom declares she has not. Was it beyond the bounds of possibility for him to take these two women and give them so thorough a going-over that at the end of an hour... or a day... or a week... he would be able to look at the evidence and declare beyond all reasonable shadow of doubt that the original answers had or had not been correct?
>
> From this was developed the technique of what is called 'the intensive interview', a breakthrough in research methodology of almost unprecedented significance not only for readership research but also for every other form of field research.
>
> Harry Henry: 'Wheels - and their re-invention',
European Research, July 1980

A key finding of Belson's work was the discovery that there were large compensating errors: several readers were classified as non-readers, and vice versa. Although these errors were individually quite large, they tended to be nearly equal in size and so cancelled out, leaving the 'true' readership figure reasonably close to the survey finding. However, in some cases, notably monthly magazines, the errors did not compensate, and the survey result was found to be some distance from the 'truth'. This finding, together with other experimental work, led to a recognition of the problem of 'replicated readership': the extent to which claimed readers actually read the same issue in different issue publication periods (e.g. Tuesday's *Times* looked at again on Wednesday). This phenomenon naturally applies more to longer-life publications, especially monthly magazines which are kept in the home perhaps for several months, and tends to inflate readership estimates, although it tends to be offset by what is called 'parallel readership' (when someone reads two or more issues of the publication for the first time within the same publication period.)

The replication problem was not merely theoretical but commercially important, if you were competing for revenue against monthly magazines whose readerships were being overestimated systematically. When Harry Henry joined the Thomson Organisation and found himself faced with exactly this problem, he conceived the idea of a competition in which the best research brains would be invited to think about the problem and propose solutions. This was the start, in 1962, of the Thomson Gold Medal, which set replication as the subject and was won by Tom Corlett, Brian Pretty and James Rothman in a classic exposition. The Thomson Medals (a gold and a smaller silver cash prize each year) were to continue for eight years and produced several seminal papers on practical media research problems.

Another landmark for the NRS was the adoption of the Extended Media List (EML) system, after long piloting, in 1984. This was in response to the pressure of a very large increase in the number of titles wanting and deserving a place on the survey. Such an increase could not be coped with if every publication's masthead continued to be looked at separately. Under EML, a grouping system was devised in which respondents could eliminate at one go whole groups of similar titles which they knew they never read; they could then concentrate only on those titles which were relevant to them. EML enabled the coverage of the NRS to be more than doubled, greatly increasing its commercial value.

A third, recent, landmark has been the adoption, since 1992, of computer-assisted interviewing, using laptop computers. This has increased the complexity of the questions which can be covered and improved the speed and accuracy of the results.

Special Readerships

The NRS is not the only syndicated readership research survey. It covers titles read by the general public, but for that very reason cannot generate a sample suitable for the needs of those publishers who target the business community. The British Business Survey was set up to fill this gap, managed by the BMRC (British Media Research Committee), a body composed of representatives of the six publishing houses who provide the funding, plus the contractor, RSL. The first survey was done in 1973, and to date (1995) there have been twelve. The population sampled is businessmen in Great Britain, defined as: 'a man or woman of middle or higher management status whose occupation implies the exercise of significant business responsibilities.'

The same methods of measuring readership are used as in the NRS. There are other business readership surveys: the Banner survey specialising in the computer field, and 'City' surveys by MORI and the *Financial Times*.

Another development was the need to measure international titles read by globe-trotting executives. The Pan European Survey (PES) has been carried out every three years since 1978; to date there have been six. Again it is sponsored by the relevant publishers, and covers 'high status' individuals defined in terms of income, qualifications, occupation and propensity to travel, across (in the 1992 survey) sixteen European countries. A rival survey, the EBRS (European Business Readership Survey), has been produced every two to three years since 1973; it has a wide sponsorship, and is published by the *Financial Times*. It covers seventeen European countries (in 1993). Its difference from the PES is that it samples from large establishments rather than the general population, so that its definition of a 'senior businessman' is more tightly focused than the PES; business and professional people who do not work in large companies will appear in the PES sample but not in the EBRS. Other special interest cross-Europe surveys include the International Air Travel Survey (IATS), and surveys of Chief Executives and Financial Managers.

The NRS covers essentially national publications. Until 1989, *regional* dailies and weeklies lacked any standard method for quantifying their audiences. Some of the larger regional dailies and Sundays are covered on the NRS, but there are substantial gaps. Yet regional papers account for a very large share of press advertising revenue. Similar research to the NRS applied on a local scale would have been prohibitively expensive, far more than the publishers could have afforded, so a system was devised which combined research with modelling. Those local papers which had done research to required standards were brought in to the system: for the remainder, mathematical models were built based on circulation figures and local demographics, and tested against the available research. A new JIC was formed: JICREG, which like JICNARS included representatives of all sides of the business. The JICREG innovation has enabled a media currency to be established for *all* publications used by advertisers.

While the NRS was being refined in Britain, national readership currencies were in place, or being developed, in many other countries in the world. Many of them were similar in concept to the NRS and were facing similar difficulties. In 1980 the two NRS contractor companies, RSL and BMRB, joined forces to promote a new initiative: an *international* Readership Research Symposium, to which those involved in readership research across the world would be invited to come and compare notes. It was an immediate success. The first Symposium was held in New Orleans in February 1981. Although 120 places were planned for, 150 delegates attended from 21 countries, many on the waiting list and latecoming gatecrashers turned away at the door. New Orleans started what was to become a biennial event, held alternately in an American and a European city (to spread the pain of long-distance travel); the most recent (seventh) Symposium took place in Berlin in 1995.

One of the highlights of New Orleans was the exposure to the outside world of the on-going quarrel in the USA between two different methods of measuring readership: the 'through-the-book' method used by the Simmons Research Corporation and the recent reading method espoused by Mediamark (a service started a few years before by the British researcher Timothy Joyce and based on the British TGI). The recent reading system produced higher estimates, especially for monthlies, exactly as had been found in 1947 when the Hulton and IIPA surveys were compared with Attwood's. In America, the two sides continued to be supported by interested publishers, with no convergence towards a 'JIC' structure of agreement, and in spite of various attempts to provide validation. It is only very recently that 'through the book' has finally been abandoned in the USA. To many observers, the situation has revealed a deep difference of approach between British and American researchers: Americans tending to believe that there exists a 'true' or 'gold standard' measure of readership and that it should be possible to find a way to replicate it, Britons being more sceptical about the inherent uncertainty of the 'reading memory' and placing a higher value on achieving agreement.

In the event, the 'recent reading' method has plainly won throughout the world, since the Americans have finally dropped 'through-the-book' and the other contender (the more recently invented 'first read yesterday' or FRY method) has also been dropped by the Dutch, who were its main protagonists.

Television Audience Measurement

Commercial television started in Britain, with its single channel, in 1955, depending from the first on advertising revenue. With the example of the newly-formed NRS before them, the television companies did not delay to set up a research system. The Joint Industry Committee for Television Audience Research (JICTAR, the first of the JICs) was formed in 1957, representing ISBA, the IPA and the ITCA (the Independent Television Companies' Association).

From the start, the buyers and sellers of TV time required a level of detail which presented special difficulties for research. It could not be simply a matter of establishing how many people viewed a channel, or even a particular programme, on any particular day. Media planners had to know what audience each individual spot is likely to attract, and what duplication there would be between any combination of different spots. Jane Perry, International Media Research Director of Young and Rubicam, explains the problem as follows:

> TV audience measurement is more complex and detailed than any other kind of media research. There are several reasons for this. The first is that the way TV is bought and sold is more varied than for any other media. There is no single way of constructing a TV rate-card, and there is an amazing diversity world-wide in the ways in which it is done. This leads to very different requirements from TV research. Secondly, TV sales are very concentrated compared to other media. The bulk of commercial TV audiences is usually found on only one or two channels, and

where audiences are more fragmented, they are usually sold through a small number of sales houses. As TV accounts for the largest share of total display advertising expenditure, this means that the amount of money spent per purchase is comparatively large. TV audience measurement therefore has to be very accurate, because there is more money at risk for every degree of error.

Finally, the TV market is in the fortunate position of being able to afford more expensive research than other media, because it has the highest revenue from advertising. This allows it to pay for the complexity it needs...

TV channels are restricted in how much advertising they can carry, when it appears, and what can be shown. In addition, there are natural limits to the amount of time people are able to spend watching TV... Both these limitations are unique to TV. Because the supply of commercial TV audiences is limited, they have to be rationed in some way. There is no standard formula for doing this. As a result, TV sales structures vary more than for any other media. This affects their need for research data, and consequently the way in which TV is measured.

> *Jane Perry: 'Television – how to measure audiences',*
> *in The MRG Guide to Media Research, 1995*

It was commonly expected that Nielsen, which had already had long experience of TV audience measurement in the USA (since the late 1940s), would win the first JICTAR tender in 1957. It was recognised that the best way of obtaining the detailed measurement required was by meter, an electronic device attached to the television set which automatically recorded when it was switched on, and what channel it was switched to. This was of course expensive, but obviated the problems of relying on human memory, whether in a day-after recall survey or a panel in which people recorded their detailed viewing day by day. Nielsen were perceived as the leaders in meter technology. But the contract went to a British system, TAM (Television Audience Measurement), run by Attwood Statistics Ltd with Nielsen (eventually) as a junior partner.

TAM came into being through the enterprise of Bedford Attwood, widely recognised as a genius as well as one of the most maddening characters in post-war British research. "Working for him", wrote Norman Webb, "was like being a member of a very skilled crew of a pirate ship run by somebody like Captain Ahab." Attwoods had been running continuous consumer panels since 1947; indeed, they virtually were the panel market. They only needed the meter, and this Bedford Attwood invented.

Norman Webb, who joined TAM at the start of its operation, wrote the following in an appreciation of Bedford Attwood following his death in 1988:

> With the advent of ITV, Bedford was invited to put up some competition to Nielsen, whose TV meters had swept the board in the States. He had a keen interest in clocks, and some superb specimens of 18th century timepieces. He produced the Tammeter, a remarkable piece of clockwork that was, properly serviced, to provide the industry with accurate minute by minute audience data for about 15 years. A generation later we have quartz watches and pocket calculators that were not available to him then, but he achieved a remarkable feat with a 200 year old technology, though he switched to electronics and computers when the time came. (Not only that, but he operated the first people meter, the Tammatic, and a London panel giving instant meter ratings, the Instammatic, and both thirty years ago!)
>
> Awarded the first contract, he was in competition with Nielsen over here... We were carrying out operations in completely uncharted territories – monitoring the growth of two channel sets, controlling the panels, introducing the concept of boundary surveys, and possibly more important than anything else, being able to report on the actual performance of commercial TV advertising schedules...
>
> By the mid 60s, with consumer panels all over Europe and TV meter operations in Britain, West Germany and Ireland, British market research was leading Europe, largely due to Attwood. But the continental Europeans were quick to learn, and as the years went by local competition grew

increasingly more powerful and this particular British empire eventually disappeared, though its effects can still be seen, for instance in our strong participation in ESOMAR.

Norman Webb, MRS Newsletter, September 1988

Analysing the data which poured from the meters was a formidable task. Nora Loader, who joined TAM in 1956, recalled:

In those days there was only one ITV station broadcasting in the London area, and our total panel was 150 households. A good thing really, because we had very few aids to our work. Not only were there no computers or calculators, there were hardly any comptometers or adding machines – they only appeared on the scene years later. Mostly we relied on mental arithmetic...

Almost the first type of special analysis I produced were coverage and frequency schedules, which in their final form looked reasonably similar to those produced today. The difference was that I had to do everything by hand and eye, seeing who had been watching at a particular time, and whether they were watching again the second time the spot appeared, and determining how many people who saw the second spot had not seen the first...

Nora Loader, interviewed in MRS Newsletter, August 1986

In 1961 the trinity of Audley, Gapper and Brown, plus Martin Maddan, split from Attwood to form AGB. But TAM continued to run the television audience service until 1968, when the JICTAR contract moved (finally) to AGB. As Norman Webb explains:

Attwoods... lacked the political and public relations acumen which was to prove its downfall when it unnecessarily lost forever the industry TV meter contract to AGB in 1967. There was no stopping AGB now, and in the fullness of time the failing Attwood consumer panel was eventually taken over by them in 1979 and absorbed. There is something inevitable and appropriate about this, since the founders of AGB learnt their trade with Attwood, profited from the pioneering activities of Attwood, and have essentially become the company that Attwoods might otherwise have been.

The JICTAR contract with AGB lasted into the 80s, based on household set-meters placed with a panel. This panel, being relatively small (since meters are expensive) had to be carefully selected; it was sampled from an establishment survey, regularly updated, which established the extent and quality of reception of each ITV company, both in its exclusive area and where it overlapped with other stations. Results were reported in periodic book form. From the metered records it was established how many households were tuned to the commercial channel minute by minute and therefore had an 'opportunity to see' the commercial break; which commercials were shown in that break were also reported. In addition, diaries were kept in the panel households recording when each individual was watching, and from these a crude estimate of the exposure probabilities of different types of people (housewives etc.) to each spot could be provided.

Are you quite sure you switched off the Research company's TV Household Usage Monitoring Eye?

The Change to BARB: Involving the BBC

The next major change occurred in 1980, when JICTAR was replaced by a new body, BARB (the Broadcasting Audience Research Board). The first benefit of this was that it integrated the two sides of television, the commercial sector and the BBC, into a single co-operative endeavour. Up to that point, the BBC had continued to carry its own daily surveys of listening and viewing behaviour, whilst JICTAR was entirely concerned with ITV. It plainly made sense to combine the two so as to afford a better instrument.

Improvement was needed, because the viewing environment was becoming more complex. Channel 4 had appeared, and TV-AM would soon arrive; together with generally longer broadcasting hours, this was to double the number of hours available for commercial broadcasting between 1981 and 1990 (Stephan Buck). There was increasing multi-set usage within homes. VCRs were beginning to appear, with their ability to postpone the viewing of live programmes or replace them altogether, and with every sign of growing fast. And the combined meter/diary technique was becoming less satisfactory for measuring the viewing of individuals, with increasing fragmentation of viewing within multi-set households, and persistent niggling questions like what to do about guests. The stage was set for the introduction of the peoplemeter, introduced with the new BARB contract for AGB in 1984.

This BARB peoplemeter was the first to be introduced, although other countries (Germany and Ireland) had been experimenting with them before that date. Peoplemeters enable individual viewing to be recorded by using a remote control handset, with push buttons allotted to each individual (plus a spare for guests). Each TV set in the house has its own monitor, which records the channel as before and also which push buttons have been pressed by individuals; the information is automatically fed down the telephone line to the central computer during off-peak hours. Thus, minute by minute (or even second by second) records can be made of each individual's viewing, enabling far more detailed analysis than was possible from the old quarter-hour diary.

After the pioneer BARB introduction in 1984, peoplemeters spread quickly through the world. According to Toby Syfret, a consultant who advises the European Association of Advertising Agencies on broadcasting research matters, each year since then has seen a number of new countries adopting peoplemeters: by the end of 1995 there were 48.

Your mother has clocked up £25 in guest viewing time on the Peoplemeter

In 1991 a revised BARB contract came into operation, in an attempt to deal with the increasing complexity of the medium. The two parts of the survey were split, for the first time, between two separate contractors. AGB would continue to operate the television panel and produce the data, using an improved peoplemeter designed to identify VCR time-shift playback as well as on-air viewing, with push buttons for household members and guests. Data would be available, if required, in much greater detail and downloaded electronically, so that users could develop their own analysis programmes. The recruitment and maintenance of the panel, and the establishment surveys on which it is based, were allotted to a new company, RSMB, jointly owned by Research Services and Millward Brown. To represent viewing patterns which had become more complex over the years, the sample was increased from 3,500 homes to 4,700 homes, sampled differentially within the various TV reception and overlap areas (the number allows for 6% non-response, so that the actual panel delivering data is 4,435 homes, yielding some 12,000 individuals). Viewing is reported for all household members and guests aged 4 and over. The establishment survey, from which the panel homes are selected, was more than doubled in size, to over 40,000 households, and carried out continuously instead of once a year.

BARB also runs an Audience Reaction Service to programmes, based on a weekly diary panel, which is a continuation of the service previously provided by and for the BBC. This service is confidential to the television companies, which want the results only for internal planning and prefer them not to affect the rate cards; much as advertisers and agencies would like to see these data, it is not permitted to them.

What we have written above is the situation at the end of 1995. It will be surprising if there have not been changes, even by the time this book is published. Television is facing, as everyone knows, more and more complexity and fragmentation. There will be a new Channel 5, and increasing satellite and cable channels, and the new world being opened up by digitisation and the consequent merging with telephones and computers. There are already calls being made for a simpler, less detailed service. Bob Hulks (formerly Chief Executive of BARB) and Ken Baker, writing in *Admap* (July/August 1995) suggest that the likely arrival of electronic trading between buyers and sellers in the airtime market "may well condition the level and nature of the new currency, with perhaps less emphasis on detail and more on speed of delivery".

The Target Group Index (TGI)

From the days of the Hulton readership surveys there was an interest in being able to link readership with product use, in order to make possible more precise targeting of schedules. Broad classifications of readers or viewers by age, class, sex or region were helpful up to a point, but, if advertisers were to improve the effectiveness of their advertising, they ideally wanted to be able to link media use with consumers' habits: especially their use of different products and brands.

Both Hulton and the early NRS included some product purchase data, as well as general TV viewing and radio listening habits. But the scope of these surveys to cover such detail was severely limited. For the most part, media planners were driven to identify targets by computer matching with data obtained from other surveys. Although some sophisticated ways of doing this were developed, the ideal was 'single-source' data in which product purchasing on a wide scale and readership data (and perhaps some viewing data) could be obtained from the same persons. BMRB was to take up the challenge, initially with an experimental service in 1966 which proved that the system could work. But, according to John Downham:

> The real break-through came with a visit to the USA in November 1967 by Jack Fothergill and Timothy Joyce. During the course of this visit they were impressed by the success of the Simmons and BRI services – but also convinced that the data collection and reporting procedures used by these organisations could be greatly improved on. Extensive pilot work proved this to be the case and led to the launch of the Target Group Index in the UK a year later.
>
> *BMRB International, 1993*

To date, the TGI has reported twenty-seven annual surveys. Being privately owned by BMRB, it is not controlled by an industry committee like the various JICs, although there is a committee of subscribers. All the field and production costs are funded by the research company, and the reports and (increasingly) other means of access to the data are sold by them to agencies, media owners and advertisers.

It is a massive database, obtained from samples of 25,000 or thereabouts each year. It aims to cover 'all major products and brands and use of services': the current questionnaire carries questions on some 3,000 brands in more than 200 fast-moving consumer product fields, together with brand usage and consumer behaviour in areas such as finance, travel, cars, holidays, grocery shopping and other retail data. Informants are also asked about their readership of about 200 newspapers and magazines, providing readership estimates which are weighted to NRS levels (so that comparability for these titles is precise), plus frequency of TV viewing, radio listening, cinema going and exposure to posters. The data obtained are, of course, basic; so wide a coverage must sacrifice detail, and the TGI is not supposed to be a substitute for individual market surveys. The questionnaire is left with informants for self-completion, using a simple, standard format for each product (whether used, how often, which brands used most often and which others used). It is a tribute to the research company's efficiency that such a huge questionnaire, numbering some 90 pages, has yielded a net response of usable questionnaires which has remained at about 62-64% with little variation during the whole history of the TGI.

As with most innovative projects, it took time and trouble, and aggressive marketing, to get the TGI established. However, as Downham says, "the significance of the TGI for BMRB's history over the last 25 years cannot be over-emphasised". Its commercial success has grown, especially since it has become possible to access the data through PC systems as well as the 30 volumes of reports, and various special market services have been added (e.g. the AB TGI, the Youth TGI). Timothy Joyce, the original director in charge, took the system to the USA and ran the US TGI from 1972 to 1978, after which it was a strong influence on the successor company, Mediamark. Other attempts to launch a TGI in Europe were less successful, although it has recently been extended into Ireland.

Radio Listening Research

Commercial radio did not appear in Britain until 1973, with the launch of LBC. Before that, there was only Radio Luxembourg (which commissioned its own periodic research), and the various pirate radio stations of the 1960s. The BBC continued to run its own, daily, survey of radio listening with a system of aided recall (1,000 persons a day, every day since 1939).

As soon as the first commercial stations came on air, a JIC was formed: JICRAR (Joint Industry Committee for Radio Audience Research), representing the prospective radio stations as well as IPA and ISBA. At first, ad hoc surveys only were done, using a specification approved by JICRAR. By 1977 there were 19 commercial stations, and the first network survey was done. The JICRAR specification was based on a one-week self-completion diary. This system remained in use until 1992, when JICRAR was disbanded and replaced by a new body, RAJAR (Radio Joint Audience Research).

RAJAR is radio's counterpart to BARB; the vehicle which brought the BBC in from its isolation to form a joint venture with commercial broadcasting, to provide a single radio audience currency. RAJAR is jointly owned by the BBC and AIRC (the Association of Independent Radio Contractors). The listening data (by quarter-hour) are collected by means of a diary placed for a week in a sample of households and completed by (or for) all individuals aged 4 or over in those households, each day during the week (including listening in the car, etc.). The sampling is complicated, because every single station's area of coverage must be represented in it, as well as every overlap area between two commercial stations or between a commercial and a BBC station. There are now over 150 independent radio services in the country, apart from the BBC ones, so the scale of the problem will be apparent. As fragmentation increases, it is scheduled to get worse.

Other Media

Cinema is measured in two ways. The Advertising Admissions Monitor, commissioned by the Cinema Advertising Association, has obtained admissions data by telephone from cinema operators since 1984. Also, there is an annual audience survey called CAVIAR (Cinema and Video Industry Audience Research), which provides a unified body of data about the whole cinema and video audience, including children, and is funded by the CAA plus a consortium of interested parties (advertising agencies, distributors and retailers, etc.).

Posters have always been a problem for audience research. People do not 'watch' posters in the sense that they watch TV or are readers of a newspaper. Posters are simply part of the background. A person could be assumed to have an 'opportunity to see' a poster message whenever he or she happened to be within sight of a hoarding, but clearly it is no good expecting anybody to remember this. And merely being able to 'see' a poster is not enough, because the visibility of a site can be very much altered by various details about it, such as how it is angled (relative to where you are standing), how high up it is, how well lit, etc. (quite apart from how well the advertising on it makes its impact).

The first attempt to measure the poster audience were the studies undertaken for Mills & Rockley Ltd by Market Information Services (specifically, J.W. Hobson and Harry Henry). In the introduction to the first Mills & Rockley study, published in 1949, there appears the following statement:

> Gentlemen,
>
> In accordance with your instructions we have carried out, inside the area which you cover, a survey designed to measure the extent to which an average poster campaign is remembered by the population exposed to it. Apart from the pilot survey..., this is the first attempt to make a statistical assessment in this way of the size and nature of the poster audience to be published in this country, or, so far as we are aware, in the world. References to American studies appear on page 12.

The American studies referred to, including the classic 'Fort Wayne Survey' of 1946, were all based on measuring the effectiveness of *particular* posters. Mills & Rockley was the first attempt to establish *general rules* for assessing the number of people who will remember any poster campaign, irrespective of the actual advertising. The survey was based on showing respondents pictures of poster designs and asking whether they remembered seeing them on hoardings, and how long ago. The results could then be compared between campaigns of different densities and durations, and between different respondent classifications (sex, age, class, work habits, etc.); not poster size, since the assumption was made of a 'normal' 16-sheet campaign. An important feature was the introduction of some bogus campaigns, to provide an adjustment factor against overclaiming.

The next development in poster research avoided memory altogether. People cannot be expected to remember seeing poster sites very accurately, but they can remember journeys taken in the past few days. In 1952, Brian Copland developed the method and formula which was to do duty for the next 30 years. Two methods were used: either showing photographs of recognisable locations and recording whether the person had been there, or (better) tracing actual journeys on street maps. In this way, it was possible to establish the average number of people in an average week who passed any particular spot where a poster site might be, and how many times they passed it. From these two statistics, plus the population of the town, Copland was able to model the coverage and frequency that a poster campaign in that town would achieve.

The Copland model began to break down by around 1980, largely as a result of increased car usage and out-of-town shopping, etc.; the model was based on people living and moving about in 'towns', and could not cope with developing patterns of travel. It was also disliked because it treated all poster sites in an area as equal, whereas everybody knew that a billboard on a main highway, say, was likely to be worth much more to an advertiser than a 48-sheet hoarding in a back street. Furthermore, merely having an 'opportunity to see' a poster was not enough: posters vary greatly in the likelihood that they will be seen (for example, you are less likely to look at them if they are too high up, or badly lit, or you are coming from the wrong direction). Coping with all these variables seemed to many impossibly complex.

Some of these points might have been dealt with through refinements of the Copland approach, but media buyers had by that time lost confidence in it. A new initiative brought together representatives of the poster contractors, together with ISBA and the IPA, in yet another JIC (JICPAR: Joint Industry Committee for Poster Audience Research). This led to the launch, in 1985, of OSCAR (Outdoor Site Classification and Audience Research), funded by the Outdoor Advertising Association.

OSCAR set out to provide something which had never been attempted before: a complete classification of every poster site in Great Britain. NOP, the research organisation which had previously had the job of inspecting poster sites, were given this new task. NOP had to collect, for every site, a range of detail including what type of area it was in (shopping, residential etc.); what type of road (main, minor etc.); plus other details including traffic access and traffic flow. Traffic counts, and estimates of vehicle and pedestrian traffic past the site were made. Details were also recorded about the visibility of the site: its height, angle, lighting, whether it was obstructed, the competition from other panels, and so on. All these data were put onto a computerised database, and regularly updated.

The second part of OSCAR was allotted to AGB. This was to develop a model for 'opportunities to see' based on analysing the relationships between the number of people passing the sites on foot or in vehicles and the various characteristics of the sites. From this they developed coverage models (estimates of gross passages per week) which could be applied to any package of sites by inputting the site characteristics from the database. An adaptation of Copland's formula was later applied to produce net coverage and frequency estimates.

The trouble with a census like OSCAR is that it quickly becomes out of date, as the face of the country changes. A new, more detailed service, OSCAR II (or POSTAR, as it has been renamed) has been introduced in 1996. The new system derives OTS estimates partly from a large travel survey and partly by neural network modelling of vehicular and pedestrian traffic estimates, and applies corrections for visibility derived from another model based on laboratory experiments at Birkbeck College.

OSCAR is not the whole of the audience research done by the poster industry. There are special systems for estimating the audiences to posters in the London Underground, and on the sides of buses and taxis.

There have also been, over the years, a number of studies of particular advertisements to see how they communicate on posters, and whether different poster types or sizes have different effects. Some of these became famous because they used mock subjects which people could not have seen before, e.g. More O'Ferrall's 'Bertie the Basset Hound ' of 1967 and 'Sheila' of 1989. Such studies have proved that posters can and do communicate, over and above any 'false memory', if they have good material.

How the Media Are Used

In this chapter we have concentrated on audience research, because its importance as the basic currency for buying and selling media has meant that it attracts the lion's share of funding, anxiety and drive for improvement. As new media come on the scene with the much-discussed 'superhighway' and the Internet, etc., there can be no doubt that pressures will increase and that change, and the development of new measuring instruments, will become faster.

However, audience research is not the only type of media research which is needed. On top of the basic counting of the audience, considerable judgement is required for the media planner to construct the appropriate schedule for the product. Some 'messages' are right for television; others would be better in the press; others again would benefit from a mixture of media, and so on. This brings in again, as with everything else in advertising, the question of consumer response. Parallel with the growing realisation that people 'use' advertising, rather than being manipulated by it, it came to be realised that they also 'use' the different media in various ways – for news, for instruction, for amusement, when travelling, when relaxed at home, etc. – and that the particular media which they select to match these different moods may well affect their response to the messages contained.

It is possible to hypothesise situations in which the context of media consumption might influence advertising communication. For example:

i)   How do housewives react to advertisements on television for gravy mixes, dog food, etc., which they might see immediately after eating their main meal?

ii) How do housewives react to advertisements for lavatory cleaners, etc., that they might see in the middle of the 'love story' they are reading in their favourite weekly magazine?

iii) How do people react to advertisements for whisky or brandy which they might see in their Sunday colour supplement whilst they lie in bed on a Sunday morning recovering from Saturday night?

Douglas Richardson: 'Measuring the Role of Media in People's Lives', Thomson Gold Medal winning paper, 1971

If these consumer responses, and their possible effects on advertising, are not studied properly by research, they tend to be decided on the basis of received wisdom, and several 'media myths' of this sort have been noted at different times: for example, that advertising is better concentrated into one medium, television gets more attention, complicated stories can only be told in print, posters are a reminder medium, or the *Times* (or *Telegraph/Independent/Daily Mail* etc.) 'has authority'.

Information is therefore sought, and provided ad hoc by various means, about the *quality* of exposure obtained from different media. This leads into areas such as how media are used within people's lives, their response to editorial and programming, what sort of advertising works best in each medium, and how different media may work effectively in combination (for instance, whether a combination of television and press may work better in some cases than television alone). Such studies have been done since the 1960s. Most of them have been (and continue to be) sponsored by specific media owners seeking to add value to their product; but there have been attempts by various consortia to acquire more general learning, such as the series of Television Attention Studies during the 1960s or, more recently, the Media Multiplier group of studies, which looked at how mixing press and television might enhance the value of a campaign. This last is an example of an initiative which originated in Britain before being taken up in a number of other countries. There have also been agency initiatives such as the JWT 'Use of Media' study in the 1970s, which took respondents through a typical day recording every time they used a medium, and the support (again by JWT) of an academic team at Leeds University who were, at the same time, engaged in an SSRC-sponsored research project studying the 'uses and gratifications' which people derive from media.

And another question which we have not touched on, but which is important to media planners, is how to assess the optimum frequency with which to advertise, because either not enough or too much wastes the advertiser's money. This is an extremely difficult question to generalise about, because one has to distinguish so many factors (what sort of response is relevant, the timing and spacing of the 'exposures', whether they are on their own or competing with other advertisements, and so on). It is only recently that we have begun to have a real clue about the general pattern of 'response' to television for fast-moving consumer goods, and that the way press attracts response is different. British (at least, British-born) researchers have been among the most proactive in this field, sometimes working with American single-source panel data; notably, Simon Broadbent's many papers on response functions, John Philip Jones's analysis of the Nielsen Household Panel, and Millward Brown's investigations of press build-up and advertising response.

★ ★ ★

8

The Future

The growth of British market research during the past fifty years has been remarkable; a tribute to the skills and inventiveness of the people who have worked in it. Because its main purpose is to describe, understand and so predict people's attitudes and behaviour, it has been exceptionally responsive to the many economic, social and political changes which have occurred since the late 1940s. Most commentators, especially in the marketing press, see the rate of change accelerating. Everybody therefore expects that market research will have to respond to these changes very rapidly; but of course there is less agreement about where the changes will lead.

Three kinds of change seem especially likely: first, changes in the consumer environment and the popular response to research; secondly, changes in the commercial demands that are made of research; and thirdly, changes in the technology which researchers can use. Some of these changes will be positive for research, whilst others will make it harder. The challenge for the Market Research Society and its members will be to accommodate these changes without abandoning the essential principles – objectivity, accuracy and integrity towards both clients and informants – which make research especially valuable to its users. There is always a danger that new demands and new technology may put a strain on maintaining these principles. Research is not peculiar in this; other professions, such as accountancy, the law and medicine, face similar strains, sometimes leading to serious questions of professional ethics. But perhaps research is in a weaker position through having a smaller backlog of precedent. People may still (after only fifty years) not understand well enough what would be lost, in these days of the information revolution, if there were no longer any ways of telling the difference between good and bad data, or sound and unsound conclusions.

The Consumer Environment

More discriminating consumers

In the early days of research, consumers still had limited choices, and were willing to buy what they were told was a good product. The item's presence in the local shop and the fact of its being regularly advertised would be taken as evidence of a 'good product', if backed up by one's own and others' experience. The aim of marketing and advertising was seen as to convert users of other brands to yours and lock them in.

With greater disposable incomes and more choice, consumers became more discriminating. Research such as the consumer panel analyses of the 1960s showed that for the most part people do not get 'converted' from one thing to another, but like variety: increasingly, this has come to be seen as a matter of *mood*. It is not that different types of people buy different brands, so much as the same people buying different brands at different times because they feel like it. Advertising came to be seen as aiming to induce a particular *response* in the consumer's mind, appealing to the appropriate mood. This moved the emphasis from measuring standard actions and responses to understanding with greater subtlety what feelings consumers have and where the item will fit into these.

Research responded to this increasing concern to understand consumers and their response to brands by both widening and deepening its approach. It is no longer enough to rely on simple measurements of sales, consumption, attitudes, brand images and the like; markets must be looked at in a holistic way, in which all of these may have their place. Qualitative studies are no longer mere preparations for the 'main' measurement, but now take their place alongside quantitative measures to deal with those aspects of the total problem for which they are particularly appropriate. Client marketing managements either buy these complementary strands from specialist suppliers, or work with a single supplier who can cover them all.

An excellent example of this holistic process in action is the case history which won the AMSO Research Effectiveness Awards for 1995, the relaunch of Harveys Bristol Cream sherry. It is quoted here to illustrate the sort of contribution market research can make when it is integrated into a company's decision processes.

The research agency involved was The Research Business, which has won a deserved reputation (and considerable growth) over the past decade from its innovative use of qualitative methods and their integration with other research. Harveys Bristol Cream had been the clear brand leader in the very substantial sherry market (in 1980, the second largest alcoholic drinks category after wine), but the problem identified by the company was that both category and brand had started to suffer, from changing perceptions among younger drinkers and competitive challenges introduced to meet them. Research was showing that Bristol Cream was becoming confined, compared with own label, to Christmas and formal occasions, and was widely perceived as inhibited, out-dated, Establishment, 'safe', ritualistic and home-based. The task was to relaunch the brand and return it to profitable volume growth.

The first requirement was to understand what constituted the brand for consumers: was it the product itself, or how far were other things involved, such as associations with types of user or occasion, the advertising, etc.? Previous research was combed through, and a specialist company (Brandformers) commissioned to explore what was suggested by the taste, aroma and presentation of Bristol Cream. It appeared that the taste and smell, and the packaging, all had certain limiting associations. It was decided that the brand needed a complete repositioning, away from the old 'sherry' associations, involving all the elements which were making up the brand.

The next stage was qualitative research by The Research Business, which involved asking a sample of sherry drinkers to try the product presented as a 'new' drink in an unbranded, non-sherry shaped bottle; informants had to keep a record of all their drinking over ten days, including occasions and the mood they were in, before being interviewed in detail. The result showed that Bristol Cream "had the capability to move out of its traditional 'box' and satisfy a range of needs, offering different rewards in different circumstances to a wide range of people". This enabled the research agency to develop a blueprint for 'reframing' the brand into a new, more widely appealing image, with more up-to-date emotional values and away from the inhibiting associations of 'sherry'. This new image could be communicated to the lighter drinkers, without alienating the core already committed to Harveys.

The communication blueprint could then be translated into a total brief for the creation of new advertising (Saatchi) and a new pack design. These were developed and tested, first in another wave of qualitative research, and then validated in a comprehensive quantified test involving four alternative pack designs. One pack, based on a new Bristol blue glass bottle, clearly came out top and was incorporated in the new campaign. The success of the re-launch was proved by subsequent waves of brand tracking research (which could be compared with two years of historical tracking data); it has "all the signs of being one of the most notable re-launches of the past few years".

The way research is used, as demonstrated by this example of Harveys Bristol Cream, is a far cry from the standard pre-testing, packaging or U & A studies which would have been the norm in the 1950s and 1960s. It is comprehensive, integrated research for a marketing problem seen as a whole, involving a full range of (qualitative and quantitative) research tools, and requiring commitment (and investment) by the client. Something like this will only be done for brands whose contribution is understood and valued. It is significant that (according to the submitted paper): "The project had the total commitment of the Board". But this kind of understanding of what a brand means will occur more often in the future, and is a sign that research, as well as marketing, has matured. In the future, it may be expected that more and more marketing companies will appreciate the need for 'holistic' research of this kind; new ways will have to be found for segmenting moods and circumstances, etc., to replace or enrich the old segmentations of people into demographic, psychological or brand-using 'types'; when there are more and more extravagant promises of 'one-to-one marketing', research will need to come to terms with this increasing flexibility.

Greater public scepticism

The increasing individuation and sophistication among consumers has been accompanied by another social trend which is worrying for research. Respondents are becoming steadily harder to interview.

Survey response rates have become an issue on which "we are letting ourselves down and something needs to be done" (Bill Blyth, paper at the 1995 AMSO Conference). Even in flagship surveys such as the National Readership Survey, response rates are now just over 60% after eight or more calls, whereas in 1954, when the survey started, they used to reach 85% after six calls, and 50% of successful interviews were obtained with only one call (Dawn Mitchell). There are several reasons for this, resulting from lifestyle as well as attitude changes. Underlying all this, there is thought to be less tolerance and good will towards research:

> The perceived value of research is becoming less. People no longer believe that giving their opinions helps manufacturers to make better goods; they probably believe instead that it leads to cheaper goods and more profit. There is less perceived social value from research; it has become a nasty word, a surrogate for governments trying to meet people's aspirations.
>
> *Bill Blyth, paper at the 1995 AMSO Conference*

Blyth's comments here may seem somewhat extreme (after all, the majority are still co-operating with surveys even on the evidence quoted above); but one does not have to go as far as that to be concerned.

The Research Development Foundation is currently sponsoring a large study of public attitudes to co-operation with market research surveys and the factors leading to non-response, with funding from the main trade associations, AMSO and the ABMRC. This indicates how seriously the industry is taking this problem and the need to repair the damage.

However, it is clear that the difficulty will not be quickly solved, if a solution is possible, and this will lead clients to look seriously at other alternatives. Surveys will continue to be important for many purposes, but will be less central to market research than they were when the industry began (and was virtually defined in terms of survey-based information). It is expected that there will be more use made of previously recruited panels and databases, lists of persons who have already given their permission to be approached for further interview; there will be a growth in the use of 'professional respondents'. Audience Selection's announcement of AS 100,000, billed as 'a large consumer database for cost-effective research among specific demographic groups', recruited by telephone to be a sample base for subsequent surveys, is a recent straw in the wind.

There is perhaps less scepticism about research in the public sector, perhaps because the topics seem more important. Things like housing, employment, health or town planning are serious concerns, about which people like to be consulted, especially if they feel they have some grievance or worry. Interviewers have always liked to be able to say they are working on a 'government' survey, because they feel it makes it easier to obtain co-operation from respondents.

Public sector research, especially for Central Government, has grown steadily in the past few years, as we saw in Chapter 3, with the appetite for departmental 'flagship surveys'. There is no reason not to expect this to continue, indeed, perhaps increase, with pressure from the European Community. A key indicator such as the Retail Price Index, based on a monthly survey of a wide range of prices, has now, wisely, been put in the hands of the professionals, instead of being conducted by semi-trained employment office staff in their spare time; Research International has held the contract for a few years now. In general, governments and government agencies will continue, perhaps increasingly, to be influenced by what they think the public wants or at least what the public is prepared to accept; the penalties of misinterpreting the views of the public will be greater and imposed more quickly. Most research for government is not publicised, and contractors, led by OPCS and SCPR, continue to take great care to uphold standards and to ensure that the surveys they conduct are publicly acceptable.

However, there may be rather more concern about research which is publicly quoted in the media, and called in evidence to support or refute a point of view. We are not thinking so much here of political opinion polls. The fact that these are now known to be fallible, as in the 1992 election, has not in the least damped the intense interest which they arouse both from the media who publish them and the politicians and public who pretend to wrinkle their noses at them. In any case the research community goes to great lengths, as they did in 1992, to investigate the errors and improve procedures.

The greater danger lies in the publication of research designed, or manipulated, to support argument, in these lobbying and litigious times. Pressure groups have long been in the habit of using fabricated 'media events' for their publicity. When research began to be publicly respectable as evidence, they began to add 'research events' to their armoury.

Such uses of opinion research have two things in common. The first is that they usually greatly over-simplify what are, properly considered, fairly complex issues; in this way they serve the demand of the media for the simple and dramatic. Secondly, they tend to rely on numbers (which way does the biggest slice of opinion go) at the expense of any depth of understanding. There is little room in such 'research events' for qualitative methods or open-ended questions. The current discussion about referenda (in relation to the European single currency, for example) illustrates this problem: it is difficult to design questions for a referendum on such a complex subject without causing it to deteriorate into a 'research event'. These published 'research events' do not represent the thought and care which go into genuine opinion research of the kind for which clients pay good money.

For example, Teletext runs a regular 'survey' of its viewers on various topical matters. A simple question appears on the TV screen; you call one number for 'yes' and another for 'no', and the following day the results are given. Some examples of questions in early 1996 were:

- *Tony Blair has promised to rid the House of Lords of hereditary peers if Labour wins power. Is he right?* (81% said yes.)

- *The TUC has launched a new campaign to get better legal rights for Britain's six million part-time workers. Do you think part-timers are unfairly treated?* (92% said yes.)

- *Should a tiny, rare snail halt the controversial Newbury bypass?* (80% said yes.)

We also learnt from Teletext that 70% thought that the National Lottery was making the poor poorer, 93% that cabinet ministers should resign after the Scott (arms to Iraq) report, and 2% that MPs deserved a pay rise.

It might be argued that this is merely a bit of harmless fun, with no pretensions to asking balanced questions of a representative sample. But it is easy to imagine how pressure groups could use such 'findings', and it is a fact that the Teletext page is headed 'Opinion Poll'. It would thus appear to most viewers to have the same sort of standing as the opinion polls reported in the papers at the same time, which told them that 60% of Germans were against monetary union, 70% of people in Northern Ireland supported the idea of an elected assembly, and 54% in the UK wanted to return to a fully selective education system.

The way to deal with the problem is to strive to improve the conduct of opinion research, and make clear what standards are being applied (at least, whenever research results are to be quoted). It has been a struggle to get survey research evidence accepted in courts of law during the last three decades; but the difficulties encountered by researchers in this alien field have at least put a spotlight on the importance of extreme rigour in the conduct of any research intended for legal consumption. The problem is to do justice, and be seen to do it, to the complexity of people's opinions on even the most apparently simple issues: the sets of ideas and feelings they have, not necessarily compatible; the potential differences between their public and private opinions.

Improving the standards of public opinion research along these lines takes constant effort. It is not primarily a matter of techniques, important though these are. It is more a matter of facing up to the need for adequate content. Guidelines suggested in 1979 for well-conducted opinion research, for example, included:

- establishing how interested people are in a topic and/or how much they know about it, before asking for their views on it;

- recognising that for most topics a variety of questions and techniques will be needed to give a full picture of opinions (because people rarely carry around pre-packaged views, and do not even know what they think until they have talked about it);

- using personal and concrete questions as well as general, abstract ones, since they may well give more accurate answers. A good example is the comparison between three questions about the effect of advertising:

		Agree	Disagree
EEC survey	*'Advertising often misleads consumers'*	78%	16%
AA survey	*'The ads you see are often misleading'*	67%	28%
AA survey	*'I am frequently misled by the ads I see'*	28%	68%

Source: *Tom Corlett – 'Advertising and the European Consumer: a review of an EEC survey', in Public Attitudes to Advertising, 1977*

- take account of people's view on what others think, which may form an important part of their own opinions;
- relate what people think wherever possible to what they do, since their behaviour may be a better guide to their real opinion than what they say in public.

Keeping up these standards is clearly a constant battle against countervailing pressures: cost constraints, lack of time to think a problem through properly, the 'soundbite' culture with which we are familiar. Nevertheless, the best quality research projects (certainly those conducted by OPCS, SCPR, the industry media surveys and many others) undoubtedly do follow these guidelines and take trouble to do so. The problem is, these efforts seldom see the light of day. The challenge confronting market researchers, and especially the Market Research Society, is to promote these vital principles successfully to business people, the public sector, MPs, journalists and the general public, and make sure they are understood. The more sceptical people become about research, the greater the challenge to do something about it.

Asking the right questions

However sophisticated respondents become, one thing will *not* change: the vital importance of good questionnaire design. Indeed, its importance can only intensify. The use of computers to administer questionnaires extends the range of what an interviewer can do, but by itself has no effect on the quality. It is even more possible, if anything, to ask silly questions and get silly answers, when the computer can multiply them. Only one thing can prevent it: the skill of the experienced research designer, knowing precisely what information his client needs, and crafting simple, straightforward, unambiguous questions which both interviewers and respondents understand and which do not irritate or bore them.

The art of question wording has always been at the core of the research profession. It has been developed surprisingly little on paper, and it is arguable that researchers have not given the attention to it which it deserves, compared to other important areas such as the statistical foundations of sampling and experimental design. There has been one classic instructional book on the subject – Stanley Payne's 'The Art of Asking Questions' – published in 1952 and long out of print. Apart from this, and Belson's pioneering 'Studies in Readership', there has been little academic treatment. Market researchers rely on custom and practice, passed down to new recruits in the Winter Schools and by the senior executives (and, not least, the field managers and supervisors) working on their projects.

There is an obvious reason for this – the fact that question design is an art, and highly variable with the subject matter. Statistics and sampling are scientific enough to be capable of description in text-books, since there are a relatively small number of common rules. Question design is much more difficult. The reluctance to address it stems not from inexperience but from the realisation of the experts just how difficult and varied it can be. As some have pointed out (notably Wendy Gordon of The Research Business) there is a large intuitive component: it is not possible to get people to

answer the question *we* want unless we have an understanding of its relevance to *them*, its emotional correlates, how *they* 'see' and feel things. Phrasing our questions right is therefore much more than simple logic; it also requires a high degree of empathy with respondents, and common sense to keep us within the limits of what an interviewer can be expected to do.

However, the subject is so important for the future of research that it would pay to have the principles of question design re-stated for the modern profession, if only to up-date Stanley Payne. The more 'research events' are based on loose thinking and special pleading, the more vital will be the precision and integrity that researchers themselves are able to show.

The Commercial Environment

The change from marketing 'functional' brands to company and service brands

This change is acknowledged by every commentator, and confirmed by a glance at the list of papers offered at any marketing conference. It has a number of aspects. One is that the idea of branded marketing, pioneered by the classic brands in packaged groceries, has been taken up by numerous other classes of business. Philip Barnard, then Chairman and CEO of the Research International Group, has written:

> For many years fmcg companies were the main users of market research. Increasingly, they have been joined by consumer service businesses, media owners, regulated industries / public sector organisations, business-to-business suppliers and others, in their commitment to market research. Of my own company's several hundred clients, 30 account for 50 per cent of our world-wide revenues – and only 12 of these are consumer packaged goods businesses.
>
> *'New Directions in World Research', Admap, October 1992*

Some of these new categories of company are self-conscious about the need for branding and the difficulties of achieving it; it coincides with the growing realisation of the importance of the customer. It has been particularly noticeable, perhaps, in the financial sector. The 'culture of authority' perhaps lasted longer with banks, building societies and the like than in most other places, and its rejection by customers voting with their feet has seemed sharper. New approaches to selling services, such as the telephone-based First Direct and Direct Line, have offered cheaper, easier and more friendly consumer benefits, and succeeded; this has convinced the traditional suppliers that they had better find some way of differentiating their product, before the erosion of customers gathers pace.

> Consumers are sufficiently disenchanted with service and price to alter their actual behaviour in favour of a new entrant that offers a better deal. The result... is that only real brands will prosper, i.e. only companies which learn to incorporate a consumer focus throughout their marketing mix, and manage to differentiate themselves from their competitors in a positive way...
>
> ... There is not a single element of the marketing mix that is not already being rethought by many financial service companies.
>
> *Dominic Owens of the Prudential Corporation:*
> *'Brand Dynamics in Financial Services', Admap, May 1995*

This again is a continuing trend. Of the seven entrants who won AMSO Research Effectiveness Awards in the 1995 competition, only the winning paper (Harveys Bristol Cream, as above) was dealing with research for a traditional fmcg product. Of the remaining winners and commended entries, two were about 'utilities' (Anglian Water and British Telecom), two were for banks (Nat West and TSB), one was about Tate Gallery business sponsorship of exhibitions, and the final one concerned television programme evaluation.

The trends towards 'company' or service brands have had a number of implications for research. Since services are about people, it is realised that the research must often be internal, covering one's own employees, as well as external. Customer and employee satisfaction research have developed as specialisms offered by certain companies or subsidiaries of larger agencies. New research methods have evolved, notably the practice of 'mystery shopping', in which interviewers pretend to be real customers in order to assess how well company procedures are being carried out at the interface between customers and staff. The change in the acceptability of this technique is as good a marker as any of the changing priorities in marketing.

Mystery shopping used to be looked at askance by the Professional Standards Committee of the Market Research Society, because it flouted the rule that informants must be free to withdraw consent to an interview: the essence of mystery shopping is that staff do not know they are being observed. Moreover, it would often be impossible to conceal who was being observed from the client. Yet, increasingly, clients were demanding it, and for the best of reasons: to improve their service. What to do? After some agonising, it was decided that it could be accepted within the terms of the Code if there was a general awareness among staff that the company would conduct mystery shopping from time to time, and that it would not be used to discriminate between people or identify 'bad apples', but simply as a guide to improving procedures.

Mystery shopping, commissioned from external agencies, is now frequently used as part of the process for checking the effectiveness and quality of service to customers, especially in types of business where the interface with staff is complex. The technique, for example, enabled a bank to discover that when a customer asked for details of the bank's mortgage services, most of the cashiers handed out a leaflet, but only 15% took the enquirer's name and address; and a survey in car showrooms found that, although it is believed that half the people who test drive a car end up buying it, only 10% of the salesmen actually offered a test drive. One of the 'highly commended' entries for the 1995 AMSO Research Effectiveness Awards included mystery shopping as part of a research-based drive to improve service in the TSB.

The concern of companies to concentrate on customer retention and adding service values is having another effect, made possible by new technology: the development of and reliance on electronic *databases*, which enable companies to single out and 'talk directly' to relevant customers, attract them and keep them loyal with special offers, etc. This tendency is likely to have a profound and possibly malign effect on research; there is a danger that the information held on such databases could replace proper research, in spite of the fact that (being self-selected) they are seldom if ever unbiased and objective. Why indulge in expensive research to get a true understanding of the market when all you need to do, to improve your business, is to continue 'talking' to the special group who responded to your initial mailing or were recruited by your telemarketing bureau (perhaps on the understanding that they were taking part in a 'research project')?

The challenge for research here is to maintain 'clear blue water' between genuine research uses of database material and other applications. As already noted, researchers are already beginning to set up 'research databases' as a way out of the problems of non-response and finding 'difficult' samples. The Market Research Society now has a special section in its Code of Conduct entitled 'Guidelines for handling databases containing personal details of respondents or potential respondents and the conduct of identified surveys'. Beyond this, there is an increasing need to ensure that research clients understand the dangers of getting false readings from a database if the research principles of objectivity, avoidance of bias or conditioning, etc., are not applied. Databases will, inevitably, be used more and more; it is up to the research industry to see that, where research is concerned at least, their use is 'ethical'.

Internationalisation

We noted in Chapter 1 that international research in the UK (meaning principally research commissioned in other countries via UK agencies) has grown faster than the total research spend for some time. "In the last two years", said Derek Martin in his Chairman's report to the 1995 AMSO Conference, "international has grown by well over 20 per cent per annum, while domestic has been around 8-10 per cent. As a result, nearly a quarter of all AMSO companies' business is now international". In the same period, research expenditure has been accelerating in most other parts of the world, especially where economies are developing fastest (such as South East Asia and the Pacific Rim). In 1985, John Goodyear estimated the world-wide value of commercially-available market research to be in the region of £3,000 million sterling. By 1991, according to Philip Barnard, it was over 6 billion dollars (£4,000 million sterling at today's rate).

What lies behind this expansion? Philip Barnard, reviewing the scene late in 1992, listed the following reasons for the 'international dimension underlying much market research':

- globalisation/regionalisation of many businesses and their branded properties;
- corporate guidelines or 'rules' for research buyers world-wide, e.g. for preferred research suppliers or techniques;

- the European Single Market and other trading bloc developments;
- opening up of Central and Eastern Europe, South and East Asia.

Barnard went on to say:

Internationalisation is not only a feature of consumer packaged goods companies. Most parts of the world provide a comfort blanket of international brands spanning many product and service categories and featuring many of the world's heaviest spenders on market research; for example:

• alcoholic beverages	• electrical goods
• business services	• electronic products
• cars	• hotels
• car rental	• luxury goods
• charge/credit cards	• tobacco products.

In Europe, the international theme is further reflected in the centralising of European businesses and the growing commitment to pan-European brands. Examples of major companies (or major divisions of these) which are now being run on a European basis, rather than as separate national units, include:

• BP	• Nestlé
• Citibank	• Philips
• Gillette	• Samsonite
• Heineken	• 3M
• Henkel	• Unilever
• J & J	• Volvo

Philip Barnard: 'New Directions in World Research',
Admap, October 1992

It is generally agreed that Britain, largely for historical reasons, has had the lion's share of this international business. David Jenkins, again at the 1995 AMSO Conference, put it this way:

Britain has about 1 per cent of world population, about 3 per cent of world economy (as measured by GDP), about 5 per cent of world advertising, but about 9 per cent of world market research.

Britain is also, at present, "the main world centre for the co-ordination of international studies". There are some obvious geographical reasons for this: English is the international language; Britain is the natural launching pad for US multinationals wishing to expand in Europe, and so on. But more importantly, British researchers have taken a leading position in developing research elsewhere, first as a profession (with a high profile in such bodies as ESOMAR) and later as a business. For example, many, if not most, of the pioneer research agencies in India, Japan and elsewhere in the Far East were founded on British investment, expertise and personnel. John Goodyear, speaking in 1992 (MRS Conference paper) said that, even allowing for Nielsen and IMS (owned by the American Dun & Bradstreet),

> the UK-based research industry occupies a very close second position in terms of its ownership of research agencies around the world and may indeed come close to equalling the United States in respect of its non-domestic international research ownership.

It is not expected that this dominance can continue. Other European countries (especially France and Germany) are becoming alive to the opportunities for investment abroad, and US companies are shedding their old isolation. Instead of the wholly outwards investment of the 1970s and 1980s (for example, the establishment of the Survey Research Group in the Far East, IMRB and JMRB in India and Japan, the entry into the Unites States of AGB (failed) and Millward Brown (succeeded)), we are now seeing this balanced by investment inwards (the acquisition of Research Services, Mark Abrams' old firm, by the French conglomerate IPSOS is a recent example). British expertise is still respected, and well placed to compete; but others are now increasingly felt to be on a par with us. It has been said that, in order to share in these growing opportunities world-wide, we will have to become more genuinely 'multi-cultural' in our attitudes and sensitive to the different concerns of other countries:

> So far, we have succeeded largely by being British Colonial, shipping out good ideas to the natives, but not fully embracing internationalism. The large research companies are far less international in their top management than their clients are. With the exception of Research International, I do not know of any agency which has a substantially multi-cultural main board. This will have to change, as the emerging markets become more and more important to us.
> *David Jenkins: 'British Research is Best',*
> *AMSO Conference, 1995*

Tougher times: concentration, competition, re-organisation and 'downsizing'

The pressures on firms to become 'leaner and fitter', as a result of static markets, fiercer struggles to retain brand share, more powerful retailers imposing deals which put pressure on margins, and so on, have been documented enough, especially since the recession of the early 1990s. These influences are unlikely to go away, even if times are more prosperous, now that the importance of productivity has been grasped. The particular way in which this has affected market research has been the 'downsizing' (to adopt this unattractive American euphemism) of client research departments.

In the early post-war period of research, those companies which took it seriously built up large departments to manage the collection of data and turn them into information for management. The days of companies like Reckitts, Mars or Nestlé running their own field operations are long gone, but the market research departments persisted, especially in the USA where they sometimes reached as many as 100 or more persons. This changed sharply around 1989-91, in a process referred to by *Business Week* (February 1991) as 'The Bloodbath in Market Research'. Barnard (1992) lists 14 major American corporations, including AT&T, Campbell Soup, Citibank, Marriott and M&M/Mars, which either disbanded or severely cut the size of their market research departments in 1990-91. The same process has been happening in the UK, although it may seem less extreme because departments have tended to be smaller. There are now several major companies in Britain where the market research function has been reduced to one person, and some, such as Heinz, which have abolished it altogether.

At the same time, as we have seen, expenditure on research has continued to increase substantially. In some ways, the downsizing phenomenon has been beneficial to researchers, at least if they work in agencies. It is not merely that more work is contracted out; that would have happened anyway. It is rather that research agencies have been forced more and more to talk and sell directly to the marketing directors and others who actually use their work.

From the late 1960s it was normal that the only contact which an agency researcher had with his client would be with the client's market research manager or someone in his department. This person would assume the responsibility for turning the results of the research into information, and for 'selling it internally'. If it failed to live up to expectations, he would carry the can. He would act as an efficient gatekeeper against both sides, translating what his bosses required into research language for the agency brief, and filtering what was reported; often the only time anyone from the agency spoke to other marketing people or to the directors would be at the formal presentation to senior management where, in the worst cases, the hapless presenter could be completely thrown to discover the questions about which senior management were really concerned. The abolition of this gatekeeping function forces agency researchers to accept briefs from, and report to, directors who know little and care less about how the research is done, but want answers expressed in terms they can understand and in which they can have confidence. This gives a substantial push to researchers learning the language of marketing and business, and becoming interpreters rather than technicians, which is what clients uniformly say they want: not to have data thrown at them, take it or leave it, but to be told what they mean. As Philip Barnard has put it:

> The leaner market research departmental structures... have provided research companies with the opportunity to develop new, and often closer, forms of relationship with clients – whilst the client also benefits in a switch from fixed to variable costs.

To sum up: the trends in what users want are requiring research to become:

- more subtle and sensitive in understanding the consumer;
- better at measuring intangibles arising from the deeper understanding of what makes strong brands, including service and company brands;
- better geared to operate on a large scale and internationally (which involves investment, and efficient, profit-making business management);

- better able to act as interpreters, who can speak to clients in their own language to provide them with actionable information.

These things are all happening. Research companies have now become, in a number of cases, major international businesses. Some have been bought into communications conglomerates such as WPP and United News & Media. They have increasingly sought to differentiate themselves by branding their own services and making these packages available world-wide through local subsidiaries or under licence. At the same time, the branding increasingly has a service element: the best companies (those which are growing and retaining clients) do not take tracking or pre-testing packages off the shelf but tailor them to the particular client's needs and do their utmost to provide an interpretative service. Specialisms are growing, as clients demand and begin to get services from agencies who are knowledgeable about their particular business.

In this way, research companies are fighting back, with some success, against the competition which began to appear in the 1980s from management consultants and accountants (the likes of Price Waterhouse, Arthur Andersen, Coopers and Lybrand) competing for profitable research contracts, often as part of a wider brief. This remains a real threat. "With higher level corporate contacts and more willingness to make clear research-based recommendations than are found in most research companies" (Barnard), these organisations have obtained some major projects which might otherwise have gone to research companies (e.g. the US Postal Service delivery performance tracker won by Price Waterhouse). But now, research companies have begun to learn how to achieve these advantages for themselves.

Technological Changes

Against this background of changing opportunities, there are significant trends in the scope of what research can deliver. The most important is probably the development in computing. We have moved in not much more than thirty years from a labour-intensive to an equipment-based industry. Many things can now be done much more quickly than before, greatly increasing the productivity of the expensive research staff in the office, and making it possible for an increasing number of home-based consultants to offer effective services. We can list some of these improvements as follows:

- Questionnaires used to be typed laboriously by hand, and every change involved retyping. Now one can set them out quickly on one's PC using software which formats them easily and saves and edits changes with little fuss.

- Data processing used to involve slow, manual labour. Now most editing and all data entry is done at a keyboard and some, especially on large surveys such as the National Readership Survey or the Target Group Index, is automated using techniques like Optical Mark Reading.

- Analysis involved manual card-sorting and counting. Calculations were difficult, and any advanced or multi-variate statistics were so painful to do that they would be avoided at almost any cost. Now, tabulations can be produced by bureau services or at clients' own PCs, if they wish, and powerful software from various houses makes advanced statistics and modelling work relatively easy, so long as you know what you are doing.

- Presentation material used to be time-consuming to prepare, with charts manually pasted up. Now, charts are produced easily by the computer straight from the tables, ready for printing onto overhead projector acetates or slides. It will not be long before presentations are routinely done direct from portable laptop computers, although this procedure currently still suffers from gremlins, as slide projection used to do in its early days.

Interviewing

As recently as 12-15 years ago (the early 1980s), most ad hoc interviewing was face-to-face (interviewers calling on people in their homes, interviewing them in the street, or recruiting them to come to a hall or central location). The period since then has seen accelerating change.

Telephone interviewing began to pick up as a serious alternative at about the time when telephone ownership reached over 90% of households, which did not happen in Britain until about 1982 (in America, of course, telephone interviewing became commonplace much earlier). Computers were important in the development of telephone interviewing methods. Interviewers could work with questionnaires on computer screens in central locations, coding the answers directly at the keyboard. This has some obvious advantages: the pre-programmed questionnaires can be more complex, because the computer can cope with the filtering, routing interviewers straight to the next question following the last answer; the answers are fed directly to the analysis record, eliminating a separate data entry stage and thus removing a potential source of errors; data can be collected 'down the line' and tabulated instantly, with almost immediate reporting possible, thus saving time. The major British agencies, it has been estimated, use CATI (Computer Assisted Telephone Interviewing) for over 95% of their telephone research.

However, there were found to be some limitations to the telephone. It is not suitable when long questionnaires are involved or when material has to be shown to respondents during the interview. Mainly for these reasons, it has not taken over from face-to-face interviewing. Currently, it is estimated that some two-thirds of quantified ad hoc interviewing (i.e. excluding panel and qualitative research) is still face-to-face. A natural development was to look for ways in which interviewers could take the benefits of computer assistance with them, when they go out into the field.

This has come about with the arrival of portable laptop computers, during the later 1980s. The procedure was, inevitably, known as CAPI (Computer Assisted Personal Interviewing). John Samuels, at the time Managing Director of BMRB International, described the progress of this development in an award-winning ESOMAR Conference paper in 1994, 'From CAPI to HAPPI'.

According to John Samuels, by 1992, CAPI was in widespread use in the Netherlands, there was one regular service in Finland, it was used on a small number of very large continuous surveys in the UK, and otherwise hardly at all in Europe. By 1992, the only large commercial market research company with wide experience of CAPI was RSL, which was using it on the National Readership Survey, and British Telecom's customer satisfaction monitor (a total of 150,000 interviews). In 1992 RSL launched the first omnibus survey using CAPI, under the name CAPIBUS. This had a major impact on the very large UK omnibus market. When CAPIBUS dropped from its original high premium to more competitive pricing, all the leading players lost share, and several other companies developed their own CAPI. By 1995, BMRB, NOP and Harris had CAPI versions, RSGB was considering one, and Taylor Nelson had adopted a bar-code system which has many of the speed advantages of CAPI without laptops.

John Samuels (writing in 1994) forecast that the equipment of interviewers with laptop computers for omnibus surveys would provide an incentive to extend their use to other ad hoc applications, in order to maximise the return on the investment involved. Besides, the very great improvement in delivery times which CAPI makes possible would prove irresistible to clients; according to Samuels, delivery time on the BMRB omnibus had been cut to less than half, by the reduction in printing, mail and data entry, so that a client could now sign up the day before fieldwork started and receive results the day after it ended. Samuels questioned for his paper the top eight commercial suppliers of quantitative face-to-face surveys, plus OPCS and SCPR, and obtained answers from nine of these: they estimated that on average 60% of their face-to-face interviewing would be using CAPI by the end of 1995, and the six companies farthest ahead averaged 80%, with an average of 750 laptops apiece.

If this 'CAPI revolution' occurs as expected by John Samuels, it will have a significant impact on the management and quality of fieldwork, on the type of people who are employed as interviewers, and on the way they are employed. Interviewing will become less of a cottage industry and more of a profession. This thought comes against the background of issues of employment legislation stemming from Europe and the 'social chapter', which may well make our traditional employment of free-lance interviewers impossible in the future. It is widely expected that the UK's present advantage of relatively low-cost interviewing will not be sustainable for long; "recent court rulings on pensions for interviewers, sick pay and maternity pay, giving part-timers the same rights as full-timers, mean that we are not very far off a sharp step change in the cost of doing research in the UK" (David Jenkins). We could see a trend to smaller, more highly trained, professional field forces, and/or a growth in specialist field interview suppliers, as in the USA.

The improvements we are seeing in the handling of data, by CAPI and other means, will probably continue, alongside traditional interviewing. The 'HAPPI' scenario postulated by John Samuels, in which most data collection would be automated from wired up panels of bespoke respondents without the aid of interviewers, may seem extreme, but

Samuels is surely right to suggest that the speed, efficiency and cost reduction which these procedures can deliver to clients will tend to outweigh concerns about defective methodology. The market research profession will continue to be challenged by these developments, and will find ways to accommodate them, as it has with mystery shopping.

Plenty of Challenges Still

Market research has been a thread running through many of the radical changes we have seen in the last fifty years.

The fundamental move has been towards a greater economic freedom. With higher disposable incomes, more individuals have felt free to choose their own life-styles and to challenge accepted wisdom. They have been open to more sources of information and ideas than ever before, and able to improve their understanding of the world around them and their knowledge of those who are trying to govern them or appeal to them. Most importantly, they have increasingly been treated as though they mattered; they have been listened to. The successful organisations, commercial or otherwise, have tended to be those with the ability to listen and respond to people's real concerns. Market research has been the only *reliable* method of doing this.

In this book, we have traced how market research in the UK has developed, in skills, techniques and coverage, in response to organisations' need to understand. Most people nowadays know something about it, and almost everyone has experienced being questioned in a survey at least once. This awareness itself has helped to broaden their own agenda: they have become more expert about marketing, advertising, product improvements, new products and services, packaging, most aspects of public administration, and what credence they should give to pronouncements in the media. As knowledge has increased, largely through research, about people's lives, aspirations and ideas, the relationship between individuals and institutions, from marketing companies, services and charities to political parties and the state, has itself changed. None of these organisations can impose; they must convince – and without an accurate understanding of those they are talking to, they cannot hope to be convincing.

The ingenuity of market research people will therefore continue to be in demand, just as it has been during the past fifty years. The market research profession will have to:

- become even more subtle and sensitive in the drive towards individualism;
- be the prime source of commercial and public understanding of an ever more complex society;
- get itself understood by an increasingly discriminating public;
- get itself seen as a benefit to society and an important means of protection against the power of organisations;
- preserve and promote its distinctive values through the Code of Practice, and ensure that these are clearly understood and contrasted with other sources of information which may be flawed;
- learn to operate successfully on both an international and a local scale;
- develop the interpretative and advisory skills which clients increasingly want, while clinging tenaciously to its old principles of integrity;
- make the best use of the new emerging opportunities of technology.

The history of market research over the last fifty years leaves one with no doubt that these new challenges will be met.

The need for sound research cannot be questioned. The journalist Peter Kellner, writing in the *Sunday Times* about the dangers of an instinctive and emotional approach to politics, said:

Understanding... takes effort, and a willingness to let evidence overturn emotion. Conversely, instincts... are easy to embrace. Yet the skills needed to inquire into instincts too are the skills of experts, sifting for facts in order to achieve understanding. Once we decide to discard those skills, we discard the facility to test prejudice...

To say that there is a tension between fact and instinct is to state the obvious. We see that tension in debates about Europe, race, capital punishment, prisons and homosexuality, and, more subtly, in arguments about schools, hospitals, taxation and public spending. But to say that tension exists is a world away from saying that conflict is either inevitable or desirable.

On the contrary, conflict does harm, and asserting the supremacy of instinct over fact does most harm of all. It elevates ignorance into a virtue...

Tolerant, inclusive societies do not come about by chance; they develop because enough people work hard to combat irrational hatreds. Politicians are not the only people who engage in this task, nor always the most effective. Yet... they largely create the climate in which social issues are debated. If they scorn the very notion of rational inquiry, the efforts of others are doomed to fail.

There could hardly be a better explanation of the need for sound market research.

★ ★ ★

APPENDIX: TIMETABLE OF EVENTS

RESEARCH EVENTS UP TO 1946

1928	Sales Research Services founded
1931	Audit Bureau of Circulation started
1933	JWT London founds BMRB
1934	Mark Abrams starts work as a researcher with the London Press Exchange
1936	BBC Research Department founded
1937	Mass-Observation founded
1938	Henry Durant founds BIPO (British Institute of Public Opinion), the British Gallup Poll
1939	Nielsen starts in UK
	IIPA Press Readership Survey
1940 -45	Mass-Observation and BIPO continue operating
	Government Social Survey founded as the 'Wartime Social Survey' under the Ministry of Information
	Over 100 surveys done by WTSS up to end of 1944, including the first continuous survey ('survey of sickness', a major influence on the development of the National Health Service)
	BMRB keeps going with work contracted by government

POST-WAR

	External Events	Research Events
1946	Bank of England, coal, telecoms, airways nationalised	Market Research Society founded
	Bread rationing introduced	Research Services Ltd founded
	$4.4bn loan from US	Central Office of Information formed, takes over Social Survey
	Arts Council set up	
	BBC TV transmissions resume	
1947	Convertibility crisis (£1 = $4.03)	Attwood Statistics founded
	Marshall Aid starts	Institute of Statisticians founded
	Britain signs General Agreement on Tariffs & Trade	Hulton, IIPA and Attwood readership surveys
	School leaving age goes up to 15	MRS introduces Associate membership
	Dior's New Look introduced	
1948	Railways and electricity nationalised	European Society for Opinion and Marketing Research (ESOMAR) founded
	'Appointed Day'– Welfare State starts	Attwood Panel set up
	'Bonfire of Controls' announced	
	Bread and clothes rationing end	
	National Service starts	
1949	£ devalued 30%, to $2.80	MRS Report on Socio-Economic Classes
	Marshall Aid ends	
	Iron, steel, gas nationalised	

	External Events	Research Events
	Clothes rationing ends. First launderette opens	
1950	Korean war starts	First MRS weekend school held at Stockport
	Petrol and soap rationing end	MRS membership reaches 90
	Sainsbury opens its first self-service store	
	National dailies peak at c. 17m circulation	
1951	Festival of Britain	ESOMAR Annual Conference held in UK
	New rearmament programme of £4.7bn	
	Churchill forms new Conservative government	
	London foreign exchange market reopens	
	Austin and Morris merge, world's 4th largest car firm	
1952	Restrictions on imports and hire purchase	Application for incorporation of MRS turned down by Board of Trade
	Identity cards abolished	Copland model introduced for estimating poster audiences
	Utility scheme and tea rationing end	
1953	Coronation	MRS incorporated as a limited company
	End of Korean war	
	Road transport, iron and steel denationalised	
	Sugar and sweet rationing end	
1954	Hire purchase controls end	Code of Standards adopted by MRS
	Food rationing ends	First MRS Annual Lunch
	Building licence system ends	

	External Events	Research Events
	First purpose-built comprehensive school opens	
	Lucky Jim published	
1955	Hire purchase restrictions reintroduced	Last Hulton readership survey
	ITV starts	Attwood form TAM (Television Audience Measurement)
	BBC demonstrates colour TV at Alexandra Palace	MRS holds first one-week summer school at Oxford
		MRS publishes *The Directory of Market Research Organisations* and *Readership Surveys*
		First signs of 'sugging'
		MRS membership passes 200
1956	Colleges of Advanced Technology set up	Market Investigations Ltd (MIL) founded
	First nuclear power station commissioned	IPA's NRS becomes the industry readership survey
	Premium Bond introduced	
	'Look Back in Anger'	
	Suez crisis, emergency petrol rationing	
1957	European Economic Community set up	Joint Industry Committee for Television Audience Research (JICTAR) set up
	Rent Act loosens rent control	National Opinion Polls (NOP) founded
	Council on Prices, Productivity & Incomes set up	Public Attitude Surveys Ltd (PAS) founded

	External Events	Research Events
	Bill Haley brings rock & roll to Europe, Tommy Steele and Cliff Richard emerge	Schwerin Advertising Research founded
		Board of Trade recognises MRS
		MRS hold first Annual Conference
		Family Expenditure Survey starts
1958	CND founded – first Aldermaston march	MAS Survey Research founded
	Race riots in Notting Hill	
	Coal rationing ends	
	Stereo hi-fi introduced	
	First 8-mile stretch of motorway opened	
1959	Credit controls dropped, income and purchase tax cut	Marplan founded
	EFTA set up	Dichter sets up UK operation
	Hovercraft invented, Austin/Morris mini launched	BMRB's Advertising Planning Index pilot work
	Pilkington Committee on broadcasting set up	First edition of *Commentary* published
1960	The Pill introduced	
	Credit squeeze and hire purchase restrictions	
	National Service ends	
	The Beatles, *Beyond The Fringe*, *Lady Chatterley*	
	News Chronicle closes	
1961	Soviet Union puts man in space and builds Berlin Wall	International Passenger Survey starts

	External Events	Research Events
	Loan from IMF makes £700m available to UK	MRS appoints General Secretary, gets own offices
	Hire purchase controls relaxed, 'Pay Pause'	First MRS Gold Medal awarded
	Sit-down demos against the Bomb, 850 arrested	
	Private Eye opens	
1962	Cuban missile crisis	Thomson Media Awards set up
	National Economic Development Council set up	Audits of Great Britain (AGB) founded, starts TCA panel
	Pilkington Committee on Broadcasting reports	RBL (Research International) founded
	Shawcross Commission on the Press set up	Schlackmans founded
	Sunday Times publishes first colour supplement	MRS membership goes over 1,000
		Dr Belson publishes 'Studies in Readership'
		First Coglan Trophy awarded
1963	Kennedy assassinated	Industrial Marketing Research Association (IMRA) founded
	British entry to EEC vetoed by France	Audience Studies Ltd (ASL) founded
	Profumo affair	Stats MR founded
	Robbins Committee recommends big expansion of higher education	
	Beeching Report on British Railways	

	External Events	Research Events
1964	Vietnam war starts	Association of Market Survey Organisations (AMSO) founded, with nine member companies
	Harold Wilson forms new Labour government	MRS publishes first *Market Research Abstracts*
	15% import surcharge, $1bn loan from IMF	National Travel Survey starts
	Resale Price Maintenance abolished	British General Election Surveys started by Butler & Stokes
	BBC2 and pirate radio stations start broadcasting	
	Miniskirt introduced, Mary Quant opens *Bazaar*	
1965	National Plan introduced and abandoned	Market Behaviour Limited (MBL) and Taylor Nelson Associates (TNA) founded
	New taxes and controls introduced	Association of Research Users (AURA) set up
	Race Relations Act and Race Relations Board set up	MRS membership approaches 1,600
	Prescription charges abolished	
	LEAs required to bring in comprehensive schools	
1966	Sterling crisis	First MRS *Newsletter* appears
	Hire purchase terms stiffened, prices and wages freeze	BARS record charts research set up
	National seamen's strike	
	Oil and gas found in quantity in North Sea	
	First British credit card, Barclaycard, launched	

	External Events	Research Events
	Colour TV introduced on BBC2	
1967	Sterling devalued to $2.40	Government Social Survey formed as separate department
	Selective Employment Tax introduced	
	Second application to join EEC vetoed by France	
	Law reform: abortion, homosexuality, family planning	
	Radio 1 and local radio start, pirate radio banned	
	National Front founded	
1968	Public spending cuts, credit squeeze, HP curbs	Opinion Research Centre Ltd founded
	Prescription charges reintroduced	JICTAR contract moves to AGB who install first in-home meters
	Commonwealth Immigration Act	BMRB launches Target Group Index (TGI)
	Theatre censorship ends	InDal launch Builders Merchant Audit
	Violent anti-Vietnam war demonstrations	MRS publishes first *Yearbook*
	Open University founded	
1969	Voting age lowered to 18	Market & Opinion Research International (MORI), Gordon Simmons Research Group Ltd, Social & Community Planning Research (SCPR) and Martin-Hamblin founded

	External Events	**Research Events**
	Divorce law liberalised	MRS publishes *International Directory of Market Research Organisations*
	Death penalty abolished	
	'In Place of Strife' dropped after TUC opposition	
	Concorde makes maiden flight	
	ITV makes its first colour transmissions	
1970	Edward Heath forms new Conservative government	Office of Population Censuses and Surveys (OPCS) formed from the Government Social Survey and the General Register Office
	Age of majority reduced to 18	General Household Survey starts
	New ministries: Trade & Industry and Environment	Polls fail to forecast election result
	Equal Pay Act	
	First conference of Women's Liberation Movement	
	Gay Liberation Front formed	
1971	Decimalisation	HMSO publishes first *Social Trends*
	Bretton Woods fixed exchange rate system ends	MRS Code of Conduct revised
	Rolls Royce bankrupt, aero-space business nationalised	
	Industrial Relations Act; TUC votes not to register	
	Labour Party conference votes against entry to EEC	

	External Events	Research Events
	Angry Brigade emerges, with bombs	
1972	US withdraws from Vietnam	RSGB founded
	£ floats, unemployment goes over 1m	MRS publishes post-mortem on election polls of 1970
	Miners strike – State of Emergency, power cuts	Retail Audits launch their National Grocers Panel
	90-day freeze on prices, statutory incomes policy	Stats (MR) launch their Licensed Trade Audit
	National dock strike	
	Housing Finance Act forces 'fair rents'	
1973	UK joins EEC. VAT introduced	Millward Brown Ltd founded
	School leaving age planned to go up to 16	BJM Research Partners Group Ltd founded
	Arab-Israeli war, oil supplies cut and prices doubled	MRS adopts Interviewer Card Scheme in principle
	Foreign exchange crisis, emergency measures	British Business Survey (readership) set up
	Green Party formed	European Business Readership Survey set up
	LBC, first commercial radio station, opens	JICRAR (radio research) set up
		Research turnover estimated at £31m
1974	Miners strike – 3-day working week, speed limits	Election polls attacked by press for poor forecasts in two 1974 general elections
	Harold Wilson forms new Labour government	
	Pay Board and statutory incomes policy abolished	

	External Events	Research Events
	Industrial Relations Act repealed	
	'Social Contract' between TUC and government	
1975	IMF loan of £975m applied for, inflation up to 25%	Industrial Research Bureau (IRB) founded
	Referendum backs staying in EEC by two-to-one	Polls forecast referendum accurately (without press comment)
	Equal Opportunities Commission set up	MRS membership passes 2,500
	British Leyland taken over by Government	
	£6-a-week pay rise limit, supported by TUC	
	Employment Protection Act, ACAS as arbitrator	
1976	Sterling crisis, £2.3bn IMF loan, £3bn bank standby	MRS survey on public attitudes to market research
	£ falls below $2 for first time, goes down to $1.71	
	£2.5bn public expenditure cuts, cash limits, indirect taxes up, minimum lending rate to 15%	
	Unemployment goes over 1.5m	
	Government abandons policy of 'full employment'	
	National Theatre opens	
1977	Grunwick strike, mass pickets and violence	Market Research Benevolent Association founded
	Stage 3 of Incomes Policy: 10% limit to wage rises	First JICRAR network radio audience survey

	External Events	Research Events
	Firemen strike for 30% pay increase	Research turnover now estimated at £55m
	Imported cars' market share goes above 50%	AMSO start producing statistics. Research turnover estimated about £60m
	National Front riots	Last award of MRS Gold Medal (superseded by new Silver Medal)
	Punks emerge; BBC bans Sex Pistols song	
1978	5% guideline for wage increases rejected by TUC and Labour Party conference	Social Research Association set up
	Youth Opportunities Scheme introduced	MRS Interviewer Card Scheme finally introduced
	'Winter of Discontent': industrial action by hospital, municipal and water workers	Pan European Survey (readership) set up
	Conservatives appoint Saatchi & Saatchi	
	Disputes stop *Times* and *Sunday Times* publishing	
1979	Mass secondary picketing in road haulage strikes	ESOMAR Annual Conference held in Bristol
	Mrs Thatcher forms new Conservative government	BMRB, Mass-Observation and MBL come under common ownership (JWT Group)
	Budget cuts income tax to 30%, top rate to 60%, puts up VAT	CACI Ltd introduces ACORN geodemographics
	£3.5bn public spending cuts announced	AGB take over Attwood panel
	11-week ITV strike, Channel 4 awarded to IBA	First of new Silver Medals awarded

	External Events	Research Events
1980	Large-scale cuts in local authority grants	Broadcasting Audience Research Bureau (BARB) replaces JICTAR
	International capital movements deregulated	Market Research Development Fund set up
	Housing Act gives council tenants the right to buy	IPA Advertising Effectiveness Awards founded
	Employment Act outlaws secondary picketing, promotes secret ballots for unions	
	Riots in St Paul's, Bristol and at National Front rallies	
1981	Unemployment goes over 2m	The Research Business founded
	Government cuts higher education budget	MRS publishes *Guide to the Practice of Market and Survey Research*
	Social Democratic Party formed	RSL and BMRB sponsor first international Readership Research Symposium
	Riots in Brixton, Toxteth, Moss Side; Scarman Report criticises police	
	Women's peace camp at Greenham Common	
	150,000 demonstrate against Cruise missiles	
1982	Falklands War	Association of Qualitative Research Practitioners (AQRP) and Association of British Market Research Companies (ABMRC) set up
	Unemployment goes over 3m	RSL takes over Burke, RI takes over Marplan

	External Events	Research Events
	Employment Act bans closed shop	British Crime Survey starts
	Channel 4 starts	First special Gold Medal award made to Dr Mark Abrams
	Animal Liberation Front raids laboratories	
1983	National Graphical Association assets seized by High Court in dispute with Stockport Messenger	SCPR starts British Social Attitudes series
	Youth Training Scheme established	Labour Force Survey moves to annual basis
	Cable Authority set up	MRS publishes *Survey*
	TV-am and BBC's Breakfast Time start	
1984	British Telecom privatised	AGB introduces peoplemeter for TV audience measurement
	Nissan sets up pilot plant in Sunderland	CAA (Cinema Advertising Association) start monitoring cinema audiences
	Government bans unions at GCHQ	OSCAR (poster measurement) starts
	Miners strike, violent clashes with police, many arrests, NUM assets seized	NRS adopts Extended Media List system
	Divorce allowed after one year of marriage	
1985	£ falls below $1.10	Dun & Bradstreet takes over Nielsen
	Miners' strike collapses	OSCAR (Outdoor Site Classification and Audience Research) set up
	Greater London Council abolished	
	Anglo-Irish Agreement signed, Ulster MPs resign	

	External Events	Research Events
	Riots in Handsworth, Brixton, Toxteth and Tottenham	
	Live Aid concert for famine relief	
1986	Big Bang – financial institutions deregulated	MRS appoints first Director-General, introduces its own Interviewer Identity Card and revised Code of Conduct
	British Gas and TSB privatised	Unilever sells Research International to Ogilvy & Mather
	New Social Security Act to reform welfare system	Research industry turnover goes over £200m in UK
	First peacetime trade deficit in manufactured goods	MRS membership goes over 5,000
	Riots over newspaper printing at Wapping	Special Gold Medal award to Leonard England
	Peacock Committee rejects advertising to fund BBC	
1987	British Airways privatised	The MBL Group Plc formed
	Community Charge (Poll Tax) proposed	MRB Group acquired by WPP through its acquisition of JWT
	Sex Discrimination Bill, prepared to EEC directives	
	Nestlé buys Rowntree for three times net asset value	
	General Synod votes for ordination of women	
	Dramatic falls in London stock market	

	External Events	Research Events
1988	Education Act sets up national curriculum, allows opting out of LEA control	Special Gold Medal award to Harry Henry
	City Technology Colleges planned	
	Immigration Act restricts rights of relatives and dependents of immigrants	
	Income Support, Social Fund, Housing Benefit replace Supplementary Benefits	
	Demonstrations at Wapping, 300 injured	
1989	Unemployment falls below 2m	Research International acquired by WPP through its acquisition of Ogilvy & Mather
	Interest rates up to 15%, trade deficit a record £20.3bn	MRS/ARF Boston conference
	Water privatised, dock labour scheme abolished	ICM founded
	Sky TV launched	
	GPs campaign against government NHS reforms	
	Berlin Wall opened up	
1990	Gulf War starts	JICREG (regional media readership) set up
	Inflation up to 11%	OPCS Omnibus survey starts
	UK joins the Exchange Rate Mechanism	
	NHS & Community Care Act, Hospital Trusts set up	
	Broadcasting Act to bring in new structure	

	External Events	Research Events
	Demonstrations against poll tax	
1991	Electricity privatised	New BARB contract split between AGB and RSMB
	Unemployment goes back over 2m	IRI starts retail auditing in the UK
	Poll Tax abandoned	Worldwide research turnover estimated at £4 billion
	Citizens' Charter launched	AMSO Research Effectiveness Awards first published
	7,000 gay rights protesters rally in Hyde Park	
1992	UK signs Maastricht treaty	National Readership Surveys Ltd replaces JICNARS to run NRS
	UK leaves ERM	NRS adopts CAPI (computer assisted interviewing), now covers c. 300 titles
	Lloyd's announce a loss of over £2bn	RSL introduces CAPIBUS, first omnibus survey using CAPI
		RAJAR (Radio Joint Audience Research) replaces JICRAR
		Special Gold Medal award to Dr Elizabeth Nelson
		RSL bought by French group IPSOS
1993	European 'Single Market' comes into force	AMSO endorses ESOMAR International Code of Practice
	Maastricht Treaty ratified; with UK opt-outs on European currency and Social Chapter	

	External Events	Research Events
	Inflation falls to 1.7%, lowest for 25 years	
	Unemployment goes back over 3m	
	Council Tax replaces Community Charge	
	Hospital waiting lists go over 1m for first time	
1994	BMW buys Rover, the last British popular car maker	OSCAR site classification updated
	Homosexual age of consent lowered to 18	45 peoplemeter systems now operational in 39 countries
	30 new universities created, mostly from Polytechnics	Foundation of Business and Industrial Group of the MRS (BIG)
	Demonstrations against Criminal Justice Bill	
	Channel Tunnel completed	
	Sunday trading now legal, National Lottery launched	
1995	£ down to lowest ever DM2.19	18.5% of all AMSO members' interviewing now by telephone
	Budget reduces basic income tax to 24%	Research industry turnover exceeds £600m in UK
	One-third of children are born outside marriage	MRS membership reaches 6,000
	University student numbers go over 1m	OPCS and Central Statistical Office merge to form Office of National Statistics (ONS)
	Labour Party drops Clause 4 and nationalisation	
	Mass demonstrations by Animal Rights activists	

COLIN McDONALD

Colin McDonald has been involved in market research for some 35 years, both on the client side (Reckitt & Sons Ltd) and several years with leading agencies (BMRB and Communication Research Ltd, finally as Chairman). In 1991 he started his own research consultancy, McDonald Research, which specialises in advertising, media and communication studies. His clients over the years have included companies in many consumer and industrial markets, government departments (including the Central Office of Information), media owners (print, television and poster), advertising agencies and media independents.

In the late 1960s Colin was responsible for the analysis and reporting of an experimental diary panel study supported by JWT (London), which for the first time related purchasing and the receipt of 'opportunities to see' (OTS) from the same persons on a single-source basis over time. A convincing relationship was found, and as a result the study became a landmark case, being published in the United States by the Marketing Science Institute and, later, in *Effective Frequency* by M. J. Naples (Association of National Advertisers, New York, 1979). Colin was commissioned by the ANA to prepare a revised and updated edition of this work, which was published in 1995 under the title *Advertising Reach and Frequency*. The JWT panel findings have been called in aid during much of the controversy surrounding the problem of frequency in media planning, including the recent work of Professor John Philip Jones based on his recent analyses of US Nielsen single-source data, which he very much supports but with some reservations about some of the implications being drawn, and a conviction that we are still a long way from seeing the end of this story. Colin is currently engaged, with the support of Carlton Television, on the further analysis of another single-source database (the Central TV Adlab), in which he is attempting to push out the boundaries farther than John Jones was able to do.

Colin has had some 50 articles and papers published, mostly on advertising research and related matters, and a recent book *How Advertising Works: a review of current thinking*, commissioned by The Advertising Association, was published in 1992. He has been many times a speaker at conferences and seminars sponsored by, among others, the Market Research Society, ESOMAR, The

Advertising Association (UK), the Advertising Research Foundation (USA), and *Admap* (for which he is a commissioning editor). He has been a full member of the British Market Research Society since 1967 and holds the Society's 1974 Gold Medal award. Colin is a graduate and MA of Christ Church, Oxford, where he read Greats. Before starting his market research career with Reckitt & Sons in 1961, he did two years National Service in the army, followed by a period in the Printed Books Department of the British Museum, and then a short time as an administrative officer with Distillers Company Ltd (Chemical Division).

STEPHEN KING

After two years with the Mond Nickel Company, Stephen King spent most of his working life at the advertising agency J. Walter Thompson in London and became a director of the worldwide company in 1985.

Over the years he worked on many of the agency's major accounts, including Andrex, Berger Paints, Guinness, Horlicks, Kellogg's, Kraft, Lever Brothers, Mr Kipling Cakes, Oxo Cubes and Trustee Savings Bank. He set up and ran advertising research and new product development groups, and in 1968 was responsible for establishing the agency's Account Planning department, the first in UK advertising.

Jobs after that included being an account director on British Bakeries and the clearing banks' anti-nationalisation campaign; being non-executive Chairman of JWT's research subsidiary, MRB Group, from 1979 to 1986; being responsible for the development of market modelling and the 'professional' use of computers in JWT London; and establishing common advertising planning methods for the agency worldwide. He retired from JWT in 1988 and for the next four years worked part-time as a non-executive director for WPP. In 1992 he was appointed a non-executive director of the Henley Centre.

He is author of *Developing New Brands* and many articles on branding, advertising and market research, and is Visiting Professor of Marketing Communications at the Cranfield School of Management.

JOHN GOODYEAR

John Goodyear is the Chairman and Chief Executive of The MBL Group of companies, a major international problem-solving market research group which has 28 offices across 19 countries, but which provides a world-wide service, having carried out assignments in more than 100 countries world-wide.

Having graduated in the early sixties in psychology and anthropology, John has spent his entire career in market research, and started his first 'MBL' (Market Behaviour Ltd) in London in January 1965.

In addition to spending some fifteen years plus as a hands-on researcher, John has spent some twenty years building one of the most successful problem-solving international research groups in some of the most interesting parts of the world.

Along the way, he has been Chairman of AMSO (the Association of Market Survey Organisations) in the UK, actively involved over some eleven years on the International and Education Committees of the Market Research Society, has been an invited speaker at four annual conferences of the Market Research Society, and the invited principal speaker at conferences in Finland, Denmark, the Middle-East, Africa, Hong Kong, the Philippines, Singapore, Australia and in both New York and Boston in the United States.

Additionally, John has lectured extensively at Market Research Society training courses, was Chairman of the MRS Residential 'Summer School', has lectured at a number of ESOMAR seminars, and was Chairman of the Programme Committee and additionally a Programme Committee member for various ESOMAR annual conferences.

John has also had papers published in various research and associated publications, including *Admap* and publications of the Market Research Society and ESOMAR.

INDEX